CONDUCT UNBECOMING

CONDUCT UNBECOMING

HOW BARACK OBAMA IS DESTROYING THE MILITARY AND ENDANGERING OUR SECURITY

ROBERT "BUZZ" PATTERSON
LT. COL. USAF (RET.)

Since 1947
REGNERY
PUBLISHING, INC.
An Eagle Publishing Company

Cataloging-in-Publication data on file with the Library of Congress

ISBN 978-1-59698-621-3

Published in the United States by
Regnery Publishing, Inc.
One Massachusetts Avenue, NW
Washington, DC 20001
www.regnery.com

Manufactured in the United States of America

10 9 8 7 6 5 4 3 2 1

Books are available in quantity for promotional or premium use. Write to Director of Special Sales, Regnery Publishing, Inc., One Massachusetts Avenue NW, Washington, DC 20001, for information on discounts and terms or call (202) 216-0600.

Distributed to the trade by:
Perseus Distribution
387 Park Avenue South
New York, NY 10016

For my parents, Bob and Sandy Patterson,
who have steadfastly supported me and stood by me
through good times and bad.

For my loving wife Nichole,
and our children Kylie, Tanner, and Chase.

I love you and the journey God
continues to bless us with.

CONTENTS

BARACK OBAMA'S DERELICTION OF DUTY

W hen I was tapped to accompany President Bill Clinton and carry the nuclear "football," which contains the top-secret codes (among other things) the president needs in case of nuclear war, I was proud and grateful. As a career Air Force officer and pilot, I'd served literally around the globe, operating in and out of sixty-nine countries, and I'd flown combat support missions in Grenada, the Persian Gulf, Rwanda, Somalia, Haiti, and Bosnia. I was honored to take on this new and awesome responsibility.

But my experiences in the Clinton White House turned my gratitude and awe into shock, revulsion, and sorrow as I saw first-hand the careless and utterly selfish way in which Clinton and his administration ran our country. So, once out of uniform, retired and able to tell my story within the constraints of the Uniform Code of Military Justice, I wrote *Dereliction of Duty*, documenting our former president's contempt for the military, his indifference to important

1

issues except insofar as they served his own political or personal purposes, and his failure to accept his responsibilities as our commander in chief.

Indeed, I lay the blame for the attacks of September 11, 2001, fully at the feet of my former boss, Bill Clinton.

Now, tragically, I see history repeating itself in the presidency of Barack Obama. Only this time the misconduct and dereliction of duty of Obama and his administration could lead to even worse devastation than we suffered on September 11, 2001. Our armed forces have done great work combating the terrorist threat, but the prospect of a nuclear Iran and some of the egregious policy decisions and priorities of the Obama administration have, in my estimation, dramatically raised the level of threat to the United States. In only a year and a half in office, Barack Obama has not only reversed much of the successful accomplishments of his predecessor George W. Bush that have kept us safe, but he's done it at lightning speed. In doing so, Obama is clearly placing the United States in an increasingly vulnerable and threatened condition. With today's struggling global economy weighing down the economies of the United States and Europe, with China's burgeoning influence and military capability, and with Islamist terrorist groups gaining footholds in regions around the world, this is obviously a dangerous time—so dangerous that it is a legitimate fear that a combination of economic and foreign policy reverses could render moot the dreams, sweat, and toil of our founding fathers and all Americans who have gone before; we could be living in a different America, a less prosperous America, a less confident America, a less dominant America.

In Barack Obama we have elected a foreigner—I don't mean in the sense that he is not a United States citizen; nor do I mean it in the sense that he is half Kenyan and spent some years growing up in Indonesia. No, it is that he seems a stranger in our midst, someone whose gut reactions are not those of an American, but of someone raised with different touchstones. We have elected in Barack Obama a man who is comfortable bowing to the Japanese Emperor

Akihito, King Abdullah of Saudi Arabia, and Chinese President Hu Jintao—something that I think most Americans, with their democratic instincts, consider wrong and even un-American, and certainly conduct unbecoming of the leader of our proud Republic. But then, how proud is he of our Republic? Barack Obama is a man who made a point of disdaining to wear an American flag lapel pin; he said he believed in American exceptionalism—only to add that all nations think they are exceptional; his wife on the campaign trail said her husband's popularity with voters made her proud of America for the first time in her adult life. I don't think many of us would consider these mainstream American opinions or actions.

Perhaps before we elected him president, we the people should have been more concerned about his relationships with the radical leftist and former terrorist William Ayers or the radical black-power preacher Jeremiah Wright. Perhaps we should have delved more into his education, his body of work as a community organizer, and his fondness for the radical teachings of Saul Alinsky.

But now Obama is in the White House, the most powerful man in the world, a man who can leave an imprint on American history forever. We need to pay far more attention to him now, to see how he is conducting our nation's foreign policy, and what his plans are to keep our country safe. I believe his foreign policy record thus far and his agenda for the future are extremely deleterious to our national security, and need to be reversed in the elections of November 2010 and 2012.

Barack Obama, I fear, remains little understood and underanalyzed. How many know, for instance, that his key California fundraiser and money bundler, Jodie Evans, is a leader of the radical organization Code Pink that delivered cash and materiel support to the terrorists killing Americans in Iraq? How aware are the American people that the administration's promise of "change" is being carried out by many of the same personalities I served with at the Clinton White House, such as Hillary Clinton, John Podesta, Harold Ickes, Rahm Emanuel, Eric Holder, Susan Rice, Leon

Panetta, and Erskine Bowles? The only difference now is that they feel liberated to move even farther to the Left. How much did the American people follow what we might call Obama's "Global American Shame Tour," in which he offered apologies for American foreign policy in such locales as Cairo, Prague, Moscow, Berlin, Ankara, Oslo, and the United Nations—giving the impression that America had been a rogue nation on the world stage, but that he would set America right?

But there's much more, if one wanted to create a bill of indictment of Obama's national security policy failures, including:

- The cessation of "enhanced interrogation techniques" that provided the United States with precious information that prevented future terrorist attacks;
- The emasculation of the Central Intelligence Agency through the release of previously classified documents and the threatened prosecution of CIA interrogators;
- The administration's ambivalent approach toward the wars in Iraq and Afghanistan, where the administration seems afraid to follow its gut and simply quit them, but cannot commit itself to winning them either;
- The announced closure of Guantanamo Bay, Cuba, and the determination to transfer committed terrorists onto American soil;
- The decision to move trials for senior Al Qaeda leaders, such as Khalid Sheikh Mohammed, from military tribunals in Guantanamo Bay to the federal court system (at one point in New York City, just blocks from Ground Zero);
- The retreat on deploying a missile defense shield in Poland and the Czech Republic, much to the dismay of our European allies;

- The dithering and feckless diplomatic efforts as Iran and North Korea build nuclear weapons and the vehicles to deliver them.

From my point of view as a military analyst, it seems that a unifying theme of Democrat presidents Jimmy Carter, Bill Clinton, and Barack Obama is a consistent underestimating of foreign policy dangers. Carter, after warning the American people of their inordinate fear of communism, was shocked to find the Soviets invading Afghanistan; he was equally shocked by the rise of Islamic fundamentalism and to find Iranian radicals holding American hostages in Tehran. Bill Clinton was shocked by the radical Islamists in Somalia, and never understood the full danger of al Qaeda, even as it attacked American targets overseas.

Barack Obama seems cut from the same cloth. He appears to believe that by sheer force of his own personality and his endless apologies for the behavior of George W. Bush's administration he can bring our enemies to drop their hostility towards us. So far, that doesn't seem to be working. If anything, it appears only to have increased our enemies' contempt, as we've seen in the dismissive reactions of Mahmoud Ahmadinejad of Iran and Hugo Chavez of Venezuela.

While Obama has declared that he will triumph over the enemy we face in our "overseas contingencies," jihadists continue to prosecute their war from Pakistan to Yemen to Fort Hood, Texas, to Detroit. While Obama spends his time attacking his predecessor and his policies, our enemy continues to plan, plot, and execute attacks on America and Americans. Barack Obama has a sacred, or at the very least a constitutional, duty as commander in chief to defend America. He is failing in that duty, and it is not at all clear to me that he even wants to succeed.

Chapter 1

MR. ALINSKY GOES TO WASHINGTON

"We are the ones we've been waiting for. We are the change that we seek."[1]

—Barack Obama

I walked out of the White House for the last time in late April 1998. It was a gorgeous, crisp spring day in Washington, D.C. It was similar in many ways to the day I first walked through the East Wing Gate two years earlier. Then, I was thrilled by the prospect of starting my new assignment. I'd been chosen by the White House to carry the "nuclear football" and serve at the side of President William Jefferson Clinton. I was proud and grateful.

On this spring day two years later, I had very different emotions. I'd been witness to scandal upon scandal and repeated national security failures in the Clinton White House that shocked me. My early feelings of excitement and gratitude had given way to profound disappointment and disgust. I'd seen first-hand the cavalier and self-serving way Clinton and his staff went about the business of running our country. Now, as I walked out of the East Wing on this bright spring day, I felt dirty and dulled.

Upon my retirement from the Air Force in 2001, I wrote my first book, *Dereliction of Duty: The Eyewitness Account of How Bill Clinton Compromised America's National Security*. As I watched the World Trade Center towers collapse on September 11, 2001, I had no doubt that Bill Clinton was the person most responsible for those tragic events. Indeed, Clinton's repeated failures to address the gathering threats during the 1990s had ultimately metastasized into radical Islam's first attack on American soil. As an airline pilot on my way to fly to New York's LaGuardia Airport that ominous morning, my personal association with former president Clinton was painfully renewed.

I wrote *Dereliction of Duty* out of a sense of obligation. I'd seen our military severely degraded and my country attacked. In the book, I detailed my many experiences serving at the side of one of the worst commanders in chief in our nation's history. My hope was that America would realize the colossal damage done to our national security and our military during those eight years and never make that mistake again.

Sadly, we have not remembered the painful lessons from our recent past. The common cause and patriotism we embraced as a nation in the days following those attacks are gone from our collective soul. Unfortunately, we have once again elected a president wholly unequipped for the responsibilities required of America's commander in chief and leader of the free world.

In truth, this time I fear it's far worse. When I left my White House position, I certainly couldn't have imagined we'd elect anyone more inept than Bill Clinton. Nor could I have predicted that just seven years after we'd been attacked and gone to war, we'd elect the most radical leftwing president in our nation's history—one with no experience in national security affairs and an apparent belief that the problem with American foreign policy was that it had been insufficiently interested in appeasement as a strategy.

Which begs the question—how did we let ourselves be so completely fooled by Barack Obama? Were we, as a nation, so beat up by and tired of the Bush years that we were willing to reach for any alternative no matter how dramatic or extreme?

As dreadful and damaging as Clinton was in his eight years in office, we now have a commander in chief whose administration is unqualified for and incapable of addressing the threats we face as a nation. Our current administration at its core refuses to acknowledge and confront our enemies. Instead, we have a president who wants to kick the "ass" of British Petroleum, but doesn't want to kick the ass of an ideological enemy sworn to defeat us, which murders innocents and suppresses human freedoms around the globe.

What we have is Barack Obama, the ultimate in radical chic: cool, beloved of the media and Hollywood, with a baby-boomer narcissism that, unfortunately, attracts support because it makes him seem like an innate VIP; a celebrity, the biggest, most powerful, wisest Twitterer or Facebooker; the perfect man to pose as a secular savior to those who have disposed with the One our forefathers worshipped and the faith that built our nation.

Few seem to have noticed, until recently, that Barack Obama is inclined to dispose with a lot of other things our forefathers valued: a robust defense of American sovereignty and our national interest for one; limited government for another; fiscal prudence for a third.

Similarly, few seem to have noticed that our new president is the most radical president in American history, with views more often associated with leftwing banana republic dictators than with a president of the United States. That is partly because so many of us have failed to see how, for a long time, the Democrat Party has had within it a radical wing that sets the agenda for the party. The party might tamp down the rhetoric, but the policy goals of the far Left pretty quickly become the policy platform of the purportedly moderate Democrat Party. And in Barack Obama, the Left in the Democrat Party has truly elected one of its own. The radical dreams of the Students for a Democratic Society, American Communists, Marxists, and Black Liberation theologians have been realized.

Other Democrats have been participants in the radical anti-war movement of the 1960s and 1970s (Bill Clinton and John Kerry, for instance), but how many had their early political careers intertwined, as Barack Obama did, with Bill Ayers and Bernardine Dohrn, former leaders of the Weather Underground, a domestic terrorist group of the 1960s and 1970s whose goal was to achieve a Communist revolution in the United States?

Many Democrats have felt obliged to seek the approval of a racial shakedown artist like Jesse Jackson, but how many actually sat in the pews most Sundays to listen to the radical—not to mention crazy—racially driven theology of the likes of the Reverend Jeremiah Wright, an admirer of the conspiracy-mongering, anti-Semitic racist Louis Farrakhan and the Nation of Islam?

Many Democrats are naturally inclined to support "peace movements," but how many have embraced the support, as Barack Obama did, of Jodie Evans of Code Pink, whose group has not only supported our nation's enemies in time of war but has gone out of its way to besmirch our nation's servicemen and their families to the point of holding unconscionably belittling protests at the Walter Reed Army Medical Center and against military families and their children attending a party at the White House?

It is astonishing but true that Barack Obama convinced the American people that he not only represented "hope" and "change," but "moderation" and "reason." Yet his biography clearly reveals the extreme leftward tilt of his intellectual formation. When Obama proclaimed, "We are the ones we've been waiting for. We are the change we seek,"[2] it was meant as populist rhetoric—inspiring to his true believers, asinine to others—but he might just as well have been talking about the aspirations of far Left progressives, socialists, and Marxists; Obama was the democratically viable—indeed, elected—champion of their values and beliefs.

To understand the man we've entrusted with our military and the keys to the nuclear arsenal, one doesn't have to look too deeply into his makeup. He is, in fact, a "red diaper baby," who grew up in a family sympathetic to the members and ideologies of the Communist Party USA. Since he was abandoned by his Kenyan father (himself a socialist), Obama's mother became the most important influence in his early life. According to Obama, she was "the dominant figure in my formative years.... The values she taught me continue to be my touchstone when it comes to how I go about the world of politics."[3] His mother, Stanley Ann Dunham, was also a radical leftist, cultural Marxist, feminist, atheist (or, as Obama himself described her "a lonely witness for secular humanism, a soldier for New Deal, Peace Corps, position-paper liberalism"), and a committed believer in multiculturalism.[4] And it is hard to escape the suspicion that her marriages as a white woman from Kansas to a Kenyan man and an Indonesian man were ways of acting on that ideological belief.

Barack Obama's father, Barack Hussein Obama Sr., was also an atheist, who left his rural village and his Muslim family in Kenya to study economics abroad. On a scholarship, he became the first African student to attend the University of Hawaii at Manoa. It was there, in a Russian language class, that he met 18-year old Ann Dunham. Two fellow Marxists, one white and one black, came together, dated, and married in early 1961. Barack Obama Jr. was born six months later.

Barack Obama Sr. and Ann Dunham divorced after he left the islands to pursue higher education at Harvard University. When she remarried, it was to an Indonesian named Lolo Soetoro whom she met at the East-West Center in Honolulu, a congressionally established organization designed to foster better relations between the peoples of the United States, Asia, and the Pacific. Soon after their marriage, Lolo and Ann Soetoro moved the family to Jakarta, Indonesia, where young Barack lived for the next four years. Changing his name to "Barry Soetoro," Obama first attended a Muslim school (his stepfather was a non-practicing Muslim) and then a Catholic school (where records show him enrolled as a Muslim). His mother not only strove to instill in young Barry the values of multiculturalism (which proclaims, in theory, that no culture is better than any other; and, in practice, teaches that other cultures are better than Western culture), but also to convince the half white, half black Barry that he was in fact black. She immersed him in the speeches of Martin Luther King and the recordings of Mahalia Jackson. Affirming Barry's black identity was a further way for Ann Dunham to put her son on the side of the "oppressed," to affirm her preference for the "other" (in the language of academic progressives), and to make him part of the great, ever-expanding civil rights crusade that so roiled liberalism in the 1960s and 1970s.

In 1971, Obama's mother sent young Barack back to Hawaii to be raised by his white, middle-class, maternal grandparents, Stanley Dunham (more affectionately known as "Gramps") and Madelyn Dunham (known to the family as "Toot"), and to attend the prestigious Punahou School. Barack Obama's grandparents raised him in the same ideological atmosphere that shaped his mother. They attended religious services at the leftwing First Unitarian Church of Honolulu, hobnobbed with socialists and Marxists, and introduced young Barry to Stanley's close friend, the poet, columnist, and avowed Communist Frank Marshall Davis.

In the 1970s, the First Unitarian Church served as safe haven and refuge for Vietnam era draft dodgers and maintained close ties with the extremist anti-war group Students for a Democratic Society (SDS). It was within the SDS organization that Bill Ayers and Bernardine Dohrn, later Hyde Park neighbors of Obama's, rose to prominence, eventually leaving SDS to form the Weather Underground, a radical terrorist offshoot seeking to use violence to accelerate the hoped-for revolution.

Obama's mother had attended a church similar to First Unitarian during her formative years as a teenager on Mercer Island in Seattle, Washington. The East Shore Unitarian Church, otherwise known as "The Little Red Church on the Hill," was a place for debate on controversial political issues, and its president, John Stenhouse, was an admitted member of the Communist Party.

Similarly, Honolulu's First Unitarian Church is where young Barry Obama attended Sunday school. First Unitarian's Reverend Mike Young boasted that his church "has always been, and to this day still is, involved in political activism."[5] In this light, it's not difficult to understand how Barack Obama would feel completely comfortable sitting in the pews at Chicago's Trinity United Church of Christ with his wife and two small children, listening to the racist, anti-American, anti-Semitic, and Marxist sermons of his pastor Jeremiah Wright years later.

It was also during these formative years that Obama's grandfather introduced him to Frank Marshall Davis, who quickly became his mentor and advisor. It is probable that Davis became the most significant person in Barack Obama's life after his mother's influence in his younger years. Davis was a black man and one that Stanley Dunham, the white paternal figure, felt could connect the young Obama to his race. It was to be, however, the Communist Party's view of race. Davis was not only a poet and a columnist who wrote for the islands' Communist newspaper, the *Honolulu Record*, but a member of the Soviet Union-controlled Communist Party USA. Davis, who had come to Hawaii at the suggestion of his friend and associate actor/singer Paul Robeson, spent at least nineteen years on the FBI's list of subversives.

In *Dreams from My Father*, the first of two autobiographies written by Obama (the other being *The Audacity of Hope*),[6] he refers to Davis as "a poet named Frank." It's an obvious attempt to obscure his relationship with Davis, but there is no denying that "poet Frank" was in fact Frank Marshall Davis, who was a close friend of his grandfather Stanley Dunham.

In describing his first meeting with Davis at the age of nine or ten, Obama fondly recalls, "By the time I met Frank he must have been pushing eighty, with a big dewlapped face and an ill-kempt gray Afro that made him look like an old, shaggy-maned lion. He would read us poetry whenever we stopped by his house, sharing whiskey with gramps out of an emptied jelly jar."[7]

In the course of their get-togethers, Davis cautioned Obama not to "start believing what they tell you about equal opportunity and the American way and all that shit."[8] When Obama sought counsel from his mentor regarding his transition from Punahou School to college, Davis defined higher education as "an advanced degree in compromise" designed to keep African-Americans in their place. In the end, Davis told Obama, "they'll yank on your chain and let you know that you may be a well-trained, well-paid nigger, but you're a nigger just the same."[9]

And Davis was not shy in writing of his admiration for communism and his disdain for Christianity and white people. Among his many poems are "To the Red Army," in which he celebrates the Soviet revolution while condemning the "rich industrialists in Washington, D.C., and London," and "Christ is a Dixie Nigger," in which he portrays Jesus Christ as just another "New White Hope."

Obama took Davis' radical counsel to heart when he attended Occidental College in California. He wrote later:

> To avoid being mistaken for a sellout, I chose my friends carefully. The more politically active black students. The foreign students. The Chicanos. The Marxist professors and structural feminists and punk-rock performance poets. We smoked cigarettes and wore leather jackets. At night, in the dorms, we discussed neocolonialism, Franz Fanon, Eurocentrism, and patriarchy. When we ground out our cigarettes in the hallway carpet or set our stereos so loud that the walls began to shake, we were resisting bourgeois society's stifling constraints. We weren't indifferent or careless or insecure. We were alienated.[10]

We also know for a fact that as he grew older, Obama became an apostle of leftwing activist Saul Alinsky, author of two books—*Reveille for Radicals*, published in 1946, and *Rules for Radicals* (originally titled *Rules for Revolution*), published in 1969 for the

Machiavellians of the Left. Symbolic of the way he and fellow radicals view America and Christianity, Alinsky dedicated his seminal piece on revolution in America to the "first radical known to man who rebelled against the establishment and did it so effectively that he at least won his own kingdom—Lucifer."[11]

Alinsky was born in Chicago in 1909 and died in California in 1972, well before Obama's ascension to the political stage. But no understanding of Obama's approach to America's military and our national security issues is possible without considering his appreciation for, and affiliation with, the radical teachings of Alinsky. A product of the Chicago streets like so many of Obama's associates, Alinsky—who has inspired many leftwing politicians, including Hillary Clinton—is the original grassroots "community organizer," who dedicated his entire life to destroying America, a country he considered oppressive and unjust and worth "burning."[12]

"The Revolutionary force today has two targets, moral as well as material," writes Alinsky in the prologue to *Rules for Radicals*. "Its young protagonists are one moment reminiscent of the idealistic early Christians, yet they also urge violence and cry, 'Burn the system down!' They have no illusions about the system, but plenty of illusions about the way to change our world."[13]

Unlike Hillary Clinton, Barack Obama never actually met Saul Alinsky, but after his graduation from Columbia University, the 24-year-old Obama went to work on Chicago's South Side to organize residents while "learning and applying Alinsky's philosophy of street-level democracy."[14] In 1985, Obama became the Director for the Developing Communities Project, and he taught workshops on the Alinsky method which were, in effect, courses in leftism, anti-capitalist agitation, and polarization. As Alinsky wrote in *Rules for Radicals*, "From the moment an organizer enters a community, he lives, dreams, eats, breathes, sleeps only one thing, and that is to build the mass power base of what he calls the army."[15]

For Saul Alinsky, "organizing" was the means to, and a smoke screen for, "revolution." In this way deception is absolutely vital to the Alinsky method, and may be the single most important aspect of his theory. Barack Obama took notes and learned well. Throughout his political career, it appears that Obama's "moderation" has always been a tactic to make his radicalism more acceptable to voters—a tactic that comes straight out of the Alinsky playbook.

So, too, has been Obama' presidency, where he has used the Alinsky philosophy and tactics to achieve goals that even Alinsky himself might not have thought easily done: such as nationalizing entire industries or taking over America's armed forces and treating them as an institution where, as commander in chief, he can enforce radical social policies in the name of "fairness." As Richard Poe writes, "Alinsky viewed revolution as a slow, patient process. The trick was to penetrate existing institutions such as churches, unions and political parties." And that's precisely what Obama and his administration are undertaking with amazing effectiveness.[16]

Immediately after the Democratic National Convention in August 2008, Saul Alinsky's son, L. David Alinsky, wrote a letter to the editor of the *Boston Globe* trumpeting his father's impact on the soon-to-be president of the United States. "Barack Obama's training in Chicago by the great community organizers is showing its effectiveness," wrote Alinsky's son. "When executed meticulously and thoughtfully, it is a powerful strategy for initiating change and making it really happen. Obama learned his lesson well. I am proud to see that my father's model for organizing is being applied successfully beyond local community organizing to affect the Democratic campaign in 2008. It is a fine tribute to Saul Alinsky."[17]

Much like my former boss, President Clinton, Obama has also surrounded himself with people proud of their animus towards all things military. In fact, in many cases, the names and the faces are the same. Just as Clinton reached out to retreads of the Carter administration to form his staff and advisors, so Obama has enlisted the services of many of the same people I worked with at the Clinton White House.

Instead of "change you can believe in," the mantra of his candidacy, Barack Obama represents a return to the Clinton years, but with a much more radical bent and with a power undreamt of even by the Clintons. Among the carryovers from the Clinton era are Hillary Clinton (secretary of state), John Podesta (Clinton White House chief of staff and key principal on Obama's transition team), Rahm Emanuel (senior advisor to President Clinton and now chief of staff to President Obama), Erskine Bowles (former Clinton White House chief of staff and now co-chair of Obama's fiscal commission), Eric Holder (deputy attorney general under Janet Reno in the Clinton administration, now Obama's attorney general), Susan Rice (foreign policy advisor to President Clinton, now America's Ambassador to the United Nations), and Elena Kagan (associate White House counsel and advisor to Clinton and now an Obama-appointed Supreme Court justice).

But such continuity shouldn't lead to complacent thoughts that Obama can't be *that* radical with so many staffers who have served in the White House before. That's only to underestimate how radical the Clinton administration would have been had it not lost control of Congress in 1994. It's also to fail to recognize that Barack Obama's own political background is far to the left of Bill Clinton's. Clinton did not have close advisors the likes of Van Jones, Obama's former "Green czar," who became a Communist while serving time in prison, and who was a "9/11 Truther," supporting the idea that the 9/11 terror attacks might have been foisted by President George W. Bush.

Many of Obama's associates are far more radical than the Bill Clinton wing of the Democrat Party. Clinton's appointees might have had similar radical political inclinations, but they were restrained by Clinton being a Southern Democrat who had a little caution in his bones, coming from a conservative part of the country. And, in the end, the bottom line for Clinton was popularity, which was another restraining check on his liberalism. Being the "rock star president" was more important than liberal policies and ideas.

Obama has no such restraints, freeing his advisors to go farther along the leftist path. Like Clinton, he has Baby Boomer narcissistic instincts, but his ideological goals and methods come directly from Alinsky: replacing the existing free-market republic with his own view of a radical, socialist utopia. Obama's judgment and character, proclivities and beliefs are reflected in the people he chooses to associate with—people like unrepentant former terrorists Bill Ayers and Bernardine Dohrn, anti-Semitic and pro-Palestinian professor Rashid Khalidi, Black Liberation theologian Jeremiah Wright, and Code Pink founder Jodie Evans.

When his relationship to Bill Ayers came to light during a Democratic primary debate in 2008, Obama attempted to spin it as a casual association with neighbors. "This is a guy who lives in my neighborhood, who is a professor of English in Chicago, who I know, and who I have not received some official endorsement from. He is not somebody who I exchange ideas from on a regular basis."[18] In reality, the relationship between Barack Obama, Bill Ayers, and Ayers' wife Bernardine Dohrn is intimate, longstanding, and representative of their shared view of the world. They are members of the same ideological team.

It was in the living room of Bill Ayers and Bernardine Dohrn in the fall of 1995 that Barack Obama began his career in politics. That night, Ayers and Dohrn sponsored a reception and fundraiser that became Obama's political "coming out" party and the launch pad for his Illinois state senate campaign. In the home of Bill Ayers and Bernardine Dohrn, Democrat State Senator Alice Palmer announced that she would be leaving her state senate seat to run for a United States congressional seat and was recommending Barack Obama to be her successor. Who is Alice Palmer? Ten years prior to the reception at the Ayers/Dohrn residence, Palmer was an official for the Communist front group U.S. Peace Council, an affiliate of the then-Soviet controlled World Peace Council. Both of these organizations were, at the time, working steadfastly to undermine the U.S. military buildup that ultimately felled the Soviet Union and the Iron Curtain.

It was in the home of Ayers and Dohrn that Barack Obama graduated from civil rights attorney, law professor, and community organizer to politician. But Bill Ayers and Bernardine Dohrn are more than just Obama's Hyde Park neighbors with mutual political views who lived three blocks away. There is evidence, in fact, that Ayers helped Obama write much, if not all, of his autobiography, *Dreams from My Father*, which was originally published in June 1995, just a few months before Ayers' and Dohrn's endorsement of Obama's state senate candidacy. Much has been written about this, and while nothing can be proven definitively, it is certainly true that Obama had previously shown little literary talent, and the book had had a troubled history with Obama apparently unable to deliver the manuscript until suddenly the literary dam burst—or Ayers stepped in to the rescue.[19] Nor is Ayers, as Chicago mayor Richard Daley characterized, just a "distinguished professor of education" and "a valued member of the Chicago community."[20] Ayers and Dohrn are unrepentant terrorists who spent years trying to overthrow the United States government: first, as the leaders of the Weather Underground, and now, as well-funded leftist activists with senior academic positions and political leverage.

The Weather Underground was a revolutionary sect of the Students for a Democratic Society which, after an internecine war, split from the SDS in 1969 in search of more violent means. Their founding document called for a "white fighting force" to work with black nationalist organizations such as the Black Liberation Movement to form "an American Red Army" with the unified goals of destroying American "imperialism" and achieving a Communist revolution.

Under the leadership of Ayers and Dohrn, the Weather Underground declared war on "AmeriKKKa" (always with capitalized "KKK") and carried out at least thirty bombings from 1969 to

1975, targeting, among other locations, the U.S. Capitol, the Pentagon, the State Department, the National Guard offices in Washington, D.C., the New York City police headquarters, courthouses, and banks.

In 1969, shortly after the "Days of Rage" riot in Chicago, a coordinated effort on behalf of the SDS and the Weathermen which injured twenty-eight policemen, Ayers and Dohrn were personally involved in the bombing of a San Francisco police station, killing one officer, Brian V. McDonnell, and injuring two others. In 1970, three members of Ayers' and Dohrn's terror cell, including Ayers' then-girlfriend Diana Oughton, blew themselves up in a Greenwich Village safe house as they were assembling a bomb they planned to detonate at a U.S. Army social dance at Fort Dix, New Jersey. The bomb that exploded prematurely was composed of dynamite wrapped with roofing nails and was designed to maximize the casualties among the Army soldiers and their dates at the dance.

In 2001, Ayers released a book entitled *Fugitive Days*, detailing his years as a radical on the run from justice, which tellingly featured a supportive blurb from his friend Barack Obama. In his memoirs, Ayers described his radical glee as he bombed the Pentagon in May 1972: "Everything was absolutely ideal. . . . The sky was blue. The birds were singing. And the bastards were finally going to get what was coming to them."[21]

In an interview for the *New York Times* following the release of his book (ironically appearing on September 11, 2001, as other terrorists attacked America), Ayers said, "I don't regret setting bombs. I feel we didn't do enough." When reflecting on whether or not he would use bombs against the United States in the future, Ayers wrote, "I can't imagine entirely dismissing the possibility."[22] Only five days after the 9/11 attacks, with the nation in deep grief, the *New York Times* again featured a fawning profile of Ayers in which he said of the United States, "What a country. It makes me want to puke,"[23] a more graphic version of the sentiment Michelle Obama gave during a speech on the campaign trail in February 2008:

"For the first time in my adult lifetime, I am really proud of my country, and not just because Barack has done well, but because I think people are hungry for change."[24] Ayers and Michelle Obama apparently agree that America was not a very nice place until Barack Obama became a presidential contender, and the bringer of hope and change.

Ayers' wife and former Weathermen comrade Bernardine Dohrn spent time on the FBI's Ten Most Wanted List and was named by the FBI's J. Edgar Hoover as "the most dangerous woman in America—La Pasionara of the lunatic left."[25] She was also a fan of Charles Manson. In a 1969 meeting in Flint, Michigan, that the Weather Underground dubbed the "War Council," Dohrn celebrated the Charles Manson Family's gruesome Hollywood murder of pregnant actress Sharon Tate, a Folgers Coffee heiress, and others by holding her fingers as if to simulate a fork and said, "Dig it. First they killed those pigs, then they ate dinner in the same room with them." And, referring to the unborn infant in the pregnant stomach of Sharon Tate, she said "They even shoved a fork into the victim's stomach! Wild!"[26]

During the Vietnam War, with American servicemen fighting and dying in Southeast Asia, Dohrn made visits to Fidel Castro's Cuba and Soviet-controlled Budapest, Hungary, to meet with North Vietnamese and Viet Cong representatives to discuss strategies for America's defeat. During her visit to Budapest, a member of the North Vietnamese delegation presented her with a ring crafted from the remains of a U.S. jet shot down over North Vietnam. Bill Ayers received a similar ring while meeting with an enemy delegation in Toronto, Canada, which so touched him that he "left the room to cry." "I realized . . . America was an evil . . . and that I was . . . living inside the belly of the beast," claimed Ayers.[27]

After the failed bombing of the Fort Dix Army dance, Ayers and Dohrn went underground for the remainder of the 1970s and, with the help of sympathetic fellow travelers and associates, successfully evaded capture by the FBI. When, in 1980, they determined that the political environment was right—during the Carter administration, after liberal Democrat senator Frank Church had successfully led the charge to eviscerate the FBI's ability to gather intelligence on domestic terrorists, and the administration had prosecuted agents who had neutralized terror groups like the Weathermen—they surfaced, surrendered to law enforcement authorities, and were set free. As a result of their successful evasion of justice, Ayers smugly proclaimed, "Guilty as hell. Free as a bird. Ain't America great?"[28]

These impenitent terrorists, once free, quickly rose in the ranks of Chicago politics and academia, Ayers taking a job in education and Dohrn working for the prestigious Chicago law firm of Sidley Austin. It was during her employment at the law firm that Dohrn first met and worked with Michelle Obama. Ayers and Dohrn have since raised three children: Malik (the Muslim name for Malcolm X), Zayd (who is named for Zayd Shakur, a Black Panther who was killed in a shoot-out with New Jersey State Troopers), and Chesa Boudin (whose natural parents Kathy Boudin and David Gilbert were serving lengthy prison sentences for their involvement in the murders of two police officers and a Brinks guard during a holdup).

In pure Alinsky fashion, Ayers and Dohrn are today continuing their work for revolution from within the system. Ayers is a Senior University Scholar at the University of Illinois, Chicago, teaching the teachers who are educating America's children, and is vice-president for curriculum for the 25,000-strong American Educational Research Association. Bernardine Dohrn is an Associate Professor of Law at Northwestern University and Director for the Children and Family Justice Center.

But Barack Obama's association with Bill Ayers and Bernardine Dohrn is not confined to their support for his Illinois state campaign and associated fundraising efforts, nor is Ayers just "a guy" who lives in Obama's neighborhood and possibly helped him write a book. In 1995, the same year as the fundraiser at the home of Ayers and Dohrn, Barack Obama, a young lawyer working for a second-tier law firm, was appointed as the first chairman for the Chicago Annenberg Challenge (CAC), a radical "school reform organization" founded by Bill Ayers. Between 1995 and 1999, Obama and Ayers—often sitting at the same table for board meetings—distributed $110 million to a variety of leftist educational organizations. Among the funds handed out were $600,000 to another organization founded by Ayers, the Small Schools Workshop, run by Mike Klonsky, a Communist activist, a leader of the Marxist-Leninist Communist Party, an SDS associate of Ayers and Dohrn, and an official blogger for the Barack Obama campaign website.

Among other groups receiving funding from the CAC were ACORN (the Association of Community Organizations for Reform Now, a radical activist group that Obama once represented as an attorney), the Arab American Action Network (an anti-Israel, pro-illegal immigration group founded by fellow Hyde Park neighbor and Columbia University professor Rashid Khalidi, which argues that the creation of Israel was a "catastrophe" for the Arab world),[29] Bernardine Dohrn's Children and Family Justice Center, and Jeremiah Wright's Trinity United Church.

The Obama–Khalidi connection is also illustrative of the circles Barack Obama and his wife Michelle frequent. They were often guests at the home of Khalidi and his wife Mona, a former PLO translator. "Khalidi and Obama lived in nearby faculty residential zones and the two families dined together a number of times," recalled a source on the University of Chicago faculty. "The Obamas even babysat the Khalidi children." In 2003, the Obamas, Ayers, and Dohrn attended a farewell party for the Khalidis, after Rashid Kalidi accepted a position at Columbia University. Khalidi, like Ayers and Dohrn, hosted a fundraiser for Barack Obama in his home.

Obama and Ayers were also paid board members from 1999 to 2002 of the Woods Fund, a Chicago-based nonprofit foundation. Here, too, they directed money to Rashid Khalidi's Arab American

Action Network and Bernardine Dohrn's Children and Family Justice Center.

Part of this cozy, radical, self-enriching circle was the Reverend Jeremiah Wright, the black liberation theologian of breathtakingly extreme views whom Obama took on as his spiritual advisor.

For almost twenty years, Barack and Michelle Obama attended services at Chicago's Trinity United Church of Christ. For almost twenty years, Barack and Michelle Obama sat comfortably in the pews of Trinity United, not only listening to the Marxist, racist, and hate-mongering sermons of Jeremiah Wright, but also contributing tens of thousands of their own dollars to the church. Perhaps more telling, and I say this as a Christian husband and father who understands the significance, the Obamas were not only married in the Trinity United Church by the Reverend Jeremiah Wright, but also chose him to baptize their daughters. Most significant of all, this is the church where Barack Obama has claimed that he affirmed his Christian faith and "committed to Christ."[30]

Just as with his friendships with Ayers and Dohrn, however, Barack Obama was quick to throw the Reverend Wright under the bus when their relationship was held to the light of day and threatened to derail his presidential campaign. His pastor was no longer an asset—as he had been in Chicago politics, where he gave Obama "street cred" with black voters and the Left—but a liability. Only then did Barack Obama claim he wasn't aware of Wright's comments and hadn't attended the church regularly. "He's never been my political advisor; he's been my pastor," Obama said. He also stated, "I don't think my church is actually particularly controversial," downplaying the extremist views of Jeremiah Wright as if they were just the goofy mutterings of "an old uncle."[31]

But Barack Obama didn't drive past hundreds of churches from his home in Hyde Park to Trinity United located in the rough neighborhood of Chicago's South Side and sit there for almost twenty years by happenstance. He chose the church and he chose the pastor, and the Reverend Jeremiah Wright represents another in the long line of openly radical friends and associates Barack Obama has chosen to get close to. Wright is not an incidental figure in Obama's life, he is a principal, and Obama is Wright's top acolyte.

Jeremiah Wright is a believer in, and proponent of, Black Liberation theology, which is basically Marxism cloaked in Christianity. As explained at DiscoverTheNetworks.org, black liberation theology "teaches that the New Testament gospels can be understood only as calls for social activism, class struggle, and revolution aimed at overturning the existing capitalist order and installing in its stead a socialist utopia where today's poor will unseat their 'oppressors.'"[32] "If you want to understand where Barack gets his feelings and rhetoric from," says the Reverend Jim Wallis, the spiritual advisor for many on the Left, "just look at Jeremiah Wright.[33]

Precisely. In fact, the title of Obama's second autobiography and the theme of his keynote address at the Democratic National Convention in 2004, *The Audacity of Hope*, comes from one of Wright's sermons, "The Audacity to Hope." Obama's other book, *Dreams from My Father*, includes an entire chapter on Trinity United Church.

In an interview with the *Chicago Sun-Times* columnist Cathleen Falsani in 2004, Obama boasted of his friendship with, and admiration for, the Reverend Wright.

"Do you still attend Trinity?" asked Falsani.

"Yep. Every week. 11 o'clock service. Ever been there? Good service. I actually wrote a book called '*Dreams from My Father*,' it's kind of a meditation on race. There's a whole chapter on the church in that, and my first visits to Trinity," said Obama.

"Do you have people in your life that you look to for guidance?" Falsani questioned further.

"Well, my pastor (the Reverend Jeremiah Wright) is certainly someone who I have an enormous amount of respect for," replied Obama.[34]

Here are a few of the radical, racist, and anti-American ideas and admonitions that Barack and Michelle Obama, and their children, would have heard from the pews at Trinity United.

In the sermon Wright gave following the attacks of 9/11, as rescue workers were pulling charred bodies from the World Trade Center wreckage and smoke continued to rise above the skyline of New York City, Wright proclaimed:

> America's chickens are coming home to roost!...We took Africans from their country to build our way of ease and kept them enslaved and living in fear. Terrorism!...We bombed [Libyan leader Muammar] Qadhafi's home and killed his child...we nuked far more than the thousands in New York and the Pentagon, and we never batted an eye!...We have supported terrorism against the Palestinians...and now we are indignant, because the stuff we have done overseas has now been brought back into our own front yards! America's chickens are coming home to roost![35]

What makes this most alarming is that Wright delivered this sermon only five days after the attacks—and from his hotel room window in Newark, New Jersey, he had personally witnessed the second plane crashing into the World Trade Center. When his country was attacked in front of his own eyes, when his fellow Americans were killed, when almost all Americans across the country were united in grief and patriotism, the Reverend Wright, Barack Obama's pastor and friend, took to his pulpit and condemned America and said that the "chickens are coming home to roost."

In a sermon he delivered in 2003, Wright shouted,

> The government gives [black people] the drugs, builds bigger prisons, passes a three-strike law and then wants us to sing "God Bless America." No, no, no. Not God bless America,

God damn America! It's in the Bible for killing innocent people. God damn America for treating us citizens as less than human. God damn America as long as she tries to act like she is God and she is supreme!"[36]

In a sermon he delivered at Howard University in January 2006, Wright made the following points:[37]

1) There are more black men in prison than there are in college in America;

2) Racism is how America was founded and how America is still run;

3) America is the number one killer in the world;

4) America put Nelson Mandela in prison and supported apartheid for twenty-seven years. Americans believe in white supremacy and black inferiority, and they believe in white supremacy more than they believe in God;

5) America shamelessly supports Zionism while ignoring the Palestinians;

6) America is conducting radiation experiments against its own people and cares nothing about human life if the ends justify the means;

7) America doesn't care if poor black and brown children cannot read and kill each other senselessly;

8) America started the AIDS virus. And now that it is out of control, America still puts more money into the military than into medicine, more money into hate than into humanitarian concerns;

9) America is only able to maintain its standard of living by making sure that Third World people live in grinding poverty;

10) America is comprised of selfish, self-centered egotists who are arrogant and ignorant and fail to make the kingdom that Jesus talks about a reality.

This is the pastor whose church Barack Obama chose to attend; this is the pastor he chose to conduct his marriage ceremony and baptize his children; this is the church where he became a born-again Christian. During the 2008 presidential campaign, Wright was shunted aside as an irrelevant sideshow; the liberal media prefer to ignore religion anyway, unless it comes to exposing a scandal in the Catholic Church or a conservative Protestant congregation. But to ignore the rantings of the Reverend Wright is to ignore a clear link to the inner radicalism of Barack Obama that tells us much about his instincts, his prejudices, and his core beliefs. He might never let himself go as far as Wright, he might discount some of Wright's loonier theories, but it is beyond belief that Barack Obama associated himself with Wright and his church, as he did by choice for twenty years, without sharing affinities with the pastor and his message.

If Wright seems a crazed, racist, Afro-centric anti-American, if Ayers and Dohrn are reformed terrorists turned mere radicals comfortably ensconced in academia, the law, and the self-serving world of the Chicago Left, Jodie Evans, an Obama fundraiser and the co-founder of the extremist anti-military organization Code Pink, shows how Obama is happy to rake in the money from a woman and an organization directly linked to America's enemies.

Don't know her? President Obama does... and you need to as well.

Well known in California's progressive Democrat social circles, Evans is a former political appointee who worked for Jerry Brown when he was the governor of California and managed his failed presidential run in 1992.

Barack Obama's first major event after announcing his long-shot run for the presidency in February 2007 was a Hollywood fundraiser co-hosted by Evans. Just as the radicals Bill Ayers and Bernardine Dohrn launched Obama's political coming out parties at their Hyde Park home in 1996, Evans introduced Obama to

Hollywood and California, and elevated him into the national spotlight as a viable contender.

Along with her partner and ex-husband, financier Max Palevsky, and Dreamworks braintrust Steven Spielberg, David Geffen, and Jeffry Katzenberg, Evans successfully pulled together the rich and the radical in Los Angeles to support the emerging *wunderkind*. The event was a breakthrough success. It provided the liftoff Obama needed to make his way to winning the Democratic nomination and eventual election to 1600 Pennsylvania Avenue.

But Evans is not just a skilled fundraiser with big time connections in the entertainment industry. She is a radical leftwing activist devoted to gutting our military and supporting our nation's enemies.

Along with fellow revolutionary extremists Medea Benjamin, Diane Wilson, and a "dirt loving" Wiccan activist who refers to herself only as Starhawk, Evans founded Code Pink for Peace as a "grassroots peace and social justice movement" in November 2002.[38] In reality, Evans and the members of the Santa Monica, California-based Code Pink are anything but pacifists.

Since 9/11, Evans and her cohorts have set their sights squarely on demoralizing the U.S. military and damaging America's war against Islamist terrorism. They've been at the forefront of an antiwar effort seeking to systematically undermine America's military and bring about defeat for American troops in Iraq and Afghanistan. Along the way, they've ruthlessly attacked our soldiers and their families on the home front, demeaned and undermined their noble and brave efforts abroad, and sided with terrorists and state sponsors of terror around the globe.

Just a few weeks prior to her Hollywood shindig for Obama, for example, Evans and her Code Pink sisters were in Havana conspiring with Fidel Castro and his government by seeking ways to put pressure on the Bush administration to release the terrorists detained at Guantanamo Bay.

In addition to Cuba's Castro, Code Pink's "evil dictator out-reach" includes collaborating with Iraq's Saddam Hussein, Iran's Mahmoud Ahmadinejad, Syria's Bashar Assad, Venezuela's Hugo Chavez, Nicaragua's Daniel Ortega, and Bolivia's Evo Morales. After a personal meeting with Ahmadinejad in New York, Evans praised the Iranian ruler as being "really about peace and human rights and respecting justice."[39] This is the same Ahmadinejad who is pursuing nuclear weapons in defiance of the United Nations, who looks forward to armed conflict that will usher in the Muslim ver-sion of Armageddon, and who has made it clear that he would like to see Israel removed from the map. In 2006, Evans met with Venezuela's Chavez and declared him a "sweetheart."[40] This is the same Chavez who has been closing down opposition media, remov-ing all obstacles to his dictatorial power, and whom even liberal Democrat House Speaker Nancy Pelosi has called "an everyday thug."[41]

Evans doesn't draw the line at snuggling up to some of the world's vilest dictators and despots. She's also forged close relation-ships with, and done the propaganda bidding of, murderous terror groups Hamas, Hezbollah, the Taliban, the Sunni insurgents in Iraq, and—the patriarch of all radical Islamic terror organizations—the Muslim Brotherhood. The Muslim Brotherhood is the world's largest Islamic promoter of jihad, inspiring, among other Islamic terrorist leaders, Osama bin Laden's deputy, Ayman al-Zawahiri, the chief strategist of al Qaeda's war with the United States and the West.

Code Pink's official website invites the Muslim Brotherhood to "join us in cleansing our country." A banner advertisement on the site titled "Arrest the War Criminals" links to another page on the Code Pink site that calls for the kidnapping of former President George W. Bush and his wife Laura.[42]

Let's be clear here: this is an American citizen who, as the head of an international antiwar organization, is attempting to rally

America's enemies. There is a word for that: some might call it treason.

That hasn't deterred President Barack Obama. Rather than distance himself from Evans and Code Pink, he has embraced her support. He even appointed Evans to be a key "bundler" for his Obama for America and Obama Victory Fund, where she collected more than $50,000 in donations for the future president. "Bundling" is collecting individual political contributions into a big donation, and Evans does it well. She and her son also contributed money of their own, each giving the maximum individual amount of $2,300 to presidential candidate Obama, and she ranked among the top 500 of Obama's campaign underwriters.

The Obama campaign must have been well aware of Evans' past, because the anti-American efforts of Evans and Code Pink are legion. Here are just a few:

In February 2003, with American troops massing for the imminent invasion of Iraq, Evans' Code "Pinkos" traveled to Baghdad to meet with Saddam Hussein's government in a transparent attempt to try to gain international support for the Iraqi dictator.

In July 2003, with American men and women fighting and dying to liberate Iraq, Evans joined the Advisory Board for the Iraq Occupation Watch (IOW). Fellow Code Pink-founder Medea Benjamin and long-time radical socialist, homosexual rights advocate, and pro-Castro activist Leslie Cagan traveled to Baghdad to establish the IOW.

The charter of the IOW, according to the watchdog website DiscoverTheNetworks.org, was to "(a) undermine the Bush administration's reconstruction efforts in Iraq through propaganda and dissimulation in the American media; (b) demoralize U.S. troops by relaying tales of wavering public support; and (c) encourage widespread desertion by 'conscientious objectors.'"[43]

Simultaneously, Evans and her colleagues smeared U.S. troops and their mission with fabricated stories of atrocities and alleged war crimes. In an interview with a publication produced by the Revolutionary Communist Party USA, Evans claimed that American soldiers were wantonly slaughtering Iraqi women and children, and that "they couldn't give a shit about an Iraqi life."[44] Another IOW Advisory Board member, Tariq Ali, called for the murder of U.S. troops in Iraq.[45]

Evans' confessed intent was to demoralize our troops and significantly undercut the war effort. As Evans explained, "As an antiwar activist, one of the things you try to do is you try to find the pillars that keep us at war and try to undermine those pillars. And one of the things: You can't go to war if you don't have soldiers."[46] Her role model might have been her close friend Jane Fonda, who had famously defied U.S. law when she visited Communist North Vietnam in 1972 and encouraged American troops to desert. Fonda recorded several radio broadcasts for Hanoi and posed for photos that show her smiling as she pretends to shoot down America's military aircraft. But not even the traitorous Hanoi Jane physically approached American soldiers at war and attempted to facilitate their desertion.

Evans and her associates also delivered more than $600,000 in cash and "humanitarian aid" to the insurgents fighting and killing U.S. Marines and soldiers engaged in bloody house-to-house combat in Fallujah in December 2004. In a press conference celebrating her organization's support for the enemy, Code Pink co-founder Medea Benjamin chortled, "I don't know of any other case in history in which the parents of fallen soldiers collected medicine for the 'other side.'"[47]

Perhaps even worse, according to the online publication *Islamonline*, Evans' entourage received logistical support from elected American politicians. In order to successfully deliver aid and comfort to America's enemy, the women of Code Pink carried letters of support and diplomatic courtesy from Democrat Senator Barbara Boxer of California and Democrat Congressmen Henry Waxman of California, Dennis Kucinich of Ohio, and Raul Grijalva of Arizona.[48]

The delegation delivering goods to support terrorists killing America's troops also included Hany Khalil, a national organizer for Cagan's international leftist organization United for Peace and Justice, which was a sponsor of Code Pink's trip to Iraq, as were Global Exchange, the Middle East Children's Alliance, Physicians for Social Responsibility, Peace Action, and Voices in the Wilderness,[49] all of which are hard-line radical leftist organizations. The founder of the Middle East Children's Alliance, for instance, "is allied with the Worker's World Party, a Marxist-Leninist sect aligned with Communist North Korea."[50]

Evans traveled to Istanbul, Turkey, in June 2005, where she participated in mock "war crimes" trials against the United States, signed a joint declaration backing the Iraqi insurgency, and said, "We must begin by really standing with the Iraqi people and defending their right to resist," said Evans. "The Iraqi people are fighting for their country, to protect their families and to preserve all they love. They are fighting for their lives, and we are fighting for lies."[51]

A year after she'd helped aid and abet the terrorists in Iraq, Evans and Code Pink again met with America's enemy, a group of pro-insurgency Iraqi parliamentarians in Jordan. The terrorist-supporting politicians appealed to the "Pinkos" to seek recognition for the so-called Iraqi resistance. Evans and Code Pink also visited Damascus, Syria. Later that summer, Code Pink went from Syria to Lebanon to provide moral support and offer a propaganda voice for Hezbollah as it rained thousands of rockets on innocent Israeli citizens.

Evans and Code Pink aren't satisfied simply with undermining America and our military abroad. Some of their most vicious and unconscionable behavior occurs here at home.

Since the inception of America's military involvement in Afghanistan and Iraq, Evans' Code Pink has routinely staged protests outside Walter Reed Army Medical Center in Washington, D.C. Walter Reed is the primary convalescent home for wounded soldiers returning from battle.

Positioning themselves directly in front of the hospital's main entrance, Code Pink held signs proclaiming the injured troops were "Maimed for a Lie." Recovering soldiers and their families were forced to walk through gauntlets lined with mock caskets and placards reading, among other things, "Enlist here to die for Halliburton."[52]

One of the soldiers treated at Walter Reed was Kevin Pannell, a member of the Army's First Cavalry Division who lost both his legs in a grenade ambush near Baghdad in 2004. Pannell recalled, "We went by there one day and I drove by and they [the antiwar protestors] had a bunch of flag-draped coffins laid out on the sidewalk. That, I thought, was probably the most distasteful thing I had ever seen. Ever. You know that 95 percent of the guys in the hospital bed lost guys whenever they got hurt and survivor's guilt is the worst thing you can deal with."[53]

Obama probably didn't have wounded soldiers in mind when in September 2008 he tapped Evans for another Hollywood fundraiser, this one a $28,500-per-plate event held at the historic Greystone mansion in Beverly Hills. Evans had been in the headlines just two weeks before when she crashed the Republican National Convention, attempting to disrupt Sarah Palin's vice-presidential acceptance speech. Two weeks after the Hollywood fundraiser, Evans traveled to New York to meet with Iranian President Mahmoud Ahmadinejad. A few weeks after Obama's election in November 2008, Evans and Code Pink traveled to Tehran at the personal invitation of Ahmadinejad. Evans represented a one-woman Hollywood-to-Obama-to-Ahmadinejad axis.

Her organization meanwhile has continued to haunt military families. In October 2009, several hundred servicemen and women and their children gathered outside the White House to attend a Halloween Party. They were met by the women of Code Pink dressed up as "zombie soldiers killed in combat" and "ghosts of war victims." The Code Pink website announced that their intent was to target the troops and their families. Dressed in fatigues with a bloody bandage circling her head, Medea Benjamin played the role of a "zombie soldier" and wailed and moaned while she carried a sign that read, "The White House is haunted by the ghosts of Bush's war."[54] Another woman dressed as a wicked witch confronted the children, saying, "More pretties to die in my war! More pretties!"[55]

That same October, Evans participated in another Obama fundraiser, this one in San Francisco, which drew more than 900 attendees and netted more than $5 million. Just a few weeks before the blockbuster Bay Area fundraiser, Evans and members of Code Pink visited Afghanistan and met with members of the Taliban. At the San Francisco fundraiser, Evans personally delivered a message from the Taliban to the president.

In December 2009, Evans and Obama friends Bill Ayers and Bernardine Dohrn traveled to Gaza to deliver tens of thousands of dollars in "humanitarian aid" to Palestinian activists in Hamas-controlled Gaza. According to the official Code Pink website, the security for and safety of the travelers was "guaranteed" by members of Hamas. Code Pink's mission in support of America's enemies came with the support of official letters from Democrat Senator John Kerry of Massachusetts and Democrat Congressman André Carson of Indiana.

The point in drawing these connections is not just to highlight Evans' role in raising money for Obama, or to point out how radical some of his sycophants are, but to make the point that, as with the Reverend Wright, it seems highly likely that Obama, our nation's commander in chief, shares much of the radical ideology of Evans and her cronies—even if he has to be more prudent and even Machiavellian in acting on them (endorsing, for instance, a brief troop buildup in Afghanistan, so that he might not appear weak on terrorism, but only with the quid pro quo of it being tied to a withdrawal date, withdrawal being his true objective).

Barack Obama's views on foreign policy and the military were not shaped in a vacuum. Unlike most Americans, patriotism does not come naturally to Barack Obama, which was why he famously disdained wearing a flag lapel pin. And unlike most Americans, he does not believe in American exceptionalism—or he affirms such a belief only to deny it: "I believe in American exceptionalism, just as I suspect that the Brits believe in British exceptionalism and the Greeks believe in Greek exceptionalism." As the historian John Steele Gordon notes, "In other words, to Obama, American exceptionalism is nothing more than casual chauvinism."[56] Obama's beliefs are manifestly the fruit of his upbringing in an environment where multiculturalism and socialism were taught as right, and America was regarded as a racist, imperialist, exploitative power that needed radical reform. With that background, it should not surprise us that, as an adult, his friends and associates have included the likes of Bill Ayers, Bernardine Dohrn, Rashid Khalidi, Jeremiah Wright, and Jodie Evans.

What is more surprising is that we've elected such a man as president, a president whose foreign policy can only be characterized as one where we give our friends the back of our hand while we bow to our enemies.

We have elected a president whose Justice Department is run by lawyers with radical resumes, who have built their reputations representing terrorists, and who pursue policies that emasculate our intelligence agencies, hamstringing their ability to collect the information needed to prevent future terror attacks, and undermining our soldiers in the field.

We have elected a commander in chief who sees the military as a place where he can enforce the most radical policies of leftist social engineering. While our country is fighting two wars, it is a priority of this administration to overturn the policies of moral conduct that guide our armed services in order to liberate homosexuals in the service and open up the military to those now referred to as "transgendered."

Simply put, we have elected the most radical commander in chief ever. Satirist P. J. O'Rourke once wrote that "giving money and power to government is like giving whiskey and car keys to teenage boys." Well, we have handed the keys to the leadership of the free world to a man whose sole leadership experience is that of a "community organizer" and whose ideological goals are apparently those of Saul Alinsky.

While we are at war, our nation's military is led by a man who has spent his adult life either on liberal college campuses, where anti military sentiments thrive, or palling around with radicals and domestic terrorists who have been his political allies in his meteoric rise through Chicago's machine politics. Barack Obama commands a force of 2.3 million young men and women in uniform. As someone who used to train Air Force officers, I would judge him, from his public record, as someone unqualified to command even a squadron of a few hundred airmen—that is, if Barack Obama had ever considered serving his country as an Air Force officer, which of course he never did. The man now collecting salutes as commander in chief is a man who never thought of giving salutes as a soldier himself. Worse, there is every reason to suspect that for the first four decades of his life, Barack Obama might have believed that our own nation's troops were on the wrong side of every foreign policy conflict in which they were deployed. Certainly it appears that is what many of his cronies and colleagues and mentors believed, and there seems little reason to think that Obama was any different.

Chapter 2

THE OBAMA REVOLUTION

"We are the ones we've been waiting for. We are the change that we seek."

—Barack Obama, February 5, 2008

The first shots in the Obama Revolution, the highly unlikely campaign that elevated an inexperienced former community organizer born in Hawaii and raised in Indonesia into the Oval Office, were fired at the Long Island Southampton beach house of billionaire hedge fund manager George Soros in the summer of 2002.

It was during that secretive meeting that Soros, Morton Halperin, (Director of Soros' Open Society Institute), John Podesta (former Clinton White House chief of staff and soon to be President and CEO of the Center for American Progress), Jeremy Rosner (former speech writer for Bill Clinton), Robert Boorstin (Democrat strategist, pollster, and also a former speech writer for Clinton), and Carl Pope (Democrat strategist, environmentalist, and Sierra Club executive director), among others, met to draft a plan to defeat George W. Bush in 2004.

In an interview with Laura Blumenfeld of the *Washington Post* in November 2003, Soros said, "America, under Bush, is a danger to the world," and removing him from office "is the central focus of my life…a matter of life and death. And I'm willing to put my money where my mouth is."[1] More troubling, perhaps, was his later comment: "The main obstacle to a stable and just world order is the United States."[2]

Soros ultimately spent more than $26 million out of his own wallet in 2004 to oust George W. Bush (his campaign included support for anti-Bush organizations and ads, and even a personal anti-Bush speaking tour). Soros failed in his attempt to remove George Bush from office and elect John Kerry—a failure he attributed to Kerry's weakness as a candidate.[3] But the Hungarian-born billionaire was not to be denied. If he could not defeat George W. Bush, he could still help choose and elect the next Democrat president, and he was determined to do that. To that end, Soros created what has been called the "Shadow Party." The excellent website DiscoverTheNetworks.org defines the Shadow Party as being "originally devised by journalists to describe '527' political committees promoting Democratic Party agendas…more specifically…the network of non-profit activist groups organized by George Soros and others to mobilize resources—money, get-out-the-vote drives, campaign advertising, and policy initiatives—to elect Democratic candidates and guide the Democratic Party towards the left. The Internet fundraising operation MoveOn.org is a key component."[4] The Shadow Party is also a "nationwide network of more than five-dozen unions, non-profit activist groups, and think tanks whose agendas are ideologically to the left.…"[5]

George Soros is the Shadow Party's spiritual leader, principal funder, and architect—and it is this Shadow Party that helped lift Barack Obama from being a state senator from Illinois, to being a United States senator, to being president of the United States.

George Soros is one of the wealthiest men on the planet, with a personal fortune of at least $7 billion and additional investments of another $11 billion or so. His collaborative group of pro-Left foundations distributes more than $400 million a year to causes ranging from underwriting left-leaning Democrat Party candidates, to legalizing marijuana, to advocating for euthanasia.

As Richard Poe adroitly wrote in *The Shadow Party*, a book he co-authored with my former colleague David Horowitz, "The Shadow Party is the real power driving the Democrat machine. It is a network of radicals dedicated to transforming our constitutional republic into a socialist hive. The leader of these radicals is... George Soros. He has essentially privatized the Democratic Party, bringing it under his personal control. The Shadow Party is the instrument through which he exerts that control.... "[6]

George Soros, a naturalized American citizen, was born in Hungary as György Schwartz in 1930 to a family of non-practicing Jews. His father later changed the family name from Schwartz to Soros to hide their Jewish heritage during the Nazi Holocaust. His family relocated to England in 1947, and Soros eventually immigrated to the United States in 1956. Through his father, young Soros became a practitioner of "Esperanto"—a language invented in 1887, designed to be the world's first "global language" for a global community that, its inventor believed, would evolve beyond nation-states.

In 1979, George Soros founded his Open Society Institute (OSI) which has, over the years, contributed more than $5 billion to predominately leftwing organizations. Among the organization's objectives, as encapsulated by DiscoverTheNetworks.org, are:

- promoting the view that America is an oppressive nation...
- opposing virtually all post-9/11 national security measures enacted by the U.S. government, particularly the Patriot Act
- depicting U.S. military actions as unjust, unwarranted, and immoral and unnecessary

- promoting open borders, mass immigration, and a watering down of current immigration laws ...
- defending suspected anti-American terrorists and their abettors ...
- advocating America's unilateral disarmament and/or steep reduction in its military spending ...
- bringing American foreign policy under the control of the United Nations ... [7]

Among the many leftist organizations that have received funding and support from Soros' OSI are the American Civil Liberties Union (ACLU), Amnesty International, the Arab American Institute Foundation, the Center for American Progress, the Center for Constitutional Rights, the Gamaliel Foundation, Human Rights Watch, the Lynne Stewart Defense Committee, the Malcolm X Grassroots Movement, MoveOn.org, the National Association for the Advancement of Colored People (NAACP), the National Abortion Federation, the National Lawyers Guild, the National Organization for Women, Planned Parenthood, the Tides Foundation, and the Tides Center.

Soros' influence wasn't solely financial. He also began moving in important political and social circles. During the 1990s, George Soros, the leftist philanthropist, became friends with Bill and Hillary Clinton, who made him their surrogate envoy to Russia and Eastern Europe, giving him the sort of real world political influence he no doubt craved, and that whet his appetite for more.

On July 7, 2003, George Soros, Morton Halperin, John Podesta, and Harold Ickes (Clinton's White House deputy chief of staff) founded the American Majority Institute just three blocks from the White House. A few months later, they changed the name to the Center for American Progress (CAP). CAP is meant to be the cornerstone organization of the Shadow Party. CAP describes itself as "a nonpartisan research and educational institute," aimed at "developing a long-term vision of a progressive America" and "providing a forum to generate new progressive ideas and policy proposals."[8] When CAP was founded, Hillary Clinton remarked, "We need some new intellectual capital. There has to be some thought given as to how we build the 21st-century policies that reflect the Democrat Party's values."[9]

CAP's founding president is John Podesta, the former White House chief of staff to Bill Clinton, who also served as leader of the Obama transition team after Obama was elected president. So it should be no surprise that the Obama administration policy can be traced along the lines developed by CAP and supported by Soros.

From 2003 to 2007, CAP received more than $15 million from grants from more than sixty foundations, with the biggest contributor being George Soros, who ponied up the first $3 million. Today, CAP has over 180 staff members and an annual budget of $27 million.

From the tenth floor at their address on H Street NW, Washington, D.C, young workers pound on desktop PCs and watch big screen televisions. The idea is to have a perpetual political war room, a command post that not only develops and communicates the positions of the Left, but that can provide an instant counterpoint to the conservative Right. For example, CAP employs eleven full-time bloggers, who write for the Center's many websites, and who develop daily feeds for radio stations across the country.

Among the other key CAP staffers and former Clintonistas are the aforementioned Robert Boorstin, Gene Sperling (Democratic Leadership Council staffer and former head of Clinton's National Economic Council), Matt Miller (former senior advisor to Clinton's Office of Management), Debbie Berger (Director of Media Strategy and daughter of Clinton national security advisor and "infamous pants burglar" Sandy Berger, who was convicted of stealing and destroying highly sensitive official documents, which he smuggled out of the National Archives in his pants), and Jennifer Palmieri (vice president for communications and former Clinton White House deputy press secretary). "Others strive to be objective, we don't," said Palmieri.[10]

The relationship between George Soros and Barack Obama goes back at least as far as June 7, 2004, when Soros hosted a fundraiser for Obama's U.S. Senate campaign at his New York home. Just a few weeks prior to the fundraiser for Barack Obama, Soros publically compared the miscreant behavior at the Abu Ghraib prison in Iraq to the terrorist attacks that killed nearly 3,000 people on 9/11.

After the 2004 election, Soros convened a secretive meeting of seventy like-minded and wealthy donors in Scottsdale, Arizona, to take a look at what had gone wrong in their campaign to elect John Kerry president and to develop a plan for the future. An eventual beneficiary of the so-called "Phoenix Group" was Barack Obama, because when the group looked for a candidate, he became the one.

In December 2006, as Obama was contemplating a run for the White House, George Soros and Barack Obama met to discuss the young senator's political ambitions. In a matter of a few weeks, on January 16, 2007, Obama announced he was establishing a presidential exploratory committee although, at that point, he'd logged a total of 143 days in service as a United States senator. Literally hours after the announcement, George Soros sent Senator Barack Obama the maximum individual contribution allowed by campaign finance law. "I recognize that there is a certain presumptuousness in this, a certain audacity to this announcement," Obama said.[11] But it was presumptuousness backed to the hilt by Soros.

Later that week, Soros publicly announced that he would be supporting Barack Obama for president rather than Hillary Clinton, whom he'd previously supported. In an interview with Judy Woodruff in May 2008, Soros was prophetic, gushing, "Obama has the charisma and the vision to radically reorient America in the world." He added, "This emphasis on experience is way overdone."[12]

In early 2008, the Shadow Party's Internet fundraising site, MoveOn.org, announced it was endorsing Barack Obama for president. On its official website, MoveOn director Eli Pariser said,

Seven years of the disastrous policies of the Bush Administration have left the country desperate for change. We need a President who will bring to bear the strong leadership and vision required to end the war in Iraq, provide health care to every American, deal with our climate crisis, and restore America's standing in the world. The enormity of the challenges require someone who knows how to inspire millions to get involved to change the direction of our country, and someone who will be willing to change business as usual in Washington. Senator Barack Obama has proved he can and will be that President.[13]

After Barack Obama's election in 2008, John Podesta and at least ten other CAP staff members were brought in to handle the White House transition, and continue to serve amongst Obama's most influential advisors. What sort of man is Podesta? His is a harder Left version of Bill Clinton. Podesta cut his political teeth in the anti-Vietnam War movement and on Eugene McCarthy's failed presidential run in 1968. He worked with Bill Clinton for anti-war candidate Joseph Duffy's unsuccessful Senate campaign in Connecticut, and they worked together again on the George McGovern presidential campaign in 1972. During the Clinton administration's first term in office, John Podesta held positions as White House staff secretary and as an assistant to the president. I first met Podesta in 1997, when he returned after a two-year leave of absence to work for Bill Clinton as deputy chief of staff, becoming chief of staff the following year. One of Podesta's jobs was handling the "bimbo eruptions" of Paula Jones and Monica Lewinsky.

Robert Dreyfuss, writing in the leftwing magazine *The Nation*, said of Podesta and CAP, "In looking at Podesta's center, there's no escaping the imprint of the Clintons. It's not completely wrong to see it as a shadow government, a kind of Clinton White-House-in-exile."[14] Or, as it turned out, the Obama administration in-embryo.

Another key player, and one that operates in the shadows, is Harold Ickes. One might think of him as Soros' unofficial director for the greater umbrella Shadow Party. Soros and Morton Halperin turned to Ickes to help Podesta launch CAP. More notably, Harold Ickes was Bill Clinton's Deputy Chief of Staff and was perhaps the Rahm Emanuel of his day, famous for playing political hardball. Harold Ickes' father, Harold LeClair Ickes, was Franklin D. Roosevelt's Secretary of the Interior. Like Clinton and Podesta, the younger Harold Ickes was active in the anti-war movement and worked on the presidential campaigns of Eugene McCarthy in 1968 and George McGovern in 1972.

Harold Ickes met Bill Clinton when both worked for a program entitled Operation Pursestrings, a grass roots lobbying effort seeking to cut off all military aid to South Vietnam in 1970 as a vehicle for forcing an end to the war. I first met Ickes during Clinton's re-election campaign of 1996. We'd often ride in the Control Vehicle during the many presidential motorcades that occurred in the next two years.

Hillary Clinton admired Ickes' ability to suppress the numerous scandals that encircled her husband and the White House, and she put him in charge of a special unit tasked with such matters. Oftentimes, I'd overhear his conversations with his subordinates as the Monica Lewinsky scandal came to full light. David Brock, in his book *The Seduction of Hillary Rodham*, refers to Ickes special unit as the "Shadow Counsel's Office." It seems an apt description to me.

Harold Ickes and Hillary Clinton had a close personal relationship, and Hillary chose Ickes to be the chief campaign advisor for her successful run for the United States Senate in 2000.

But Ickes also developed a close working relationship with George Soros. Ickes launched six of the seven original core organizations of the Shadow Party: the Center for American Progress (CAP), the Thunder Road Group, America Coming Together, America Votes, the Media Fund, and Joint Victory Campaign 2004. Though Ickes fought hard for Hillary Clinton to win the Democrat nomination for president in 2008, he remains a key Soros ally in the Democrat Party and is apparently reconciled to Barack Obama.

Another key figure emerging from the Shadow Party is Anthony K. "Van" Jones, who made a brief but notorious appearance in the Obama administration. Obama appointed Jones as his "green jobs czar." There are at least thirty-two "czars" in the Obama administration. Among these positions that operate outside the formal executive structure of the government, and report directly to Barack Obama, are the AIDS Czar, the Auto Recovery Czar, the California Water Czar, the Car Czar, the Climate Czar, the Domestic Violence Czar, the Faith-Based Czar, the Great Lakes Czar, the Guantanamo Closure Czar, the Pay Czar, the Regulatory Czar, the Science Czar, the Sudan Czar, the TARP Czar, the Weapons Czar, and the WMD Czar. As "czars," they are not subject to confirmation hearings, which can be a convenient way to cloak radical backgrounds, but in Jones' case, he couldn't survive the media's scrutiny.

A self-described black nationalist, Jones graduated with a law degree from Yale Law School and found his niche as an activist in Oakland, California. Jones became politically active when he was arrested and briefly jailed in the Los Angeles riots that followed the verdicts in the Rodney King case. That experience "radicalized" Jones. "I met all these young radical people of color. I mean really radical: communists and anarchists," recalled Jones. "And it was, like, 'This is what I need to be a part of.' I spent the next ten years of my life working with a lot of those people I met in jail, trying to be a revolutionary."[15]

Jones formed a radical socialist group called Standing Together to Organize a Revolutionary Movement, or STORM, a Bay Area Communist collective. During this time, Jones also headed the Ella Baker Center, a "social justice" group. Between 1999 and 2009, the Baker Center received more than $1 million in funding and support from George Soros' OSI.

Following the attacks of 9/11, Jones joined a group of fellow radicals in signing the "9/11 Truth Statement," claiming that the attacks in New York and the Pentagon had been perpetrated by President George W. Bush.

On March 10, 2009, Barack Obama named Jones to be his green jobs czar, but Jones was forced to resign six months later when his radical background came out. In 2010 Jones became a "senior fellow" at the Center for American Progress.

Finally, in the same ideological vein as George Soros and the Shadow Party, there is Rahm "Rahmbo" Emanuel, Barack Obama's Chief of Staff. Emanuel and I worked together in the Clinton White House where he was a senior policy advisor, but even then he acted like he was in charge of White House operations.

Every morning, Emanuel would head downstairs to the White House Mess, the restaurant in the basement of the West Wing staffed by Navy chefs and cooks, and start his newspaper reading ritual. He'd breeze through the *New York Times*, the *Washington Post*, and the *Los Angeles Times*, among others, looking for the next potential scandal or a crisis he could capitalize on, throwing the papers on the floor when he was finished—and leaving them for the Navy staff to pick up after he left. I'll confess, I found him narcissistic and pompous, and I didn't appreciate his penchant for profanity. Nobody could throw more four-letter words around as effortlessly as Rahm Emanuel—not even Hillary Clinton. More troubling, in my two years at the White House, Rahm Emanuel never paid his Mess bill, leaving the U.S. Navy to pick up his tab.

Emanuel is an important figure in the Democrat Party. Getting his start in hardball Chicago politics, he worked on Clinton's presidential campaign, worked in the White House, and then left to make a financial killing as an investment banker. In 2000, Clinton appointed Emanuel to the Board of Directors for the Federal Home Loan Mortgage Corporation (Freddie Mac). During his time on the board, Freddie Mac was besieged with accounting and fraud scandals, and Emanuel resigned in 2001, to successfully run for Congress in Illinois.

In spite of his young tenure in Congress, Emanuel was elected as Chairman of the Democratic Caucus, elevating him to number four in the Democratic leadership pecking order. He quickly became a close advisor to Barack Obama and, on November 6, 2008, Obama named Emanuel to be the White House Chief of Staff, where he soon became famous for saying, "Rule one: Never allow a crisis to go to waste."[16]

That Obama would appoint Emanuel as his chief of staff was the first clue, for many, that Obama might not govern as the post-partisan independent that they were hoping for—it certainly did not presage a "kinder, gentler" presidency. But it might have taken a little longer to realize the even grimmer political truth: Obama was committed to playing tough, Chicago-style politics against his domestic opponents, but such toughness would have no role in his foreign policy decisions against our enemies.

In foreign policy Obama is a true disciple of the Soros Democrats—a globalist, an internationalist, someone who thinks that the nation state is passé and that America's pursuit of its national interests is detrimental to world order. His foreign policy is only a more leftist, radical replay of Bill Clinton's foreign policy, shaped by some of the very same advisors. I doubt that's what the American people thought they were voting for when they elected Barack Obama president, but that indeed is what they've gotten.

Chapter 3

THE COMMANDER-IN-COOL

"The Dems have a war room for everything but war."[1]

—Dennis Miller

Barack Obama is a solipsist, a self-assured Commander-in-Cool. He views himself as the personification of a completely new American foreign policy that will redress our manifold sins in the world. He likes to position himself as the cosmopolitan savior we've needed after all those years of blundering, parochial, ignorant, near criminally aggressive foreign policy—when what the world needed was a president with a better, more multicultural understanding. He's hip, he's hot, he's our first post-racial, post-American president. He's the global healer for a world hungering for his touch.

How does he heal the world? By making serial apologies for America, bowing to our enemies, and snubbing our allies. But when he makes his apologies, it is clear that he sees himself as distinct from the America for which he is apologizing. Nothing is actually his fault; it's all the fault of the bad old America that once was, the America he is going to transform into a new, better, less nationalistic global citizen. His favorite target for blame of course is his predecessor, George W. Bush. No president in memory has so incessantly attacked his predecessor. But if Obama likes to dish it out, he's shown himself to be remarkably thin-skinned about taking any form of criticism of his sanctity. To listen to Obama, it seems impossible that he could do anything wrong; it seems impossible to believe that his predecessor did anything right. The president I worked for, Bill Clinton, was, like many baby-boomers, a narcissist, but not to the extreme degree we see in Barack Obama. And Bill Clinton, for all his many flaws (for which I make no apologies) was at least someone who viewed politics as a matter of give and take. He didn't see his role as the spiritual (and socialist) cleansing of a corrupt (and capitalist) America.

As Newt Gingrich, who had to negotiate with Bill Clinton, has noted, Obama seems to lack centrist instincts or even a willingness to compromise in a centrist way; he is truly a man of the hard Left. "He's not like Bill Clinton. Bill Clinton was an Arkansas, Southern Baptist, sort of understood middle America. While he had some Yale overtones being liberal, the truth is Bill Clinton was quite happy to move to the right."[2] For Obama such a move would be an utter betrayal of who he is.

Obama's father and stepfather weren't Americans, and he spent part of his life in Indonesia. These experiences have given him a different set of reference points than most Americans. He is embarrassed by, and quite frankly probably doesn't understand, notions of America's exceptionalism, as in the interview where he famously said: "I believe in American exceptionalism, just as I suspect that the Brits believe in British exceptionalism and the Greeks believe in Greek exceptionalism." As Charles Krauthammer has noted, "If we're all exceptional, no one is."[3] But that really is the point—Obama does not see America as exceptional; he sees America as just another country. Or actually it's worse than that, given his leftist ideology. He believes that America is a typical Western imperialist country that is the cause of many of the world's problems; he believes that our history abounds with recklessness and arrogant interventionism. These are the views he imbibed from his mother, from Frank Marshall Davis, from Bill Ayers, Bernardine Dohrn, and Jeremiah Wright.

If we think of Barack Obama as the "cool" president—the president who can move easily in leftist academic circles and in Hollywood, who is at one with the leftist Zeitgeist—what does that entail?

Obama grew up with leftist mentors in the 1960s and 1970s, and he has inherited much of that baggage. Just as the New Left of the 1960s marked a radical break with the more mainstream liberalism of leaders like Harry Truman, John F. Kennedy, and Lyndon Johnson, so too does Obama's leftism mark a new development, an expansion of the radicalism of the 1960s and 1970s.

The New Left itself grew out of a radical student movement led by Tom Hayden and his comrades in the Students for a Democratic Society (SDS)—the same SDS that produced the Weather Underground of Obama's later friends Bill Ayers and Bernardine Dohrn. The ideological manifesto of the SDS, 1962's Port Huron Statement, asserted that America was responsible for global conflict and the social ills of racism, materialism, militarism, poverty, and exploitation. By 1968, Hayden and the New Left were staging riots outside the Democratic National Convention in Chicago in order to undermine the candidacy of the Democrats' pro-military, anti-Communist Hubert Humphrey.

By 1972, New Left activists had burrowed deeply into the Democrat Party. The leftists pushed George McGovern to the Democrat presidential nomination and used antiwar fervor to elect seventy-six new Democrats to the House of Representatives and eight to the Senate. Included among the new congressmen were radicals Ron Dellums (an open socialist), Bella Abzug (an anti-war feminist), Robert Drinan (an anti-war, pro-abortion priest who finally left office after Pope John Paul II demanded it), and former Black

Panther Bobby Rush. Hayden himself, who had spent the previous decade preaching revolution, was elected to office in California that year.

The antiwar New Leftists took command of the Democrat Party, and they have not relinquished it. In the Carter administration and since, the Democrat Party has been the party of foreign policy appeasement and apology. Jeane Kirkpatrick spoke of this transition in her famous speech at the 1984 Republican convention. Kirkpatrick was a lifelong Democrat herself until 1985, after she had served as President Ronald Reagan's ambassador to the United Nations. In her speech she praised the earlier generations Democrats who had helped shape NATO, the Marshall Plan, and the Alliance for Progress, who defended American interests and ideals. But she was appalled at how liberals, whom she dubbed "the San Francisco Democrats," had come to "blame America first"—no matter the good we tried to do in the world, and no matter the culpability of the terrorists, Communists, and thugs we opposed. As she said, in part, "When Marxist dictators shoot their way to power in Central America, the San Francisco Democrats don't blame the guerrillas and their Soviet allies, they blame United States policies of 100 years ago. But then, they always blame America first."[4]

The 1960s and 1970s antiwar movement was the formative political experience for the Clinton generation of Democrats. They came to power doubting American motives and seeing moral superiority in war protesters with radical ideals (like themselves) over crew-cutted war fighters who believed in simple patriotism, obedience to duty, self-sacrifice, and opposition to communism. Obama comes from the next generation and takes what Ambassador Kirkpatrick called the "blame America first" mentality a step further.

Unlike the Greatest Generation, the generation that endured the Great Depression and fought in World War II and Korea, Obama comes from an ideological starting point entirely different. America needs a radical reformation; it is not at its core essentially good; it is a country that throughout its history has been fundamentally racist and sexist and in constant need of internal liberation movements. America's military defense of South Vietnam was not a selfless, noble action to protect a people from Communist aggression; it was war of foreign domination by America over the popular, progressive forces of (the Communist) Ho Chi Minh. These are the views of the 1960s radical Left, and these are the views Obama has inherited, and they color his every action today. He believes that America is racist, sexist, and imperialist, and that it is his role to rein in America abroad and reform her at home. If you understand this, you understand why his number one priority in Afghanistan is not to win the war, but to withdraw American troops by a definite deadline; why he is pressing the gay civil rights agenda on the military as a top priority (at a time when the military is under stress enough fighting two wars); and why his Justice Department has declined to pursue an obvious case of voter intimidation against black nationalists who patrolled a polling place in Philadelphia.

To be cool, Obama will be on the side of Hollywood and the academic Left on every major issue. He will be inclined to think the best of leftist or anti-American dictators around the world—that they are working for progressive ends and that their anti-Americanism is a rational response to American arrogance, stupidity, and imperialism. He will never criticize or condemn radical Islam, because that would violate the tenets of multiculturalism; just like the Hollywood and academic Left, Obama will not criticize Muslims who murder in the name of jihad—even when they target groups, like homosexuals, who are among the sanctified to liberals—but he will, at least in private, mock traditional, conservative Christians as in his famous comment on the campaign trail in 2008: "You go into these small towns in Pennsylvania and, like a lot of small towns in the Midwest, the jobs have been gone now for 25 years and nothing's replaced them. And it's not surprising, then, they get bitter, they cling to guns or religion or antipathy to people who aren't like them or anti-immigrant sentiment or anti-trade sentiment as a way to explain their frustrations."[5] Once again, at bottom, Obama sees Americans as fundamentally bitter and bigoted.

So it's perhaps not surprising that he thinks he needs to be constantly apologizing for his countrymen who all too readily cling to their guns and their religion and their small town narrow-mindedness when they should think of themselves of citizens of the world, as he does. Obama went to Europe and told the Europeans that "America has shown arrogance and been dismissive, even derisive" of our European allies. British columnist Toby Young said that Obama's speech "went further than any United States president in history in criticising his own country's actions while standing on foreign soil."[6] Obama also thought it important to remind the Europeans that while America had gotten "sidetracked on Iraq"—an interesting way to refer to taking down one of the most anti-American dictators on the planet, one whose forces routinely fired on American planes patrolling the no-fly zones in Iraq, and who harbored terrorists who murdered Americans—"I think it is important for Europe to understand that . . . I am president and George Bush is not president."[7]

When Obama spoke at the United Nations, he again inevitably apologized for "America acting alone" rather than as a good global citizen, but he was quick to offer the hope that is Obama, saying that he was "well aware of the expectations that accompany my presidency around the world."[8] As Nile Gardiner, a former foreign policy aide to Margaret Thatcher, noted, it is no surprise that Obama is popular at the United Nations. The United Nations "loves Barack Obama because he is weak." As Gardiner wrote, "Obama's popularity at the UN boils down essentially to his willingness to downplay American global power. He is the first American president who has made an art form out of apologizing for the United States, which he has done on numerous occasions on foreign soil, from Strasbourg to Cairo. The Obama mantra appears to be—ask not what your country can do for you, but what you can do to atone for your country. This is a message that goes down very well in a world that is still seething with anti-Americanism."

Gardiner went further, arguing that Obama's refusal to stand up for traditional American values and America's interests, in a word, his multiculturalism, made him popular at the United Nations but should not make him popular with those who believe in a strong America and its defense of freedom and human rights. "It is natural that much of the UN will embrace an American president who declines to offer strong American leadership. A president who engages dictators like Mahmoud Ahmadinejad and Hugo Chavez will naturally gain respect from the leaders of the more than 100 members of the United Nations who are currently designated as 'partly free' or 'not free' by respected watchdog Freedom House."

Gardiner concludes, "The UN is not a club of democracies—who still remain a minority within its membership—it is a vast melting pot of free societies, socialist regimes and outright tyrannies. Obama's clear lack of interest in human rights issues is a big seller at the UN, where at least half its members have poor human rights records."[9]

Nowhere, perhaps, has Obama been keener to apologize than to the Muslim world. On January 27, 2009, Barack Obama's very first television interview as our newly inaugurated president was with the Saudi-funded Arabic network Al Arabiya, during which he told millions of Muslims that his job as he saw it was "to communicate that the Americans are not your enemy. We sometimes make mistakes. We have not been perfect,"[10] and that America must once again establish "the same respect and partnership that America had with the Muslim world as recently as 20 or 30 years ago."[11]

Let's recall that thirty years ago, Iranian Muslims were holding American diplomats hostage in Tehran; that the new Islamic Republic of Iran was a state sponsor of terror; that its radical leader the Ayatollah Khomeini declared war on the United States; and that Tehran's streets were packed with revolutionaries shouting "Death to America." Thirty years ago, the Palestinian Liberation Organization was conducting its continuing campaign of terror. Thirty years ago, Saddam Hussein ruthlessly seized control of Muslim Iraq and launched his own murderous reign of terror. Twenty-seven years ago, Hezbollah, the terror group created and financed by Iran, bombed the United States Embassy and U.S. Marine Headquarters in Beirut, Lebanon, killing 257 Americans and 58 French soldiers. Twenty years ago, Saddam Hussein's Iraq was invading its Muslim neighbor Kuwait to seize control of its oil fields and other riches.

Completely contrary to Barack Obama's view of America and the Muslim world, the last thirty years have been marked by one radical Islamic attack after another on Americans and American interests, while America has consistently come to the aid of threatened Muslims in locales ranging from Somalia to Bosnia to Kosovo to Kuwait to Iraq to Afghanistan. Obama is too much of a multiculturalist to note the distinction, but as president of the United States and commander of our armed forces, he should be obliged to.

But that is not Obama's way, as former White House speechwriter and terror expert Marc Thiessen noted after Obama's speech in Cairo on June 4, 2009, a speech that was touted as a speech to the Muslim world and titled "A New Beginning." In that speech, Thiessen writes, Obama

> threw the men and women of our military and our intelligence community under the bus when he declared, in front of a Muslim audience, that the attacks of 9/11 "led us to act contrary to our ideals." On foreign soil, he accused our intelligence professionals who stopped the next 9/11 of committing torture—validating years of al-Qaeda propaganda. He talked about closing GTMO [the detention facility at Guantanamo Bay, Cuba] without any defense of the good men and women who run it—even though his own attorney general, Eric Holder, has admitted it was a model prison. If he was going to discuss these topics in the Middle East, he at least owed it to our troops and intelligence professionals to say what dozens of investigations have proven: that there was no systematic abuse of detainees at

GTMO or anywhere else. Instead, Obama echoed al-Qaeda's calumnies against them—and did so in a foreign land. This is unprecedented. It is shameful. And they deserve better.[12]

But not only does Barack Obama come from a radical past, he comes from a radical tradition that has nothing but contempt for the military and military values. He is only the second president to occupy the Oval Office in the last sixty-five years with absolutely no military experience to draw from. The first was Bill Clinton, who dodged a Reserve Officer Training Corps commitment he had made during the Vietnam War solely to maintain his "political viability." Clinton is the first commander in chief to have written of how "so many fine people have come to find themselves still loving their country but loathing the military."[13]

Obama was too young to have served during the Vietnam War, but it is clear that he never had any interest in serving the military at all. In fact, his derision toward the military is remarkably similar to Clinton's.

On March 10, 1983, just prior to his graduation from Columbia University, Obama wrote an article for the school's magazine, *Sundial*. In "Breaking the War Mentality," young Obama offered a glimpse into the psyche of the man who would one day command the greatest military the world has ever known. His poorly written article, dotted with misspelled words and awkward grammar, decries the "relentless, often silent spread of militarism in the country." He was critical of the "military-industrial interests" and "their billion dollar erector sets," while he promoted a "nuclear free world" (an ambition that he retains now that he is president of the United States).[14]

For support in the article, Obama cited Rastafarian reggae musician Peter Tosh as his foreign policy expert. "When Peter Tosh sings that 'everybody's' asking for peace, but nobody's asking for 'justice,' one is forced to wonder whether disarmament or arms controls issues, severed from economic and political issues, might be another instance of focusing on the symptoms of a problem, instead of the disease itself."[15] Somebody pass the ganja.

Twelve years later, in his autobiography *Dreams from My Father*, his anti-military sentiment hadn't waned. Even in the wake of 9/11, Obama seemed to imply that what was needed was more understanding of, to use the 1970s jargon, "where the terrorists came from" rather than responding militarily and legally to a murderous threat. Obama wrote,

> I know, I have seen, the desperation and disorder of the powerless: how it twists the lives of children on the streets of Jakarta or Nairobi in much the same way as it does the lives of children on Chicago's South Side, how narrow the path is for them between humiliation and untrammeled fury, how easily they slip into violence and despair. I know that the response of the powerful to this disorder—alternating as it does between a dull complacency and, when the disorder spills out of its proscribed confines, a steady, unthinking application of force, of longer prison sentences and more sophisticated military hardware—is inadequate to the task.[16]

It takes some doing to start with the terrorist outrage of 9/11 and to turn it into a condemnation of "the powerful" (read: the United States) for its "dull complacency" and its reliance on law enforcement and the military to combat crime and terrorism.

When Obama campaigned for the presidency in 2008, he promised,

> I'll stop spending $9 billion a month in Iraq. I'm the only major candidate who opposed this war from the beginning. And as president I will end it. . . . I will cut tens of billions of dollars in wasteful spending [on national defense]. I will cut investments in unproven missile defense systems. I will not weaponize space. I will slow our development of future combat systems. And I

will institute an independent "Defense Priorities Board" to ensure that the Quadrennial Defense Review is not used to justify unnecessary spending. . . . I will set a goal of a world without nuclear weapons. To seek that goal, I will not develop new nuclear weapons; I will seek a global ban on the production of fissile material; and I will negotiate with Russia to take our ICBMs off hair-trigger alert, and to achieve deep cuts in our nuclear arsenals.[17]

While no one is in favor of wasteful spending, one has to ask whether the appropriate time to cut military spending is while fighting two wars (and Obama has still not pulled all our troops out of successfully liberated and democratic Iraq, a transformation he opposed). Or whether the appropriate time to cut investments in missile defense systems is while rogue states like North Korea and Iran are bent on developing nuclear weapons. Or whether the appropriate time to slow our development of future combat systems is when we are facing threats from a Communist China looking to expand its influence in the Pacific; from Latin American dictators like Hugo Chavez making common cause with Iran; and from other potential enemies, including radical Islam (an enemy that the Obama administration prefers not even to name).

One of the essential tenets of military leadership is that you can't order someone to do something that you yourself are unwilling to do. Soldiers want to know that their commanders understand what it is like in the trenches, that the sacrifices they are making are not lightly regarded or treated with disrespect. But it is hard to imagine that many in the military can believe this of Barack Obama (any more than they could of Bill Clinton, a sad fact I know all too well and personally). They know that Obama never served in the military, and he knows little about it—even mispronouncing the word "corpsman" as "corpse man" in a speech at the National Prayer Breakfast on February 4, 2010.[18] The men and women serving in our military know that Obama opposed their mission in Iraq.

And many of them have to wonder what he supposes their mission is in Afghanistan.

When Obama was asked to define "victory" in Afghanistan on ABC's *Nightline* in July 2009, Obama responded, "I'm always worried about using the word 'victory' because, you know, it invokes this notion of Emperor Hirohito coming down and signing a surrender to MacArthur."[19] Notwithstanding the fact that Emperor Hirohito was not at the armistice ceremony and did not sign the surrender—a mistake that, if George W. Bush had made it, the media would have ridiculed—can you imagine a commander in chief even saying this sort of thing with his country at war? He has hundreds of thousands of young Americans putting their lives on the line daily, fighting and dying in Iraq, Afghanistan, and elsewhere, and he chooses not to talk in terms of "victory."

On the other hand, Obama had no problem crowing about "victory" when it came to cramming government-controlled health care down our collective gullet. Speaking in the East Room of the White House shortly after signing the Health Insurance Reform Bill into law, he blustered, "And of course, this victory was also made possible by the painstaking work of members of this administration, including our outstanding Secretary of Health and Human Services, Kathleen Sebelius—(applause)—and one of the unsung heroes of this effort, an extraordinary woman who led the reform effort from the White House, Nancy-Ann DeParle."[20] In "Obamaland"[21] it's perfectly acceptable to celebrate "victory" in a health care bill that the majority of the American people didn't want; but it's a mistake to think of victory over a foe that has targeted the United States for destruction. Ronald Reagan and George H. W. Bush were able to achieve victory over Soviet communism; Obama prefers to rule out such an eventuality against radical Islam, perhaps because he can't even confess that radical Islam is the enemy.

When Obama became president, his ambition was to "reset" America's relations with the world, particularly in the Middle East, in the war on terror, and with Russia (where Hillary Clinton presented Russian Foreign Minister Sergei Lavrov with a box with a red button on it and the Russian word "peregruzka," which the Clinton delegation presumed meant "reset"; in fact, as Lavrov pointed out to her, it means "overcharge").[22]

On Obama's very first day in office, he announced his willingness to have talks with rogue state Iran "without preconditions" (a concession that won him nothing but Iranian contempt). The following day he signed Executive Orders 13491 and 13492 closing CIA detention facilities and ordering that terrorist detainees held at Guantanamo Bay, Cuba, be released, transferred, or tried in civilian courts.

Following up on a campaign promise to shift the focus and the fight from Iraq to Afghanistan, Obama announced an increase in troop levels of 17,000 to "stabilize a deteriorating situation in Afghanistan," an area he said had not received the "strategic attention, direction and resources it urgently requires"[23] (although the commanding general in charge of the Afghanistan theater, General David McKiernan, had requested between 20,000 and 30,000 additional troops). Shortly thereafter, Obama replaced General McKiernan with General Stanley McChrystal, though McChrystal would have to resign in June 2010 after his staff made disparaging remarks about the administration and its understanding of the war.

In March 2009, continuing his Iranian outreach program that has borne no fruit, only scorn, Barack Obama videotaped a message for "Nowruz," the traditional Persian New Year, to the people and government of Iran, a supposed olive branch that was quickly rebuffed by Mahmoud Ahmadinejad. As the London *Daily Telegraph* reported, "In an unusually swift reaction to Mr Obama's overture, Aliakbar Javanfekr, an aide to President Mahmoud Ahmadinejad, said Iran welcomed 'the interest of the American government to settle differences.' But he said that the US government 'should realise its previous mistakes and make an effort to amend them.'"[24]

Of course, Obama was willing to make apologies for every alleged American "mistake." In fact, his "Bash Bush, Apologize for

America Tour" began in April 2009 in Strasbourg, France. "In dealing with terrorism, we can't lose sight of our values and who we are. That's why I closed Guantanamo. That's why I made very clear that we will not engage in certain interrogation practices. I don't believe that there is a contradiction between our security and our values. And when you start sacrificing your values, when you lose yourself, then over the long term that will make you less secure."[25]

Obama apparently preferred not to know the facts, rather than the leftist rhetoric about what actually went on at Guantanamo and exactly how American interrogators conducted themselves. Not only did the interrogators develop intelligence that led to the successful thwarting of American attacks, they did so fully within the confines of the law and within the confines of objective moral reasoning, as Marc Thiessen has shown in his masterful and authoritative book *Courting Disaster*. In fact, in Thiessen's words, "Barack Obama arguably did more damage to America's national security in his first 100 days of office than any president in American history. In shutting down the CIA program, Obama eliminated our nation's most important tool to prevent the terrorists from striking America. And in releasing highly sensitive documents describing the details of how we have interrogated captured terrorists—and the limits of our interrogation techniques—Obama gave critical intelligence to the enemy." And, as Thiessen goes on to illustrate, that was only the tip of the iceberg.[26]

But defending America is less important to Obama than apologizing for America's sins. In a speech to the Turkish Parliament in Ankara, Turkey, he announced, "The United States is still working through some of our own darker periods in our history. Facing the Washington Monument that I spoke of is a memorial of Abraham Lincoln, the man who freed those who were enslaved even after Washington led our Revolution. Our country still struggles with the legacies of slavery and segregation, the past treatment of Native Americans."[27]

In April 2009, Obama delivered a speech in Prague where he stated America's commitment to a world without nuclear weapons. Also in April, he delivered an apologetic speech on Latin America in Trinidad and Tobago, where he promised that "the United States will be willing to acknowledge past errors where those errors have been made." Shortly after, he lifted the travel restrictions to Cuba.

On June 4, 2009, he delivered his now famous speech at Cairo University in Egypt, calling for "a new beginning" in relations between the United States and the Arab world, and he suggested that America, Europe, and Israel were sources for the problems in the Middle East while downplaying the obvious root causes that have plagued the region for centuries: authoritarianism and corruption, not Western democracy. As historian Victor Davis Hanson noted, "The great colonizers of the Middle East were the Ottoman Muslims, who for centuries ruled with an iron fist. The 20th century movements of Baathism, Pan-Arabism and Nasserism—largely homegrown totalitarian ideologies—did far more damage over the past half-century to the Middle East than the legacy of European colonialism."[28]

Obama also dramatically misrepresented the nature of the conflict between radical Islam and the West. "Islam has a proud tradition of tolerance," he said. "We see it in the history of Andalusia and Cordoba during the Inquisition." Actually, we don't see it in the history of Andalusia and Cordoba during the Inquisition, because these were Christian-run cities in that time period—and it rather glosses over the fact that Islam was the great aggressor religion, not Christianity, which launched its crusades in self-defense. Nor have we seen much tolerance in the Islamic Middle East within our lifetimes, or certainly since the Iranian Revolution of 1979.

In August 2009, French President Nicolas Sarkozy was so taken aback by Obama's performance on the world stage, he asked his staff, "Est-il faible? (Is he weak?)." Professor Eliot Cohen, reviewing "the first year of President Barack Obama's foreign policy," seemed to agree, saying that if it "were a law firm in Charles Dickens's London, it would have a name like Bumble, Stumble and Skid." In partial summary,

> It began with apologies to the Muslim world that went nowhere, a doomed attempt to beat Israel into line, utopian pleas to abolish nuclear weapons, unreciprocated concessions to Russia, and a curt note to the British to take back the bust of Winston Churchill that had graced the Oval Office. It continued with principled offers of serious negotiation to an Iranian regime too busy torturing, raping and killing demonstrators, and building new underground nuclear facilities, to take them up. Subsequently Beijing smothered domestic coverage of a presidential visit but did give the world the spectacle of the American commander in chief getting a talking-to about fiscal responsibility from a Communist chieftain.[29]

On September 17, 2009, Barack Obama shocked and surprised our allies in Eastern Europe when he announced that he was reversing President George W. Bush's decision to deploy anti-missile systems in Poland and the Czech Republic. Once again, President Obama seemed to get matters exactly backwards: somehow the answer to the problem of nuclear proliferation was not to deploy defensive shields, but to remove them—and Obama overturned America's promise to deploy these systems without getting a return commitment from Iran or anyone else. The Obama style of negotiation was simple surrender—and springing a nasty surprise on loyal allies.

On September 24, 2009, Obama became the first sitting president ever to preside over a meeting of the United Nations Security Council with a presentation themed around his youthful utopian dreams of a planet without nuclear weapons. This was where Obama modestly announced, "I am well aware of the expectations that accompany my presidency around the world." But among those unimpressed, again, was French President Nicolas Sarkozy. "President Obama dreams of a world without weapons ... but right in front of us, two countries are doing the exact opposite.... What good has proposals for dialogue brought the international community?" asked Sarkozy. "More uranium enrichment and declarations by the leaders of Iran to wipe a U.N. member state off of the map."[30]

Sarkozy went further: "We are right to talk about the future [of arms control]. But the present comes before the future, and the present includes two major nuclear crises [the nuclear programs of Iran and North Korea]. We live in the real world, not in a virtual one."[31] It is ironic that the president of France has a better appreciation than does that president of the United States that American leadership and military might have been a stabilizing force in the world, not a threat. America's nuclear deterrence has been a safeguard of world peace and a defender of freedom. America's nuclear arsenal is not the problem—the proliferation of nuclear weapons to rogue regimes is the problem.

In 1972, nine countries had stockpiles of ballistic missiles; today there are at least twenty-five. It is open to serious question whether such fanatic regimes as Iran and North Korea will be deterred in the classic sense, or whether they might slip weapons to terrorist organizations, assuming that there will not be enough evidence for a president, especially a president like Obama, to retaliate. But Obama seems to have a very thin understanding of American nuclear doctrine.

In April 2010, Barack Obama reversed sixty-five years of U.S. nuclear weapons policy. In the administration's Nuclear Posture Review, the United States promised not to use nuclear weapons or threaten the use of nuclear weapons against any nonnuclear states that are in compliance with the nonproliferation treaty—even if those states attack America with chemical or biological weapons of mass destruction. He also announced the previously highly classified size of America's nuclear arsenal.

"We think it is in our national interest to be as transparent as we can about the nuclear program of the United States," explained Secretary of State Hillary Clinton. "We think that builds confidence." For whom? North Korea? Iran? Hillary Clinton called the new doctrine a "milestone," but toward what end?

As Obama said in his speech in Prague in April 2009: "I state clearly and with conviction America's commitment to seek the peace and security of a world without nuclear weapons. I'm not naïve. This goal will not be reached quickly—perhaps not in my lifetime. It will take patience and persistence. But now we, too, must ignore the voices who tell us that the world cannot change. We have to insist, 'Yes, we can.'"[32] As with so much else, it appears Obama expects our national security to rest...on him. But what else should we expect of our Commander-in-Cool. As the brilliant columnist Mark Steyn writes, "There are millions of people like Barack Obama, the eternal students of a vast lethargic transnational campus for whom global compassion and multicultural pose are merely the modish gloss on a cult of radical grandiose narcissism."[33] That narcissism was on display even during the 20th anniversary commemoration of the fall of the Berlin Wall in November 2009. Obama declined to appear in person, but sent a video. In his remarks, he managed to make no reference to Ronald Reagan's famous "tear down this wall" speech, but did manage to observe that "few would have foreseen...that [Germany's] American ally would be led by a man of African descent."[34]

One problem with that narcissism is that while Obama loves to rail against an arrogant America, it's hard to imagine a more arrogant national leader than Barack Obama—a man utterly convinced of his moral and intellectual superiority, who seems to care not a whit for our allies, even as he tries to cozy up to dictators. In June 2009, during an official visit to France, Obama declined to dine with French President Nicolas Sarkozy and his wife, Carla Bruni, even though they were essentially neighbors. Obama was apparently showing his pique at what he considered Sarkozy's condescending attitude. (Well, Sarkozy's French, after all). But the Germans, on the same European trip, thought they had been snubbed as well, because Obama apparently does not like German Chancellor Angela Merkel.[35] When visiting Norway to collect his Nobel Prize, Obama cancelled a lunch date with King Harald V, a dinner in his honor, and several other ceremonies the prize winners normally attend.

Particularly troubling is Obama's treatment of America's closest ally, Great Britain. The United States and Britain have fought side by side in two world wars, in Korea, in the Persian Gulf, in Iraq, and in Afghanistan. The British and American "special relationship" is one of kinship and common values, values that have linked FDR and Winston Churchill, Ronald Reagan and Margaret Thatcher. In the immediate aftermath of 9/11, in a show of solidarity and support, Great Britain loaned America a bust of Sir Winston Churchill and, appropriately, President George Bush placed it in the Oval Office. One of Barack Obama's first acts in office was to send the bust packing back to Britain—presumably because he regards Winston Churchill as a wicked imperialist.

Other Obama gaffes speak to his narcissism and arrogance. When he visited the United Kingdom and met the Queen of England for the first time, he presented the Queen Mother with the gift of an Apple iPod...containing recordings of his own speeches for her enjoyment, and, no doubt, edification. On another occasion, after he'd turned down several requests for a personal meeting with the British prime minister, Barack Obama presented Gordon Brown with a box set of twenty-five DVDs featuring some of America's most acclaimed films...in a format that doesn't work in British DVD players, and which Brown, who is vision-impaired, might have had a hard time watching in any event. And it certainly seemed a cheap and tawdry gift compared to the what the prime minister gave to Obama: an ornamental penholder made from wood from a British ship that fought the slave trade, the HMS *Gannet*, and that was a sister ship to the HMS *Resolute*, which provided the wood for a desk that's been in the Oval Office since 1880.

Most recently, Secretary of State Hillary Clinton, while visiting Buenos Aires, Argentina, called for negotiations between Britain and Argentina over the Falkland Islands, the British territory off the Argentine coast. Although Britain has both international law and the Falkland Islanders on her side, Clinton remarked, "Now, we cannot make either one [negotiate], but we think it is the right way to proceed. So we will be saying this publicly, as I have been, and we will continue to encourage exactly the kind of discussion across the table that needs to take place."[36] It might be worth reminding Hillary that Britain actually fought a war in 1982 to defend the islands from Argentine aggression.

But the Obama administration is dismissive of British interests. An anonymous State Department official expressed the new administration's approach toward our traditional ally with blunt clarity: "There's nothing special about Britain. [It's] just the same as the other 190 countries in the world. [It] shouldn't expect special treatment."[37]

In reality, Britain has been a very special ally and continues to be. Currently, Britain has about 10,000 troops in Afghanistan, far more than any other U.S. ally.

David Manning, former British ambassador to the United States, summed up the American president from his country's point of view: "He [Obama] is an American who grew up in Hawaii, whose foreign experience was of Indonesia and who had a Kenyan father. The sentimental reflexes, if you like, are not there."[38]

Sometimes we have to wonder whether Obama's sentimental reflexes are with America, either.

Chapter 4

IT'S THE ENEMY, STUPID

"Far from being moribund, Mohammedanism is a militant and proselytizing faith.
It has already spread throughout Central Africa, raising fearless warriors at every step;
and were it not that Christianity is sheltered in the strong arms of science,
the science against which it had vainly struggled, the civilization of modern Europe
might fall, as fell the civilization of ancient Rome."

— Winston Churchill, 1899

Barack Obama has a thin skin. He is so used to fawning votaries in the media and in the public, and is so certain of his own intellect and judgment, that he has a tendency to lash out angrily at his opponents, assuming that those who do not fall in line—Rush Limbaugh, FOX News, Tea Partiers, Republicans, health care insurance companies, "fat cats" on Wall Street, British Petroleum, and the state of Arizona, to name a few—must be motivated by base prejudices like racism and greed.

But when it comes to identifying America's real enemies—the ones who are trying to kill us and are killing Americans every day—he just can't muster an interest in the fight, except to try to get out of it. The problem is there is no getting out of it. The battle between the West and radical Islam is the great ideological battle of the twenty-first century. It is a new battle in the sense that radical Islam is resurgent, and has been waging a new, long war on the West at least since the Iranian Revolution of 1979. But it is an old war in the sense that it is very nearly as old as Islam itself, which, as any familiarity with history will show, has often been a religion of military aggression against any people they consider infidels. The conflict between Islam and the West is hardly new—it goes back to Islam's conquest of Christian North Africa, Spain, and the Middle East, and its siege of the Byzantine Empire, and the consequent Christian response with the Crusades.

It's not all ancient history either. The British Empire, of necessity, was well familiar with Islam. Winston Churchill's observations, written after having fought Muslim fanatics in the Sudan in 1898 (he also knew them from India), can hardly be bettered:

How dreadful are the curses which Mohammedanism lays on its votaries! Besides the fanatical frenzy, which is as dangerous in man as hydrophobia in a dog, there is this fearful fatalistic apathy. The effects are apparent in many countries. Improvident habits, slovenly systems of agriculture, sluggish methods of commerce, and insecurity of property exist wherever the followers of the Prophet rule or live. . . .

Individual Moslems may show splendid qualities. Thousands become the brave and loyal soldiers of the Queen; all know how to die; but the influence of the religion paralyses the social development of those who follow it. No stronger retrograde force exists in the world. Far from being moribund, Mohammedanism is a militant and proselytizing faith. It has already spread throughout Central Africa, raising fearless warriors at every step; and were it not that Christianity is sheltered in the strong arms of science, the science against which it had vainly struggled, the civilization of modern Europe might fall, as fell the civilization of ancient Rome.[1]

One might quibble with whether Christianity vainly struggled with science—there's plenty of evidence that Christianity gave birth to modern science[2]—but we can only wish that President Obama were as forthright in discussing militant Islam. But instead Obama prefers his usual multicultural waffle, as though the millennium-long conflict between Islam and the West is a mere misunderstanding that can be swept under the rug. Like the proverbial ostrich, the Obama administration buries its head in the sand whenever radical Islamic terror strikes, preferring to fall back on any explanation for the violence than the one that is obviously apparent.

When U.S. Army recruiter Private William Long was gunned down in front of his office in Little Rock, Arkansas, by a jihadist named Abdulhakim Mujahid Muhammad, Barack Obama could only call it a "senseless act of violence."[3] The prosecutors assigned to the case say that Muhammad's motivation was to target soldiers "because of what they had done to Muslims in the past."[4]

When Army Major Nidal Malik Hasan shot forty-three fellow soldiers, killing thirteen and wounding thirty, at Fort Hood, Texas, as he shouted "Allahu Akbar" ("Allah is Great"), Barack Obama could only gather that it was a "horrific outburst of violence."[5] Al Qaeda spokesman Adam Gadahn called Hasan a "pioneer, a trailblazer and a role-model."[6] The Army's Chief of Staff, General George Casey, was more concerned with not offending Muslims than he was about a terrorist attacking his soldiers at one of his largest Army posts. "Our diversity, not only in our Army, but in our country, is a strength," General Casey—the Army's top general—was quick to point out. "And as horrific as this tragedy was, if our diversity becomes a casualty, I think that's worse."[7] Aside from its outrageous insensitivity to the victims' families, General Casey's comments betray the incredible, but politically correct, stupidity and meaningless obfuscation that is virtually required by the reigning liberal orthodoxy. As a matter of logic—not to mention experience of the world, including, in my case, a military deployment in the Balkans—one would think that unity rather than diversity is our strength: the unity that comes from all Americans sharing basic, fundamental, traditional American values and beliefs; and that a lack of unity is a danger, a risk, not a strength. And as far as "diversity" becoming "a casualty," it's worth noting that General Casey said this while forty-three of his soldiers were real casualties, not metaphorical ones. And just how precisely would diversity become a casualty? There is no undoing the melting pot of America; it cannot be undone and no one is seeking to undo it. But we might ask that our leaders not be so crippled by political correctness as to harbor anti-American enemies, terrorists, and killers in our midst in the name of "diversity."

In fact, illustrative of today's politically correct Pentagon under the command of Barack Obama, the Department of Defense's 86-page report following the massacre did not contain a single reference to "Islam," "Muslim," "Sharia," or "Koran," although Major Hasan had a history of anti-American statements based on his radical Islamic beliefs and is a known follower of the Muslim cleric Anwar al-Awlaki, himself an American terrorist inciting jihad from his hole in Yemen.

Similarly, the Pentagon's 2010 Quadrennial Defense Review, the 128-page report that lays out America's future military strategy and the force structure necessary to fight the nation's wars, contains not a single mention of "Islam," "Islamic," or "Islamist."

In an e-mail sent out to Pentagon staff members, the Department of Defense's Office of Security Review noted that the Obama administration "prefers to avoid using the term 'Long War' or 'Global War on Terror.' Please use 'Overseas Contingency Operation.'"

Similarly, the Obama administration's official National Security Strategy, issued May 2010 (reproduced in an appendix to this book), while targeting "climate change" as a national security priority, makes no reference to radical Islamic terrorism, preferring more generic labels.

As if that weren't bad enough, the Department of Homeland Security Secretary cannot even bring herself utter the phrase "terrorism," preferring to say "man-caused disasters."[8]

How can you win a war when you are unwilling to identify the enemy? The answer is simple: you can't. But the war will be fought against us whether Barack Obama and his advisors want to acknowledge it or not.

When Umar Faruk Abdulmutallab, the "Underwear Bomber," attempted to explode a bomb onboard a Delta Air Lines jet which, if successful, would have killed 300 people on Christmas Day 2009, Obama, while vacationing in Hawaii, called the terrorist trained in Yemen and also an adherent of al-Awlaki an "isolated extremist." Further highlighting his administration's inability and unwillingness to focus on the threat of Islamist terror, Obama's aides waited more than three hours before waking up the vacationing president to tell him the news. The vacationing president then waited three full days before making his first public statement on the attempted terror attack, and even that was limited to a quick statement before heading off to the golf links and more recreation. The Obama administration simply does not take the threat of radical Islam seriously, because in their self-imposed, politically correct, multicultural ignorance, they are not allowed to; they refuse to acknowledge that any anti-Western creed can be dangerous—it is only different and probably misunderstood by a bigoted, parochial America full of people who cling to their Bibles and their guns. Indeed, on April 7, 2009, the Department of Homeland Security, so sensitive about not offending Muslims, issued a report warning of the dangers of domestic rightwing extremists, including "groups and individuals that are dedicated to a single issue, such as opposition to abortion or immigration,"[9] as well as defenders of gun rights and returning veterans. In other words, our nation's servicemen and women might be a risk, but radical Islamists—not so much, or at least we can't say so or we'd risk making a casualty of our diversity.

I'm reminded of my former boss Bill Clinton's response immediately after the World Trade Center was bombed for the first time by Islamist terrorists in 1993, killing six Americans and wounding more than 1,000. He couldn't face the reality either. In an interview with MTV, he described that attack as having been perpetrated by someone who "did something really stupid."[10]

Indeed, with Barack Obama, we have returned to the 1990s mindset and the failed anti-terrorism policies of the Clinton administration that directly resulted in the attacks of 9/11. It's a mindset that treats radical Islam as a law enforcement issue and that presumes that terrorists are not inherently evil, they are merely victims of circumstances. Seventeen years after the first World Trade Center bombing, we're back to square one. Eric Holder, Barack Obama's attorney general, even boasts that law enforcement is now "the backbone of our national-security efforts."[11] The Justice Department's website proudly proclaims "the criminal-justice system as a counterterrorism tool."[12]

Now don't get me wrong—law enforcement and the justice system have an obvious and important role to play in counterterrorism. But it is a simple fact that we are involved in two hot wars in Iraq and Afghanistan that are part of a global war against Islamic terrorism, and that as part of that war, American special forces are spread from the Philippines to West Africa. Winning the long war means fighting the long war. It was George W. Bush's recognition after 9/11 that we were a nation at war that is responsible for all the gains—and they are big gains—we have made against radical Islamic terror. Barack Obama and Eric Holder, in their arrogant assumption of moral and intellectual superiority, think there is no such thing as radical Islamic terrorism; there are only terrorists with multiple motivations, as Holder said in testimony before the House Judiciary Committee in May 2010,[13] performing random acts of individual violence, and who are likely misunderstood in any event.

As such, American troops should come home as quickly as possible, and the primary counterterrorism tool should be lawyers and law enforcement. Obama is a wartime president who shuns the mantle of responsibility that entails.

Surprisingly, it was Hillary Clinton who made national security an issue during the Democrat presidential campaign, when one of her television ads challenged Obama's lack of experience and asked the question, "Who would you want answering the phone at 3 AM?" At the time, Obama was given a pass by the mainstream media. When Obama's call came, following the attempted bombing by underwear bomber Abdulmutallab, he didn't answer it, apparently rolling over and hitting the snooze button.

"Our enemy is not terror because terror is a state of mind and, as Americans, we refuse to live in fear," says John Brennan, the president's closest adviser on counterterrorism. "Nor do we describe our enemy as jihadists or Islamists because jihad is holy struggle, a legitimate tenet of Islam meaning to purify oneself or one's community."

As Brennan says, "The president's strategy is absolutely clear about the threat we face. Our enemy is not terrorism because terrorism is but a tactic. Moreover, describing our enemy in religious terms would lend credence to the lie propagated by al Qaeda and its affiliates to justify terrorism, that the United States is somehow at war against Islam." Brennan concludes, "The reality, of course, is that we have never been and will never be at war with Islam. After all, Islam, like so many faiths, is part of America."[14]

During the course of this speech, given at the Center for Strategic and International Studies on May 26, 2010, Brennan played the "root causes" card. Obama's national security priority, said America's chief counter-terror adviser, "includes addressing the political, economic and social forces that can make some people fall victim to the cancer of violent extremism.... And I think there's more work we need to do to understand the psychology behind terrorism. But a lot of times, the psychology is affected by the environment that has those political, social, economic factors that contribute to that."[15]

However, it is clear that America is fighting a war with radical Islamists and has been since 1979, as I show in one of the appendices to this book, titled "The Long War." According to former Attorney General Michael B. Mukasey, there have been more than twenty Islamist terror plots aimed at this country since 9/11—and that is undoubtedly a conservative figure—including plots against commuter airlines, railroads, and subways; plots against military personnel stationed here in America; and others.[16]

You would think that this continuing threat would lead an incoming president to be cautious in changing the policies of his predecessor, which had kept this country safe from subsequent attack after 9/11. But before the furnishings for his new office on 1600 Pennsylvania Avenue had even been delivered, newly elected president Barack Obama took aim at George W. Bush's policies and America's war with radical Islamists. He signed Executive Orders 13491 and 13492 announcing the closure of the U.S. military incarceration facility at Guantanamo Bay, Cuba, and directing the terrorist detainees held there be released, transferred, or tried in civilian courts. This, his first official act in office, one of enormous consequence to America's national security, was delivered without any consultation with the senior military leadership across the Potomac at the Pentagon. One can only assume, then, that it was a decision made for ideological, rather than pragmatic national security, reasons. That too seems to be the norm for the Obama administration.

On the campaign trail, to prove he could be trusted on national security issues, Obama made a point of sounding hawkish on the Afghanistan War—it was another way to bash the Bush administration, which had allegedly ignored this war while pursuing the wrong and unnecessary war in Iraq. But once Obama was elected president, he dithered. He gave every impression of not wanting to fight the war in Afghanistan at all and delayed announcing that he was sending more troops to that front until nearly a year into his admin-istration. In a speech he delivered at the Eisenhower Theater at West Point on December 2, 2009, Barack Obama announced his long-awaited decision to deploy an additional 30,000 troops in Afghanistan. Immediately following his hawkish rhetoric he announced, "After 18 months, our troops will begin to come home."

He also outlined, for these future officers who will be tasked with fighting America's wars, that under his command military force will give way to diplomacy and "stronger international standards and institutions." Commander in chief Obama also told these young men and women that they'd soon have to look for another career, as battling our nation's enemies will give way to "combating a changing climate and sustaining global growth, [and] helping coun-tries feed themselves," even as their citizens achieve their "univer-sal rights."[17]

Since assuming office in January 2009, Barack Obama has accomplished the following in his handling of the war on terror. He blamed America for fueling mistrust of Islam. In his speech to the Muslim world in Cairo, Obama said, "The attacks of September 11, 2001, and the continued efforts of these extremists to engage in violence against civilians has led some in my country to view Islam as inevitably hostile not only to America and Western countries, but also to human rights. . . . This has bred more fear and distrust."[18]

It was apparently to dispel this "fear and distrust" that Obama thought it a good idea to close down the detention facility at Guan-tanamo Bay, Cuba, where we held some of the most dangerous enemy combatants. This, too, appears to be par for the Obama course—to ignore objective reality, the reality that there are danger-ous terrorists out to kill Americans, in preference for a vague but high-minded belief that with appropriate gestures and understand-ing we can make the world, including radical jihadists, think better of us.

You could chalk this up to naïveté, but it appears more likely that in the Obama administration it is based on sheer arrogance—the arrogance that the previous administration was so witless and moronic and hamfisted in its response to the attack on the Twin Towers and the Pentagon that it drove more Muslims to extremism. But if that were true, why is it that the Bush administration kept our country safe for eight years? Why is it that immediately after 9/11, before Bush had done anything, Palestinians were dancing in the streets at news of the attacks? Why is it that between 1981 and 2001, there were 7,581 terrorist attacks worldwide, many of them driven by Muslim extremism? As the late Professor Samuel P. Huntington pointed out in his now classic book *The Clash of Civilizations and the Remaking of World Order*, "Muslims have problems living peaceably with their neighbors.... Muslims make up about one-fifth of the world's population but in the 1990s they have been far more involved in intergroup violence than the people of any other civilization.... In the early 1990s Muslims were engaged in more intergroup violence than non-Muslims, and two-thirds to three-quarters of intercivilizational wars were between Muslims and non-Muslims. Islam's borders *are* bloody, and so are its innards."[19]

In other words, even before 9/11, even before, in Obama's view, Cowboy Bush rode off crazily blasting everything in sight, Islam had shown itself to be a violent civilization, not only in its ancient past, but in the present. That violence was waged against other countries as well as within its own borders. Huntington breaks down the data in painstaking detail. But it is such facts that Obama merely dismisses out of hand. If there is indeed an ongoing clash of civilizations, it is merely a misunderstanding that he, knowing the world's devotion to him and the hopes the world has for him to bring change, will dispel in his best community organizer style. Such hubris is breathtaking. Moreover, we have already seen how American efforts on behalf of the Islamic world have been greeted with hatred and contempt. In 2002, 72 percent of Kuwaitis, whom we had liberated from the invading Saddam Hussein in 1993, expressed their dislike for the United States. Two-thirds of the Arab world, a good portion of which, in Saudi Arabia and the Gulf, we had defended from Saddam Hussein, were convinced that Osama bin Laden had nothing to do with the attacks of 9/11.[20] It does not appear that America's efforts to defend Muslims in the Balkans, in Somalia, and elsewhere have won us much praise at all.

If the United States has acted as a recruiting tool for Islamic terrorists, it is less because of our foreign policy—or even our defense of democratic Israel against its undemocratic enemies—than it is because we represent a civilization that radical Islam has targeted as an enemy just as surely as communism targeted bourgeois capitalism as its enemy—an enemy to be overthrown, subverted, and destroyed around the world. Islam, like communism, has global ambitions. It seeks submission. It is less a peaceable missionary faith than a militantly aggressive one. The real recruiting tool for the radical Islamists is radical Islam itself, which breeds spitefulness toward the West, a frustration at Western global dominance, and a ferocious sense of grievance at Western values that are not its own.

As long ago as 1990, eleven years before 9/11, Bernard Lewis, one of our foremost scholars of Islam, wrote in *The Atlantic Monthly*, "It should now be clear that we are facing a mood and a movement far transcending the level of issues and policies and the governments that pursue them. This is no less than a clash of civilizations—that perhaps irrational but surely historic reaction of an ancient rival against our Judeo-Christian heritage, our secular present, and the worldwide expansion of both."[21] The title of Lewis's essay should have been a warning for Obama: "The Roots of Muslim Rage: Why So Many Muslims Deeply Resent the West and Why Their Bitterness Will Not Be Easily Mollified." We are not the problem—unless we are to submit to Islam—they are; they cannot deal with a Western-dominated world.

But it is a knee-jerk reaction of liberalism always to look for blame in ourselves rather than in the actual enemy. More damning, for instance, than any Islamic criticism of the detention facility at Guantanamo Bay, Cuba, was the criticism that came from liberals at home who might as well have been writing press releases for al Qaeda. In perhaps the most celebrated case, Democrat Senator Dick Durbin of Illinois ripped into the American servicemen at Guantanamo, comparing them to Nazis and the Khmer Rouge, and comparing the detention facility to the Soviet Gulags. He did this on the basis of an e-mail that alleged detainees were subjected to loud music, extreme temperatures, and the rough handling of a Koran. When Durbin made these charges on the Senate floor in June 2005, he was the second-ranking member of the Senate's Democrat leadership.

Durbin charged,

On one occasion, the air conditioning had been turned down so far and the temperature was so cold in the room, that the bare-footed detainee was shaking with cold.... On another occasion, the air conditioner had been turned off, making the temperature in the unventilated room well over 100 degrees. The detainee was almost unconscious on the floor.... On another occasion, not only was the temperature unbearably hot, but extremely loud rap music was being played in the room and had been since the day before, with the detainee chained hand and foot in the fetal position on the tile floor. If I read this to you and did not tell you that it was ... describing what Americans have done to prisoners in their control, you would most certainly believe this must have been done by the Nazis, Soviets in their gulags, or some mad regime—Pol Pot or others—that had no concern for human beings. Sadly, this is not the case. This was the action of Americans in the treatment of their prisoners.[22]

One has to ask what kind of moral calculus it takes to connect mass starvations and executions, gas chambers and genocide, mounds of skulls and the attempt to eliminate whole classes and races of people, with hot and cold temperatures and loud music. One voice of reason was Republican Senator John Cornyn of Texas, who said, "Clearly, that's over the top. That is not what is happening at Guantanamo Bay. What is happening at Guantanamo Bay is we're trying to treat people humanely, recognizing that these are terrorists."

Another voice of reason was Senator John Warner of Virginia, who said,

> I was trained as a lawyer, [and for] many years as a prosecutor dealt with the [FBI], [and I] have the highest respect [for the FBI]. But I do not accept at face value everything they put down on paper until I make certain it can be corroborated and substantiated. And for you to come to the floor with just that fragment of a report and then unleash the words "the Nazis," unleash the word "gulag," unleash "Pol Pot"... it seems to me that was a grievous error in judgment and leaves open to the press of the world to take those three extraordinary chapters in world history and try to intertwine it with what has taken place, allegedly, at Guantanamo.

In fact, as FOX News reported at the time,

> The military operates under strict guidelines that are widely distributed. Only mild non-injurious physical contact is allowed, such as light pushing. Sleep deprivation is used along with stress positions, but they are limited in time. One knowledgeable official familiar with the memo cited by Durbin as well as other memos said the FBI agent made no such allegation and that the memo described only someone chained to the floor. Anything beyond that is simply an interpretation, the official said.[23]

But within minutes, Durbin's comments were broadcast across the Arab world and posted on the Internet. An American soldier voiced his outrage. "What the hell is that all about?" he asked. "Doesn't he understand how this crap hurts us? Doesn't that S.O.B.

have a clue about morale? God, Osama couldn't pay enough to get that kind of free propaganda. Zarqawi is cackling with glee! We have to stop this diarrhea of the mouth—someone is going to get killed! And it might be me or one of my buddies!"[24]

As a reporter, I spoke to a number of soldiers in Iraq about Durbin's comments. Over and over I heard similar expressions of shock and outrage. Air Force Major Eric Egland told me, "Senator Durbin's remarks about Gitmo were an insult. The false reporting by the media and irresponsible remarks by Durbin and crew had a tremendous negative effect on us. It inflamed the Iraqis at a time when we were really making strides in their confidence and willingness to help. We were relying on their help in rooting out the bad guys . . . [and] comments like these made our job much more difficult. . . . He set us back immeasurably."[25]

An Army specialist in Baghdad put it more bluntly. When I asked the specialist about Durbin's comments, he said of the senator, "I don't know who he is—but I hate him."[26]

Similar reactions came from U.S. forces assigned to Guantanamo. A female Army private working at Gitmo remarked, "We try to do as good a job as possible down here. The detainees are dangerous. They try to kill us every time we get close to them and would certainly kill Americans if released."[27] Another said, "We hear all that, of course. But we try not to let it get us down."[28]

Sadly, but not surprisingly, Democratic leaders did not rush to condemn Durbin's treasonous behavior. In fact, some echoed his claims. House Democratic leader Nancy Pelosi declared, "The treatment of detainees is a taint on our country's reputation, especially in the Muslim world, and there are many questions that must be answered."

Former president Jimmy Carter committed the spineless act of criticizing his country overseas, telling an international conference of the Baptist World Alliance in Birmingham, England, "I think what's going on in Guantanamo Bay and other places is a disgrace to the USA. . . . I'm embarrassed about it, and I think it's wrong."

Al Jazeera wasted no time in airing his subversive comments.

Former president Bill Clinton called for shutting down the detention facility at Gitmo. "It's time that there are no more stories coming out of there about people being abused....If we get a reputation for abusing people, it puts our own soldiers much more at risk." Senator Hillary Clinton, in a fundraising letter to supporters, wrote, "Who knew Vice President Cheney would start lobbying for the right to torture?"

So Democrats run around screaming about "torture" committed by Americans at Guantanamo. But this is just another leftist myth, as Marc Thiessen proves beyond any shadow of a doubt in *Courting Disaster*. He concludes, after a thorough review of the evidence, more thorough than any other book on the subject, with access to more information (he was a former White House speechwriter), and with a firm grounding in Catholic moral teaching (which he uses as one standard of measurement in the book): "The CIA's actions were not only necessary and effective—they were also moral and just."[29]

One of the antiwar Democrats' favorite talking points about Guantanamo was that the United States was guilty of "torture" because the government had concluded that captured al Qaeda fighters were not covered by the Geneva Conventions. (The Left even began referring to the Justice Department memorandum on this matter as the "torture memo.")

Jimmy Carter led the charge in his 2005 book *Our Endangered Values*, saying that the Bush administration had "decided to violate" the Geneva Conventions in the war on terror because it considers the enemy to be "subhuman."

But the fact is that it's not the United States who violated the Geneva Conventions; *it's the terrorists*. The Geneva Conventions embody the idea that even in as brutal an activity as war, civilized nations should obey humanitarian rules: no attacking civilians and no retaliation against enemy soldiers once they fall into your hands. Destruction is to be limited as much as possible to professional soldiers on the battlefield. That rule requires, unconditionally, that soldiers distinguish themselves from civilians by wearing uniforms and carrying arms openly. Any soldier captured on a battlefield *wearing a uniform* is a *prisoner of war* and is entitled to all the rights of the Geneva Conventions.

A jihadist captured in Afghanistan, Iraq, or Pakistan, in contrast, is an *unlawful combatant* and is entitled to no protections under the Geneva Conventions. Why? Because he cheated. He violated the principle of sanctuary. Not only did he hide behind civilians, he targeted them. He eliminated any distinction between himself as a legitimate target and the innocent people around him—between the battlefield and the world of civilians.

Keep in mind, the people detained at Guantanamo weren't innocent foot soldiers or innocent victims. They represented some of the most high-value detainees out of the more than 70,000 al Qaeda and Taliban jihadists captured on battlefields and vetted since 9/11. Most of these terrorists were well educated, with advanced degrees in law, engineering, and medicine. Some were experts in demolition and some had been trained in former Soviet camps. They were murdering terrorists who, if allowed to fight another day, would come after Americans once again, as indeed some of them already have, an estimated one in five.[30]

During their incarceration, the detainees regularly attacked the Gitmo guards by throwing "cocktails" of feces, urine, and semen, and by shouting death threats, such as, "One day I will enjoy sucking American blood." They used their blankets as garrotes and attempt to construct weapons out of anything they could get their hands on.

All that aside, there is this elemental fact: what went on at Guantanamo simply does not constitute torture, no matter what Obama and Company insist. The truth is that Gitmo was the most culturally sensitive detention center in the history of warfare—to a fault, in my opinion. Terrorists who would otherwise be killing or plotting to kill were guaranteed prayer rugs, skullcaps, and Korans, five broadcasts of Muslim prayer each day, painted arrows pointing to

Mecca in each cell, access to a jihadist library, and superb medical care. Each detainee received three hot halal meals a day in accordance with Muslim regulations on food. The United States government spent more than $2.5 million a year to feed the detainees at Gitmo, which averaged $12.68 a day per prisoner. Meanwhile, the Pentagon spends $8.85 per day to feed each of the soldiers deployed to Iraq and Afghanistan; convicts in U.S. federal penitentiaries average $2.78 per day.

In reality, nothing happens to the world's most extreme and dangerous terrorists that most U.S. military warriors haven't endured in training. In my first few years as an Air Force pilot, I was required to attend Survival, Evasion, Resistance, and Escape training (SERE), which prepares Air Force pilots and crew members who might someday be shot down and captured by America's enemies. We learned how to survive off the land, to evade to a rescue site, and ultimately how to resist and survive in a prisoner-of-war situation. Individually we were subjected to the anticipated practices and techniques of America's enemies. It was a miserable experience, but invaluable training.

The specific techniques the U.S. military uses in training its own people are classified, but without violating that I can tell you that the techniques share strong similarities with those used by the military at Guantanamo Bay and the CIA. Grabbing the prisoner for attention, slapping him to create fear, forcing him to stand for long periods of time and in cold cells, making him disrobe, splashing him with cold water, blaring loud music or distorted noise, and "water boarding" are all common methods of "coercive interrogation."

Water boarding is the most extreme of these; the prisoner is placed on an inclined board, his feet above his head, his face is wrapped, and water is poured over him, which induces a drowning sensation. As Marc Thiessen has pointed out, the CIA used this technique on only three high value terrorists: Khalid Sheikh Mohammed, the mastermind of the September 11 attacks, and two others.

In their rush to condemn the United States, liberals miss a critical point about such interrogation techniques: sometimes they represent the only way to get vital information out of the terrorists. The moral relativism of those on the Left prevents them from appreciating this crucial need in the war on terror; and if they were true multiculturalists rather than posturing anti-Americans, they would recognize that, for Muslim terrorists, such interrogation techniques provide a face-saving rationale for cooperating with interrogators, as Marc Thiessen reported after interviewing the interrogators themselves.[31]

To be sure, the need to acquire information from terrorist suspects does not justify any and all techniques to induce such testimony. But it should be clear to anyone who bothers to investigate the record that in fact our military and the Defense Department have taken great pains to determine precisely which techniques are warranted and well within objective legal and moral criteria. The truth is that most of what the Left calls "torture" actually amounts to anything from sophisticated pranks to standard coercive interrogation.[32]

That's a truth you won't learn from the hysterical Left. It sounds much better to them to equate the U.S. military with Nazis and the Khmer Rouge.

Of course, since the presidential election of 2008, the rhetoric has been ratcheted down, because their man is now president. All that remains now is for Obama to execute his promised withdrawal of American forces—a promise based on the premise that the problem is not global Islamic terrorism; the problem is us.

Chapter 5

THE WRONG GAY LINE

"There are ways in which a ruler can bring misfortune upon his army:
... by attempting to govern an army in the same way as he administers a kingdom,
being ignorant of the conditions which obtain in an army."

—Sun Tzu, *The Art of War*

When presidential candidate Barack Obama proudly announced that, if elected, he was going to "fundamentally change the United States of America," it was a warning shot across the bow of the United States military, its culture, and the men and women who bravely serve every day.[1] As Sun Tzu said in the quote that opens this chapter, taken from his classic *The Art of War,* President Obama is seeking to govern the military as he governs his "kingdom," along the New Left lines, using the tactics of Saul Alinksy. As commander in chief, that kingdom includes the United States military—and President Obama is essentially at war with the traditional culture of our military which has been, in the past, deeply grounded not only in effective warfighting doctrine, but in traditional virtues—such as courage, duty, honor, and patriotism—and Judeo-Christian principles.

Barack Obama's culture war against our own armed forces is being conducted on several fronts: including pursuing the pet social engineering projects beloved of the Left at the expense of readiness and capability of our forces; dictating the rules of engagement (ROE) that hinder our troops' ability to fight an enemy that doesn't wear traditional military uniforms, hiding behind women's burqas, and operating from schools and mosques; and, slashing the necessary funding for force modernization and sustainability.

Former president and five star general Dwight D. Eisenhower once said, "Morale is the greatest single factor in successful wars."[2] This is a concept that Barack Obama seems incapable of grasping. Instead, Barack Obama has been virtually systematically undermining the morale of the United States military. He has done so, first, by giving the impression that he has no strategy for Iraq and Afghanistan except scuttling and running; second, by showing no concern for the sacrifices made by our armed forces, and taking this most inappropriate time to attempt to shove through the integration of openly gay men and women in the armed forces, which is sure to be a disruptive force at a time of the highest possible stress; and finally, as commander in chief, he seems to have no grasp of the necessity of funding our forces at a wartime level and investing in force modernization efforts that will avoid the hollowed out military that we have suffered during previous defense cutbacks.

It is hauntingly familiar to those of us who served in uniform during the 1990s under President Bill Clinton, and, I would imagine, also familiar for those who served in the armed forces during the 1970s under the feeble leadership of President Jimmy Carter. My personal experience comes from having served under the pro-military, principled leadership of Ronald Reagan and George H. W. Bush during the 1980s, during which time I served on the front lines of some of our conflicts and fought with military units where morale and confidence in the commander in chief was high, and then serving at the White House during the 1990s as the close personal aide of a man who, to my distress, I saw as having no character, no principles, no understanding of the United States military, and whose cynicism I saw seeping into and undercutting the institution that guards our nation. That man was Bill Clinton. I was saddened, but not surprised, at the exodus of good men and women from our armed forces under his watch. For many, having him as commander in chief seemed almost a stain on our own personal honor.

Only three days into his infant presidency, in 1993, Clinton announced that he was going to lift the fifty-year ban on homosexuals in the military. The original policy had been developed out of necessity during World War II and was reaffirmed by Congress in 1982 when it declared that "homosexuality is incompatible with military service because it undermines discipline, good order and morale."[3]

Bill Clinton's first order in office was directing then Secretary of Defense Les Aspin to stop enforcing the ban on recruiting homosexuals and to halt prosecutions of homosexuals already in the services. He did so without consulting the military leadership in the Pentagon. The result was that he ran headlong into the protestations of then Chairman of the Joint Chiefs of Staff General Colin Powell. The compromise that came out of that collision was the Department of Defense's policy we now know as "Don't Ask, Don't Tell." The *policy*, however, is often confused with the *law* passed by Congress in 1993, which expressly forbids open homosexuality in the ranks. The "Don't Ask, Don't Tell" policy is actually the implementing Department of Defense regulation. The law itself, Section 654, Title 10, U.S.C., otherwise known as *The Military Personnel Eligibility Act of 1993*, was passed by Congress in 1993 with veto-proof majorities, and the federal courts have upheld the law as constitutional several times since.

Among the findings and provisions in the law, Congress dictated, and the courts have upheld, that "there is no constitutional right to serve in the armed forces"; "success in combat requires military units that are characterized by high morale, good order and discipline, and unit cohesion"; "military life is fundamentally different from civilian life"; "military society is characterized by its own laws, rules, customs, and traditions, including numerous restrictions on personal behavior, that would not be acceptable in civilian society"; and, "the potential for involvement of the armed forces in actual combat routinely make it necessary for members of the armed forces involuntarily to accept living conditions and working conditions that are often spartan, primitive, and characterized by forced intimacy with little or no privacy." Ultimately, open homosexuality, they concluded, would present an "unacceptable risk" to good order, discipline, morale, and unit cohesion.[4]

Just as Clinton attempted to socially engineer the military to fit his ideological views and placate the gay and lesbian voting bloc in 1993, Barack Obama is attempting to do precisely the same thing seventeen years later with his announced intent to lift the ban and make good on his quid pro quo with what is now called the LGBT Left (the lesbian, gay, bisexual, and "transgendered" Left). "I will work with Congress and our military to finally repeal the law that denies gay Americans the right to serve," Obama said in his 2010 State of the Union address. Just a week later, Secretary of Defense Robert Gates testified, "We have received our orders from the commander in chief, and we are moving out accordingly."[5]

Outraged by the Obama administration's attempt to reengineer the military culture into one in which the openly (and perhaps even flamboyantly or aggressively) gay, bisexual, and even "transgendered" could serve, 1,167 retired flag and general officers personally signed a statement calling for the current law to be retained. Among their arguments were: 1) the findings in the 1993 law remain valid; 2) the proposed legislation would require acceptance of professed (not just discreet) sexual minorities, with retroactive affect; 3) the LGBT law would affect all military branches and communities, to include Army and Marine infantry, Special Operations Forces, Navy SEALS, surface ships and submarines, on a constant (24/7) basis; and 4) unit commanders would be burdened with personnel turmoil, accusations of bias, and potential career penalties that will weaken trust and team cohesion.[6] In the end, there is no value added by overturning the ban. Quite to the contrary, recent polls of United States military personnel indicate that 10 percent of those in uniform will leave the service or "vote with their feet" if the law is changed. Another 15 percent say that they will seriously consider doing so.[7]

In time of war, can we accept that sort of devastating impact? It is said that by not allowing openly gay personnel to serve, we are losing their potentially valuable contributions. But that logic is almost exactly backwards: if the law is overturned, we will likely lose 10 to 25 percent of our current, already overstretched force—a loss that would be truly devastating to our military, and that's before factoring in the impact on unit cohesion of an almost inevitable flurry of lawsuits accusing commanders or other serving personnel of bias. Moreover, is it really too much to ask that those serving in uniform who are gay keep their sexual preferences under wraps, as under the "don't ask, don't tell" policy? Is it too much to ask them to understand that while they have their sexual preferences, many of their fellow serving soldiers would see cross-dressing, or changing one's sex, or pursuing members of one's own sex as evidence of a psychological disorder or even immoral behavior? And is it too much for them to acknowledge that the military insists on certain moral standards for heterosexuals as well—adultery, for instance, remains a crime under military law for the very same reasons that open homosexuality is prohibited: because it is deemed harmful to the good order, discipline, and honor of the services.

The bottom line is that social engineering should not be the priority of the nation's commander in chief. The purpose of our military is to fight and win our nation's wars. The military is under command of the president, but the military is not meant to be his personal plaything, where he can pursue a leftwing social agenda. If it comes to be seen that way, that too will undermine morale, as well as good order and discipline.

Certainly, the American people have every right to expect that the president and the administration be capable of commanding the military. Article II, Section 2 of the U.S. Constitution provides that "the President shall be commander in chief of the Army and Navy of the United States, and of the militia of the several states, when called into the actual service of the United States." As I experienced, President Bill Clinton was most definitely not capable of executing these duties to a basic minimal standard. As our first draft-dodging president, that should have been no surprise. The sum total of his understanding of, and respect for, the military and national security seemed to come straight out of the antiwar movement of the 1960s and 1970s.

In fact, my experiences in the Clinton administration taught me that he and his staff saw the military more as a social service project than as an instrument of national defense. For Clinton, the military existed for whatever ends his administration might have in mind. The preferred norm was operating under the United Nations banner of humanitarian relief and peacekeeping operations. National defense was not the priority of the Clinton administration; "feel-good" operations that got him good coverage on CNN and that propped up his image as the "rock star president" dispensing global good was the goal.

Indeed, when it came to actual matters of national defense, Clinton, like President Carter before him, took a knife to the armed forces and military readiness: cutting manpower by almost a third, cancelling the procurement of major weapon systems, and destroying morale. He had no hesitation in slashing the military, while concurrently deploying it all over the world on missions that often had very little, if anything, to do with our national security.

In his first two years in office, Barack Obama has adopted a similar approach, chopping the Department of Defense budget to below pre-9/11 levels even as the Pentagon fights two hot wars, conducts humanitarian relief efforts around the world, guards the ever dangerous Korean border, patrols the Pacific against an expansion-minded China, and conducts global operations against radical

Islamic fundamentalism, Latin American drug cartels, and other threats.

There is certainly no requirement for our presidents to have military service in their background—and, I can tell you, given their own professionalism and integrity, career military officers and enlisted personnel have complete faith and belief in our Constitution's mandate of civilian control of the military. It matters less that a president has served in uniform than that he shows that he understands his role as commander in chief. No one doubted, for instance, Franklin Roosevelt's authority as commander in chief, though he had not served in uniform. But it is also painfully obvious to our men and women in the armed services that, while some former serving military have pushed for or supported overturning the don't ask, don't tell policy, it seems that the effort to overturn the ban comes overwhelmingly from an ideological belief and from special interest groups divorced from any understanding of military life or any concern about military effectiveness.

In fact, it is not too much to presume that the Left sees the overturning of the don't ask, don't tell policy as a way to reform the military. The Left that spent the 1960s and 1970s attacking the military as bloodthirsty, racist predators of the underprivileged, servants of a neo-colonialist empire, run by bigoted rightwing fanatics with stars on their shoulders is of course eager to socially engineer the military in a more liberal direction. The idea that the antiwar movement, with all its excesses, represents a higher morality is part of the Left's own self-mythologizing.

Robert Bork, in his excellent book *Slouching towards Gomorrah*, calls the social agenda that liberals push at the expense of national security "radical individualism."[8] Progressives and leftists such as Bill Clinton and Barack Obama are attracted to the military as a foundation for social change precisely because of the military's hierarchical command structure. It's the same reason that liberals are attracted to academia and to "reforming" the nation's churches.

The hierarchy and authority of these institutions make them valuable targets for those who want to effect "social change" and seek "social justice." The case of the military is unique, however, because it is the one American institution that progressives would like to seize and redirect without ever actually serving in it.

For decades, the Left has tried to emasculate the armed forces. Under the Clinton administration, the Pentagon was seeded with like-thinking progressives in positions of influence, intent on "reforming" the military for the social good. For example, when the Marine Corps balked at allowing females to assume combat roles during the 1990s, Assistant Secretary of the Army Sara Lister, a Clinton appointee, characterized the Marines as "extremists" and "dangerous" for not complying with the newfound need for integration of women into what were historically male roles. She also proceeded to make a joke about the Marine uniform.[9]

Madeline Morris, a Pentagon consultant on "gender integration," suggested that the United States military should eliminate "masculinist attitudes," "assertiveness," "aggressiveness," "independence," "self-sufficiency," and "willingness to take risks."[10] I, for one, can't imagine a military where we de-emphasize the qualities of, among other things, "assertiveness," "independence," and the "willingness to take risks."

Barack Obama is having his own politically correct impact on the Pentagon. For example, Obama's top policymaker at the Pentagon, Undersecretary of Defense Michele Flournoy, selected one Rosa Brooks to be a "principal adviser." In her position, Brooks is counted on to make recommendations on vital Defense Department programs, including the acquisition of weapon systems and troop deployments, as well as budgetary matters.

What are Brooks' qualifications? Well, other than the fact that she's a Georgetown University law professor who once worked for liberal billionaire George Soros and his Open Societies Institute, and is a leftist who's written a number of anti-Bush screeds for the *Los Angeles Times*, not much. Certainly nothing that would qualify her to make important decisions on issues that have a direct impact on our troops and our national security.

For some insight into her views, we can look at her *L.A. Times* columns, in which she refers to then President George W. Bush as the "torturer in chief" and the Bush administration as "our local authoritarians," comparable to the leaders of North Korea and Iran.[11] "George W. Bush and Dick Cheney shouldn't be treated like criminals who deserve punishment," Brooks wrote. "They should be treated like psychotics who need treatment." She also asserted that "the Bush administration's big legal lies paved the way for some of the most shameful episodes in our history, including the official authorization of torture."[12]

These are the attitudes that define the administration's defense policy—America has been guilty of torture against Middle Eastern criminals, the Bush administration was full of psychotics, and the United States has been led by anti-democratic authoritarians. Not to mention of course—and this comes from Obama himself—the United States fought a war in Iraq, which the Bush administration, he said in a speech on October 2, 2002, launched to distract the American people from economic problems at home.

So the United States has, in this view, plenty to apologize for—and Obama has been a champion apologizer for the alleged sins of his predecessor—and not a lot to be proud of. In fact, we could do with a lot less American patriotism, because this could be dangerously nationalistic. So, when America's military responded to the horrific earthquakes that devastated Haiti, the Obama administration specifically forbade U.S. troops from flying the American flag outside their operational bases and facilities. While other countries contributing to the humanitarian effort proudly displayed their colors, the Obama administration banned the American military from unfurling Old Glory. "We are not here as an occupation force, but as an international partner committed to supporting the government of Haiti on the road to recovery," explained a representative from the U.S. government's Joint Information Center.[13]

This is Barack Obama's Pentagon. Perhaps we should have seen the signs of his disdain for, and ignorance of, the military sooner. In August 2007, Senator Obama said, "We've got to get the job done [in Afghanistan] and that requires us to have enough troops so that we're not just air-raiding villages and killing civilians, which is causing enormous pressure over there."[14] A future commander in chief might have noted all the precautions that go into anti-terrorist air strikes—and how the enemy has a strong motive for lying about their results; and he might have noted that far from "just air-raiding villages and killing civilians," we did in fact have boots on the ground working to win hearts and minds and hunt down the terrorists.

When Senator Barack Obama gave a commencement speech at Wesleyan University on May 25, 2008, he advocated careers in public service. "I ask you to seek these opportunities when you leave here, because the future of this country—your future, my future, my children's future—depends on it," said Obama. "At a time when our security and moral standing depend on winning the hearts and minds in the forgotten corners of this world, we need more of you to serve abroad. As President, I intend to grow the Foreign Service, double the Peace Corps over the next few years, and engage young people of other nations in similar programs, so that we work side by side to take on the common challenges that confront all of humanity."[15] Notice anything missing from his advocacy for public service? What about encouraging elite college graduates to enlist or seek a commission in the armed services? Or, like Obama, are they "too good" for that? Or does the military and national defense just not interest him?

As commander in chief, Obama neglected to meet with his general in charge in fighting the war in Afghanistan, General Stanley McChrystal, until almost nine months in office. He only managed to find the time for one phone call to General McChrystal, whom he had nominated as "his general," during this time.

And then there are the Afghanistan War rules of engagement. Troops are patrolling without bullets in their rifles, aircraft are prohibited from shooting at targets during the night (when they are least vulnerable to anti-aircraft attack) because of an exaggerated fear of hitting civilians, and the Pentagon has created a medal for not firing your weapon. This politically correct approach is killing American troops.

In an Afghanistan Marine base near Marjah, a Taliban stronghold, a Marine unit was ambushed and two Americans were killed. As Lance Corporal Mark Duzick says: "We were attacked treacherously. We came under fire from everywhere, but the rules of engagement prevent me from doing my job."

Outside a tent housing a Marine unit stands an improvised cross with the words: "Here lies the 81st, death by stand down."[16]

But it's not just Obama thrusting his leftist ideology on America's fighting forces, it is the impact his senior appointments have on military policies and morale—put in this category Supreme Court nominee (as of this writing) Elena Kagan.

Kagan served in the Clinton White House in a variety of roles: Associate White House Counsel, Deputy Assistant to the President for Domestic Policy, and Deputy Director of the Domestic Policy Council. She was named Dean of Harvard Law School in 2003. It was in her role at Harvard that her animus towards the military came to light.

In Kagan's view, the armed forces should be forced to accept lesbians, gays, bisexuals, and the transgendered into their ranks. In an e-mail she sent out to the entire Law School staff and student body in October 2003, she wrote, "I abhor the military's discriminatory ('Don't Ask, Don't Tell') recruitment policy," and she characterized the policy as "a profound wrong, a moral injustice of the first order... a wrong that tears at the fabric of our own community."[17]

She's also been a long-time opponent of the Solomon Amendment, a law that denies federal funding to colleges or universities that have "a policy or practice...that either prohibits, or in effect prevents" military personnel "from gaining access to campuses, or access to students...on campuses, for purposes of military recruiting."[18]

At one time, our most prestigious colleges embraced the military and proudly featured Reserve Officer Training Corps (ROTC) detachments, which produced the overwhelming majority of America's officers. Columbia University became one of the first to host an ROTC program in 1916. Harvard and Yale established their programs in 1917, Princeton in 1919; by 1955, every Ivy League school hosted its own detachment. During World War I, World War II, and the Korean War, institutions such as Columbia, Harvard, Yale, and Princeton were vital training grounds for military officers.

As the Left marched through and took control of the institutions of higher learning, they went to enormous lengths to guarantee that campuses would be rid of any association with the military. Two key elements of the Left's effort to subvert America's armed forces were to disband and outlaw ROTC units at the elite schools and to prohibit on-campus visits from military recruiters.

This once vibrant and thriving conduit for military officers was closed. Columbia University, which at one time produced as many officers as the Naval Academy, hasn't allowed a U.S. military presence on its campus since 1969. That year, Students for a Democratic Society (SDS) launched major antiwar protests at Columbia, seized school buildings, and tossed Molotov cocktails into the ROTC offices. Soon thereafter, university faculty banished all ROTC from campus, and the prohibition has stood ever since. So bitter is the disdain for military service that even if Columbia students choose to take ROTC classes elsewhere (which a handful do at Fordham University and Manhattan College), the university prohibits their transcripts from reflecting participation or credit.

In the mid-1990s, the Republican Congress decided to attempt to counter the growing trend across the nation of universities denying the military access to their campuses for recruiting. Congressman

Gerald Solomon of New York proposed, and Congress passed, an amendment so that taxpayers no longer had to subsidize the anti-American and anti-military agenda that has existed on university campuses since the late 1960s. The original version of the Solomon Amendment denied Department of Defense funding to schools if they refused access to military recruiters.

Not surprisingly, however, the Clinton administration and Janet Reno's Justice Department ignored the Solomon Amendment. Consistent with Bill Clinton's disdain for the military, the government did nothing to enforce the amendment or to compel universities to allow recruiters on campus.

In 1996, the Republican-controlled Congress attempted to up the ante by adding funding from the Departments of Labor, Education, and Health and Human Resources to the law—that is, if a school prohibited military recruiters from coming on campus, those schools could kiss goodbye money coming to them from any of these sources. Still, the Defense Department did little to enforce the statute, as it reeled from the devastating budget cuts and the numbing malaise of the Clinton years.

Things changed during the Bush administration, especially after the attacks of 9/11. Facing a long, global campaign against terror, the Pentagon in the spring of 2002 began turning the screws on federally subsidized schools that continued to deny access to recruiters. The Air Force sent letters to dozens of law schools informing them that unless the prohibitions on military recruiters were lifted, the federal government would withdraw all funding. The administrations at these institutions relented...for a while. Apparently, even ivory tower academic administrators have their price. Harvard, given the choice of either permitting the military on campus or losing its annual intake of $300 million in federal funds, opted for the money.

Thirty-one law schools participated in a lawsuit against the government, including Georgetown, Boston College, George Washington, Stanford, and, not surprisingly, Harvard. In short, instead of working to close the gap between the academy and the military, many of America's prestigious schools sought to widen it. Congress again strengthened the Solomon Amendment in March 2004 by explicitly requiring institutions to afford military recruiters the same access to students as recruiters from any other employer—including corporations like Microsoft, Ford, and AT&T.

But in December 2004, the Third U.S. Circuit Court of Appeals ruled the Solomon Amendment unconstitutional. Dean Elena Kagan and the Harvard Law School then became the first in the nation to officially ban military recruiting on their campus. At Harvard, discrimination against homosexuals was utterly unacceptable, but discrimination against the military was deemed perfectly fine.

On February 2, 2005, the House of Representatives voted to uphold the Solomon Amendment, though eighty-four members of the House, eighty-three of them Democrats and one of them an independent, voted against the resolution. To put it plainly, these Democrats voted during a time of war to allow federally subsidized colleges and universities to bar military recruiters from campus. Among those who voted "nay" were Speaker of the House Nancy Pelosi, Charles Rangel, John Conyers, Rahm Emanuel, Barney Frank, Maurice Hinchey, Sheila Jackson Lee, Dennis Kucinich, Jerry Nadler, and Henry Waxman.

It's interesting to note that Rangel and others on that list have beaten the tired drum that our military is made up only of the sons and daughters of the poor and oppressed. But when the military wanted access to elite college campuses—where, ostensibly, the sons and daughters of the rich reside—they voted no.

Kagan then filed an amicus brief urging the Supreme Court to declare the Solomon Amendment unconstitutional. In March 2006, the U.S. Supreme Court unanimously overturned the lower court's ruling, and rejected Kagan, showing that she and her associates were incapable of properly interpreting the clear language of the First Amendment. Chief Justice John Roberts wrote in the decision, "A military recruiter's mere presence on campus does not violate a law school's right to associate, regardless of how repugnant the law school considers the recruiter's message. . . . The Solomon Amendment neither limits what law schools may say nor requires them to say anything."[19]

In January 2009, Barack Obama nominated Elena Kagan to be U.S. Solicitor General, even though she had never, as a lawyer, argued a case at trial or presided as a judge in court. On May 10, 2010, Obama named Elena Kagan to replace the retiring Justice John Stevens on the Supreme Court of the United States. Think what sort of message it sends to our military when America's commander in chief nominates to the highest court in the land someone who aggressively sought to bar military recruiters from Harvard.

Today's military is built completely from willing and capable volunteers. Our nation is fortunate that this is true. Indeed, even in the face of decades of efforts by the Left to reduce and denigrate the United States military, our Army, Navy, Air Force, Marines, and Coast Guard remain the most capable and motivated force the world has ever known.

Given that so many antiwar activists protested Vietnam because they didn't want to put their own butts on the line, it's not surprising that today they can't conceive of someone deciding to join the military of his or her own free will. But it's true, our soldiers, sailors, airmen, and Marines join because they want to.

They join the military for many reasons—adventure, education, career opportunities, and, yes, patriotism. They don't do it for the money, or fame; there isn't enough money in the federal budget to compensate military members for their family's sacrifices, their long and arduous duties, their frequent and difficult geographic relocations, and a substantially increased likelihood of injury or death. Nor are they coerced into service or forced to join because they have no other alternative.

They come from a generation that trusts the institution of the military, quite unlike the Baby Boomer generation that spawned the New Left and the radical ideologies of Barack Obama.

A post-Vietnam 1975 Harris Poll reported that only 20 percent of people between the ages of eighteen and twenty-nine had a great deal of confidence in the military.[20] In contrast, a recent poll by the Harvard University Institute of Politics found that 70 percent of college undergraduates trust the military to do the right thing either all or most of the time.[21] As a veteran, I know that those 70 percent of college undergraduates today are right, and that their 1975 compatriots were wrong.

For many in the armed forces, their reasons for joining evolve into reasons to stay. Initial training in the armed forces emphasizes the virtues of courage, honor, duty, discipline, loyalty, and adherence to a professional code of conduct, all of which can have a profound impact on individuals. "Even if you don't have it when you enlist," explained Army Sergeant Kevin Blanchard, "they breed it into you to be a better person. When you go home you see how you're different than the people you grew up with."[22]

It's a bond that defies description, a kinship and an understanding that only those with common experiences and common losses can truly understand. U.S. Army First Sergeant Jeff Nuding explained it this way from his post in northern Iraq:

> I [had] never fully understood the devotion expressed by survivors of past wars and conflicts. I must have thought somehow that such attachment of sentiment had to have something to do with something unique about the individuals or the units, or even the war. The Greatest Generation was great, wasn't it, because of the depth of their sacrifice or magnitude of their struggle or the great consequence of their triumph? I don't think that anymore. I think I now understand the bond that veterans speak of, the bond of common experience, of course, but a bond of common sacrifice and loss as well. We have shed blood here. We leave a piece of the whole here. Innocence lost, some scarring in a place that had for most of us not known wound before. But we will never share with others outside, that

connection to the past that does not travel with us forward in time. There are memories that will stay locked in OIF III [Operation Iraqi Freedom], in 2005, in the Month of June, in the sweltering heat of the Iraqi summer.[23]

When I spoke with soldiers and Marines in Iraq during the summer of 2005, I asked them what kept them going in the difficult combat conditions they faced. The most frequent response was "supporting my friends" and "protecting each other." One young soldier told me, "Sir, I'm fighting for my buddies and my buddies are fighting for me." Another described the intense relationship he felt for his fellow soldiers: "The guy next to you means more to you than anybody. He's got your back and you've got his. It has to work that way. And I know that if I mess up he'll get hurt . . . and that isn't going to happen."[24]

Marine Corporal Michael Pinkney looked around at the dust and deprivation in Iraq and said, "I don't want to be anywhere else but Iraq. . . . This is what manhood is all about. I don't mean macho shit either. I mean moral character."[25] Staff Sergeant Jamie McIntyre of Queens, New York, told *American Enterprise* magazine, "I look at faces and see fellow human beings, and I say, 'O.K. This is the sacrifice I have to make to bring them freedom.' That's why I joined the military. Not for the college money, for doing what's right. Fighting under our flag. That's what our flag stands for. I believe in that stuff. Yeah, we might lose American soldiers, but they are going to lose a society, lose a people. You've got to look at the bigger picture. I've lost friends, and it hurts. It definitely hurts. But that's even more reason why I say stay. It's something that has to be done. If we don't do it, who will?"[26]

I wish these soldiers, sailors, airmen, and Marines had a commander in chief worthy of them, who appreciates their sacrifice, and is devoted to helping them achieve the mission they were assigned. But right now it seems the Obama administration is at war with the military, more concerned with foisting its radical beliefs on our men and women in uniform than in helping them in their vital and hazardous duty, and in protecting our nation from its enemies abroad.

THE ABANDONMENT OF HOPE

In the darkness with a great bundle of grief the people march.
In the night, and overhead a shovel of stars for keeps, the people march:
"Where to? What next?"

—Carl Sandburg, *The People, Yes*

In the nearly forty years since counterculture leftists, the SDS, and similarly minded radicals seized the Democrat Party moderates, the Democrats have elected only three presidents: Jimmy Carter, Bill Clinton and, most recently, Barack Obama. From where I sit, and based on my military experience, these are the three worst commanders in chief this nation has ever had to endure and survive. Their national defense failures are undeniable: from the fall of the Shah of Iran, to the failure to engage the war on terror when Osama bin Laden first declared it, to the gutting of the policies of President George W. Bush, which kept this country safe from attack after September 11, 2001.

All three of these Democrat presidents liked to pose as "citizens of the world" rather than stepping up to their leadership roles as elected citizen-leaders of America. In Barack Obama's case, this appears to be more than a pose, it seems be what he actually feels—indeed, part of the "change" he promised to deliver to existing American policies. For all three of these presidents, American nationalism was, or is, embarrassing, if not downright dangerous. The responsible thing to do, the liberal thing to do, is prevent America from asserting herself on the global stage, to play second fiddle to the United Nations, to play down our own national interests, and to pretend that we don't have serious enemies.

The consequences of their policies have been catastrophic. In betraying the Shah of Iran, a longtime American ally, and in failing to recognize what the Ayatollah Khomenei and his revolution represented, must rank as one of the worst, if not the worst, foreign policy disasters in American history. That colossal miscalculation created the first Islamic state-sponsored terror base, led directly to the humiliating Iranian hostage crisis and a tragically bungled rescue attempt, and to the creation of Hezbollah, the terror group that has been killing Americans routinely since 1983.

Twelve years after Carter left office, Bill Clinton inherited a maturing jihadist threat which he failed to respond to after at least eight separate attacks on America and its citizens, from the first World Trade Center bombing in 1993 through the bombing of the USS *Cole* in 2000. Clinton's first director of Central Intelligence, R. James Woolsey, aptly summed up Bill Clinton's impotence when he described the former president's "PR-driven" approach to terrorism: "Do something to show you're concerned. Launch a few missiles in the dessert, bop them on the head, arrest a few people. But just keep kicking the ball down the field."

Eight years of Clintonian faux diplomacy, appeasement, and feigned resolve encouraged and emboldened our enemies while making America appear weak and vulnerable. With the grossly mistaken belief that the end of the Cold War was the end of armed conflict, liberals and some neo-conservatives viewed the crumbling of the Soviet Empire as "the end of history," as an influential book by the foolish neo-conservative Francis Fukuyama put it. For the Left, it was easier that way.

With history supposedly over—*No more war!*—Bill Clinton swept into power and immediately began pursing social experimentation in the armed forces at the express cost of military capability and morale. And now we have his wife as our secretary of state.

The Clinton years are best characterized by Mogadishu and the "Black Hawk Down" atrocity; inconsequential excursions into Haiti, Rwanda, and Bosnia; and the failure to respond effectively to Islamist terrorist attacks.

The Islamists were taking notes. In May 1998, Osama bin Laden, referring to Clinton's decision to cut and run in Somalia, told ABC's John Miller: "After our victory in Afghanistan [over the Soviets] and the defeat of the oppressors who had killed millions of Muslims, the legend about the invincibility of the superpowers vanished. Our boys no longer viewed America as a superpower. So, when they left Afghanistan, they went to Somalia and prepared themselves carefully for a long war. They had thought that the Americans were like the Russians, so they trained and prepared. They were stunned when they discovered how low was the morale of the American soldier. America had entered with 30,000 soldiers in addition to thousands of soldiers from different countries in the world. . . . As I said, our boys were shocked by the low morale of the American soldier and they realized that the American soldier was just a paper tiger."

Osama bin Laden, as he's learned to his cost, was wrong about the American soldier, but he was right about America's commander in chief Bill Clinton. I fear that he might be equally right about our new commander in chief Barack Obama. Obama does not seem to be the sort of man one would count on to assert America's national interests, to aggressively defend America at home and abroad. He seems far more comfortable apologizing for America, arguing that we need to understand our enemies and not provoke them, and encouraging a multiculturalism that, in his view, might just make the dangers of aggressive American nationalism fade away over time. The fundamental danger of the Obama administration seems to be that it sees itself as a good citizen of the world rather than a guardian of American interests—and that is not what America needs now or ever.

THE "LONG WAR" TIMELINE

One of the biggest blind spots of the Obama administration, just as it was for the Clinton administration, is not recognizing the Long War against radical Islamic terror is not something the United States opted into, nor is it something we can opt out of. Radical Islam has been waging war against America at least since 1979.

I've compiled a list of some of the highlights of the war we face as a reminder that this is not a war of our choosing—it's also a war we cannot lose. There have been far too many attacks against America and American interests abroad to concisely list them in a single chapter. The following, while not completely inclusive, is offered to underscore the nature of our enemy and its relentless aggression.

FEBRUARY 1, 1979—
THE FIRST RADICAL ISLAMIC TERROR STATE IS BORN:

With encouragement from President Jimmy Carter, Iranian shah Reza Pahlavi, a longtime American ally, is forced from power. Radical cleric Ayatollah Khomeini assumes the Iranian leadership. "We will export our revolution to the four corners of the world," Khomeini declares only ten days later. "Islam makes it incumbent on all adult males, provided they are not disabled or incapacitated, to prepare themselves for the conquest of countries so that the writ of Islam is obeyed in every country in the world. But those who study Islamic Holy War will understand why Islam wants to conquer the whole world." Carter's decision to support Khomeini's ascension leads directly to the first radical Islamic state-sponsored terrorism and will launch a series of cataclysmic events in the Middle East.

FEBRUARY 14, 1979—ISLAMIC EXTREMISTS KIDNAP
AND KILL THE U.S. AMBASSADOR TO AFGHANISTAN:

Ambassador Adolph Dubs is taken hostage by Islamic extremists attempting to secure the release of several "religious figures." He is killed in a rain of gunfire between Afghan police and his captors.

JULY 16, 1979—
SADDAM HUSSEIN BEGINS HIS MURDEROUS REIGN IN IRAQ:

In a ruthless coup within his Baath Party, Saddam Hussein seizes power from his frail older relative President Ahmed Hassan al-Bakr. His first act of leadership is to identify all "spies" and "conspirators" among his party and have them assassinated—the first of some 2 million people his regime will murder or torture.

NOVEMBER 4, 1979—
KHOMEINI DECLARES WAR ON THE UNITED STATES:

Under Ayatollah Khomeini's direct control, a mob of approximately 500 Iranian students calling themselves the "Imam's Disciples" overrun and seize the American Embassy in Tehran. Sixty-six American diplomats are taken hostage in this act of war, and one of the most humiliating foreign policy disasters in American history unfolds over 444 days. Carter's bumbling foreign policy and betrayal of the Shah has launched a series of cataclysmic events in the Middle East, and Islam's war with America has begun. Immediately Iran positions itself on the front lines in the conflict between the Palestinians and the Israelis, establishing the terror group Hezbollah ("The Party of God") in Lebanon. It also begins attacks on the United States. "We are at war with America as our Prophet was at war against the corrupt regimes of his time," Khomeini declares. "Because we believe that Islam is the one and only true faith, it is incumbent on us to fight until the entire humanity either converts or submits to Islamic authority."

NOVEMBER 20, 1979—ISLAMIC FUNDAMENTALISTS SEIZE
THE GRAND MOSQUE IN MECCA, SAUDI ARABIA:

Just days following the storming of the American Embassy in Tehran, hundreds of well-armed Islamic fundamentalists seize the Grand Mosque, the holiest site in Islam. Juhayman al-Utaybi, the leader of the insurgents, is a direct descendant of the Wahhabi warriors who helped the Al Saud family assume power in the 1920s. Al-Utaybi's radicals call for a return to pure Islam and denounce modernization, accusing the Saudi royal family of corruption and loss of legitimacy because of dealings with the West. Saudi and French forces eventually retake the mosque in a battle in which 250 are killed and 600 wounded. Iran's new ruler, Ayatollah Khomeini, blames the United States for the takeover, inflaming the Muslim world. The U.S. embassies in Pakistan and Libya are attacked and torched, and four people are killed. The House of Saud is forced to increase its religious standing in the kingdom by implementing a more fundamental Islamic agenda. Saudi Arabia begins pumping millions of dollars into religious education, creating new theological schools designed to produce large numbers of Wahhabi clerics.

DECEMBER 25, 1979—THE SOVIET UNION INVADES AFGHANISTAN:

Once the United States loses its strategic foothold in Iran, the Soviets invade neighboring Afghanistan. The war will last until 1989, when the Soviet Union finally is forced to retreat. More important, the conflict will establish the epicenter for young Muslim jihadists from across the world. Between 1980 and 1989, approximately 35,000 Muslim radicals from forty Islamic countries will come together in Afghanistan to fight the Soviet Union. Tens of thousands more will come to study in Pakistani madrassas. Eventually, more than 100,000 foreign Muslim radicals will be directly influenced by the Afghan jihad, including Saudi national Osama bin Laden.

DECEMBER 26, 1979—OSAMA BIN LADEN GOES TO AFGHANISTAN TO FIGHT THE SOVIETS:

Only days after the Soviet Union invades Afghanistan, bin Laden sets up a base in Peshawar, Pakistan, and begins raising funds to provide the mujahedeen with logistical and humanitarian aid. He forms the Maktab al-Khadamat (the "Office of Services") with his mentor Abdullah Azzam. From 1986 on, bin Laden fights in numerous battles as a guerrilla commander, including a fierce battle at Jalalabad that ultimately leads the Soviets to withdraw. It is in Peshawar that bin Laden first meets Egyptian doctor Ayman al-Zawahiri.

OCTOBER 6, 1981—ISLAMIC EXTREMISTS ASSASSINATE EGYPTIAN PRESIDENT ANWAR SADAT:

Three years after making peace with Israel, President Sadat is assassinated by Muslim extremists as he presides over Egypt's annual military parade. Cleric Sheikh Omar Abdel Rahman, the "Blind Sheikh" (who will later be convicted for his involvement in the 1993 World Trade Center bombing), issues the fatwa sanctioning Sadat's assassination.

JANUARY 18, 1982—LEBANESE TERRORISTS MURDER U.S. ARMY LIEUTENANT COLONEL CHARLES RAY:

Ray, a military attaché to the American Embassy in France, is shot and killed outside his Paris apartment by the Lebanese Armed Revolutionary Faction.

AUGUST 11, 1982—PALESTINIAN TERRORISTS BOMB PAN AM FLIGHT 830 TO HONOLULU, HAWAII:

A Pan Am jet traveling from Tokyo, Japan, to Honolulu, Hawaii, explodes at 36,000 feet as the plane prepares to descend. A Japanese student is killed and fifteen people are injured. The bomber is Mohammed Rashid, a member of the radical Palestinian organization known as the 15 May Organization. Rashid will eventually be captured and tried for his role in the 1986 bombing of TWA Flight 840 near Athens, Greece.

APRIL 18, 1983—HEZBOLLAH BOMBS THE U.S. EMBASSY IN BEIRUT, LEBANON:

Sixty-three people, including the CIA's Middle East director and sixteen other Americans, are murdered, while 120 are injured, when an explosives-laden vehicle is detonated in the U.S. Embassy compound. U.S. intelligence intercepted a preattack cable from the Iranian foreign ministry to the Iranian Embassy in Syria approving payment for a terrorist attack in Beirut. The attack is carried out by Iranian-backed Hezbollah guerrillas operating in Lebanon using

"Islamic Jihad" as a cover name. This marks the first of several Hezbollah attacks on the United States.

OCTOBER 23, 1983—
HEZBOLLAH BOMBS THE U.S. MARINES HEADQUARTERS IN BEIRUT:

Hezbollah terrorists send a large truck loaded with 2,500 pounds of TNT through the main gate of the U.S. Marine headquarters in Beirut, killing 241 Americans. The Marines are part of a multinational force sent at the request of the Lebanese government to assist in separating warring factions. Two minutes later, another truck packed with explosives slams into a French paratrooper base two miles away, killing fifty-eight soldiers and the driver. Thirteen individuals are connected to the attack, including Mohammed Hussein Fadlallah, the leader of the Hezbollah group, and Hussein Musawi (Mousavi), a leader of the Islamic Amal group, also linked to Iran. Syrian officers and the then-Iranian ambassador to Lebanon, Ali Akbar Mohtashami, are also implicated in the bombings.

DECEMBER 12, 1983—IRANIAN-SPONSORED TERRORISTS BOMB
THE U.S. EMBASSY ANNEX IN KUWAIT:

An explosives-laden truck crashes into the compound of the U.S. Embassy Annex in Kuwait, killing six and wounding eighty. The Embassy Annex is one of six installations attacked in Kuwait that day, including the French Embassy, the control tower at the airport, the country's main oil refinery, and a residential area for employees of the American corporation Raytheon. Seventeen terrorists who are members of the Iranian sponsored Al Dawa ("The Call") Party are arrested and convicted for the attacks. One of those convicted is Mustafa Youssef Badreddin, the cousin and brother-in-law of Hezbollah senior officer Imad Mughniyah. Saddam Hussein's forces will release all seventeen terrorists after Iraq invades Kuwait in 1990.

1982 to 1992—HEZBOLLAH KIDNAPS AND MURDERS NUMEROUS U.S. OFFICIALS IN LEBANON:

The kidnapping of American University of Beirut president David Dodge in July 1982 commences a series of kidnappings and murders of Americans conducted by Hezbollah. In all, thirty Westerners are kidnapped over ten years, including Americans Dodge; William Buckley, the CIA Beirut station chief; Terry Anderson, a journalist; Peter Kilburn, an American University of Beirut librarian; Benjamin Weir, a Presbyterian minister; Edward Tracy, a businessman; Jesse Turner; Thomas Sutherland; and Alann Steen. One of the most gruesome atrocities is the abduction, torture, and killing of U.S. Marine Lieutenant Colonel Richard Higgins, a United Nations official observing the peace in Lebanon. Higgins is kidnapped in February 1988 and is interrogated and tortured before his murder. In a videotape distributed by the terrorists, Higgins' body is shown hanging from a rope. Hezbollah dumps his body onto the street in Beirut in 1991.

JANUARY 18, 1984—HEZBOLLAH MURDERS AMERICAN UNIVERSITY OF BEIRUT PRESIDENT MALCOLM KERR:

Two Hezbollah gunmen shoot and kill Kerr while he walks to his office.

SEPTEMBER 20, 1984—HEZBOLLAH BOMBS THE U.S. EMBASSY ANNEX IN AUKAR, LEBANON:

The Iranian-sponsored terror group strikes once again, sending an explosives-laden van into the compound at the U.S. Embassy, which has been relocated from Beirut. The resulting explosion thirty feet from the embassy annex kills nine and injures fifty-eight.

APRIL 12, 1985—TERRORISTS BOMB A RESTAURANT NEAR
TORREJON AIR BASE IN MADRID, SPAIN:

A bomb is detonated in a restaurant popular with American servicemen near the U.S. Air Force Base outside Madrid, Spain, killing eighteen and wounding eighty-two (including eighteen Americans). It is the worst act of terrorism in Spain since the end of the Spanish Civil War in 1939. Spanish authorities determine that Hezbollah is responsible. No arrests are ever made, however. According to Spanish officials, it is the only major terrorist attack in the country's modern history that has not been solved.

JUNE 14, 1985—TERRORISTS HIJACK TWA FLIGHT 847:

TWA Flight 847, bound for Rome with thirty-nine Americans aboard, is hijacked over the Mediterranean Sea by members of Hezbollah and forced to land in Beirut, Lebanon. The hijackers, demanding the release of hundreds of Shiite Muslim prisoners held by Israel, single out U.S. Navy diver Robert Stethem, beat him, shoot him in the head, and throw his body onto the tarmac. The four hijackers are eventually set free after being offered transportation to Damascus and the release of the 435 Lebanese and Palestinian Shiite prisoners in Israel. In 1987, German officials arrest hijacker Mohammed Hamadei at the Frankfurt airport with a suitcase containing liquid explosives. German authorities convict Hamadei and sentence him to life imprisonment for the murder of Stethem. The remaining three terrorists are never captured and their whereabouts remain unknown. Hamadei is later released by Germany, in 2005.

AUGUST 8, 1985—LEFTWING TERROR GROUP BOMBS
RHEIN-MAIN AIR BASE IN FRANKFURT, GERMANY:

A car bomb detonates at the main U.S. Air Force base in Germany, killing two and wounding twenty. The next day, a U.S. serviceman's body is found; he apparently was killed for his identification card. The terrorists responsible for the bombing come from the Red Army Faction, or Baader-Meinhof Group, a radical leftwing German terror organization that trained at a Palestinian terror camp in 1970.

OCTOBER 7, 1985—PALESTINIAN TERRORISTS HIJACK THE ACHILLE LAURO:

Four Palestinian hijackers commandeer the Italian cruise liner *Achille Lauro* off the Egyptian coast and hold more than 700 tourists hostage. Demanding the release of Palestinian prisoners held in Israel and elsewhere, the terrorists shoot and kill elderly wheelchair-bound New Yorker Leon Klinghoffer and push his body overboard. The Palestine Liberation Front's Abu Abbas facilitates the terrorists' surrender and release. The four hijackers and Abbas fly out of Egypt for safe haven, but are intercepted by four U.S. Navy F-14 Tomcat jets and forced to land at Sigonella Naval Air Base in Sicily, where U.S. special operations forces await them. Italian authorities arrest the four hijackers but refuse to hold Abbas, who is allowed to fly to Belgrade, Yugoslavia, under diplomatic cover. Abbas will be arrested by U.S. forces in Baghdad in April 2003.

NOVEMBER 23, 1985—TERRORISTS HIJACK EGYPT AIR FLIGHT 648:

The Abu Nidal Organization hijacks Egypt Air Flight 648 en route from Athens to Cairo, forcing it to land on the island of Malta. The terrorists shoot three Americans and two Israelis in the head and dump their bodies onto the tarmac. Egyptian commandos storm the plane, and sixty more are killed in the ensuing battle. Abu Nidal, perhaps the most ruthless terrorist in the world and "the father of the struggle," will receive safe haven in Saddam Hussein's Iraq in 1999. But in late 2002, Saddam's security forces will assassinate him, because they know the United States is coming and want to cover up their terror ties.

DECEMBER 27, 1985—THE ABU NIDAL ORGANIZATION ATTACKS
AIRLINE COUNTERS IN ROME AND VIENNA:

Terrorists from the Abu Nidal Organization storm airports in Rome and Vienna, tossing hand grenades and firing automatic weapons at TWA and El Al airline ticket counters. They kill twenty and wound 110. Airport security forces kill four of the seven terrorists. In January 1986, Italy issues an international warrant for the arrest of Abu Nidal for mass murder. He will be tried in absentia and sentenced to life imprisonment in 1988.

APRIL 2, 1986—THE ARAB REVOLUTIONARY CELL
BOMBS TWA FLIGHT 840:

A terror group calling itself the Arab Revolutionary Cell, with ties to Abu Nidal and Yassir Arafat, detonates a bomb on board TWA 840 as it descends into Athens for landing. Four Americans, including an infant, are sucked out of the fuselage to their deaths. Five others are injured.

APRIL 5, 1986—ABU NIDAL, WITH THE HELP OF THE LIBYAN REGIME,
BOMBS A WEST BERLIN DISCO:

A bomb placed in the restroom of a discotheque frequented by U.S. military personnel explodes, killing three and injuring more than 200, including forty-four Americans. Libya and Abu Nidal are responsible for the attack, and in response President Ronald Reagan launches Operation El Dorado Canyon, sending U.S. Air Force and Navy fighters and bombers to attack Tripoli and Benghazi, Libya. Forced to fly around French airspace, Air Force F-111s accidentally bomb the French Embassy in Tripoli.

SEPTEMBER 5, 1986—
ABU NIDAL HIJACKS PAN AM FLIGHT 73 IN KARACHI, PAKISTAN:

Four terrorists from the Abu Nidal Organization storm Pan Am Flight 73. Jordanian terrorist Zayd Hassan Safarini shoots American passenger Rajesh Kumar in the head, execution-style, and pushes Kumar's body onto the tarmac. After dark, Safarini and the other hijackers order all of the passengers to the center of the aircraft, then say a martyrdom prayer and unleash a barrage of hand grenades and automatic weapons. Twenty passengers are killed and more than 100 are injured in the attack.

1988—BIN LADEN ESTABLISHES AL QAEDA ("THE BASE"):

Bin Laden starts al Qaeda, seeing the need to shift the fighting away from the Soviets and toward an international jihad that will reunite the Muslim world under a single leader and reestablish "the Caliphate." According to the CIA, al Qaeda will eventually establish terror cells in more than eighty countries.

APRIL 14, 1988—TERRORISTS BOMB THE USO CLUB IN NAPLES, ITALY:

A car bomb explodes outside the United Service Organization club in Naples, killing five (including one U.S. naval sailor) and injuring fifteen (including four U.S. sailors). The terror group Japanese Red Army, working at the direction of the Popular Front for the Liberation of Palestine, is responsible for the attack.

DECEMBER 21, 1988—PALESTINIAN TERRORISTS AND THE LIBYAN REGIME BOMB PAN AM FLIGHT 103:

En route from London to New York, Pan Am Flight 103 explodes over Lockerbie, Scotland, killing 270 innocent people, including 189 Americans. The bomb was packed into a Toshiba radio-cassette recorder in the luggage compartment. The Popular Front for the Liberation of Palestine and the Libyan government are responsible for the attack. Libyans Abdelbaset Ali Mohmed Al Megrahi and Al Amin Khalifa Fhimah will be indicted for murder. Libyan president Muammar Qaddafi will turn over the terrorists in 1999 and formally accept responsibility for the attack in 2003.

1989—OSAMA BIN LADEN RETURNS TO SAUDI ARABIA:

After the Soviets pull out of Afghanistan, bin Laden returns to Saudi Arabia as a hero. He opposes the Saudi monarchy while working for his family's construction firm, the Bin Laden Group.

JANUARY 18 to 19, 1991—IRAQI AGENTS ATTEMPT BOMBINGS OF AMERICANS IN INDONESIA, THE PHILIPPINES, AND THAILAND:

In Indonesia, an Iraqi posing as a contractor plants a bomb at U.S. ambassador John Monjo's residence. The bomb is discovered by a gardener before it detonates and is immediately defused. In the Philippines, two Iraqi agents target Manila's Thomas Jefferson Cultural Center, but as they prepare the bomb it explodes, killing one of the terrorists. Iraqi diplomat Muwafak al-Ani is deported after Philippine investigators discover that an embassy car dropped the bombers off at the target and find al-Ani's card in the pocket of one of the terrorists. Later, the Iraqi Embassy's second secretary, Husham Z Hussein, will also be expelled after it is determined that he was in close contact with members of the al Qaeda-associated terror organization, the Abu Sayyaf Group. In Thailand, two Iraqi diplomats are deported after they are found smuggling explosives into the country. According to former UN weapons inspector Richard Butler, their targets were the U.S., Israeli, and Australian embassies in Bangkok.

APRIL, 1991—BIN LADEN FLEES SAUDI ARABIA FOR SUDAN:

Bin Laden flees Saudi Arabia after his opposition to Saudi Arabia's alliance with the United States lands him in detention. After briefly staying in Afghanistan, he relocates to Khartoum, Sudan, where in 1992 he reestablishes al Qaeda headquarters. Hundreds of suspected terrorists and former mujahedeen also relocate to Sudan for safe haven, and bin Laden establishes a number of camps for training in firearms and explosives. In 1994, Saudi Arabia will revoke bin Laden's citizenship, and his family will disown him.

MARCH 17, 1992—ISRAELI EMBASSY BOMBED IN
BUENOS AIRES, ARGENTINA:

A car bomb is detonated in front of the Israeli Embassy, a Catholic church, and a school, killing twenty-nine and wounding 242. The terror group the Islamic Jihad Organization, with ties to Iran and Hezbollah, is responsible. Most of the dead and wounded are children.

DECEMBER 29, 1992—AL QAEDA'S FIRST ATTACK:

A bomb is detonated in a hotel in Aden, Yemen, where U.S. troops stayed on their way to the humanitarian mission in Somalia. The soldiers depart the hotel prior to the attack, but two Austrian tourists are killed. Two Yemeni Muslim militants who trained in Afghanistan are injured in the blast and arrested. They will eventually be released, only to collaborate in the bombing of the USS *Cole* in 2000.

JANUARY 25, 1993—A LONE GUNMAN ATTACKS
CIA HEADQUARTERS IN LANGLEY, VIRGINIA:

Pakastani Mir Aimal Kasi jumps from a car outside Central Intelligence Agency headquarters in Langley and fires an AK-47 assault machine gun, killing two CIA employees and wounding three others. Kasi trained with Afghani jihadists during the war with the Soviet Union. After the attacks at Langley, Kasi quickly boards a flight to Pakistan. After years of investigation, in 1997 the FBI will apprehend Kasi on the border between Afghanistan and Pakistan and return him to the United States to stand trial. He will be convicted of murder and killed by lethal injection on November 14, 2002. In retaliation for Kasi's guilty verdict, four American oil company employees and their driver will be gunned down in the Pakistani port city of Karachi.

FEBRUARY 26, 1993—THE FIRST WORLD TRADE CENTER BOMBING:

Thirty eight days into President Bill Clinton's presidency, an explosive laden Ryder van is detonated in a hotel parking garage beneath New York's World Trade Center, killing seven people (including an unborn child) and wounding 1,040. The blast creates a 100-by-100- foot crater.

Al Qaeda associate Ramzi Yousef, also a veteran of bin Laden's camps in Peshawar, Pakistan, planned the attack. The morning after the blast, Yousef escapes to Pakistan, disappointed he hasn't had more success. He vows to return and finish the job. "Our calculations were not very accurate this time. However we promise you that next time it will be very precise and the Trade Center will be one of our targets." Eventually, Yousef will move on to the Philippines at the direction of bin Laden and begin early preparation for Operation Bojinka—the precursor to the 9/11 attacks. In the first of his many failures to confront terrorism, President Clinton cautions Americans not to overreact to the World Trade Center bombing, and in an interview for MTV, he attributes the attack to someone "who did something really stupid." At first Clinton even downplays the possibility that terror was involved, preferring to believe that the explosion was the result of an electric generator—even though several radical Islamic groups claimed responsibility. Fortunately, bomber Mohammed Salameh's stupidity tips off law enforcement. His incessant demands for a refund of $400 for the van give the FBI the lead it needs. Salameh becomes the first of eight terror suspects arrested. Some are actually caught in the act of mixing explosive materials for attacks on the United Nations, the George Washington Bridge, and two tunnels into the city. In July 1993, Sheikh Omar Abdel Rahman, the blind cleric who was behind the assassination of Egyptian president Anwar Sadat, is indicted along with fourteen other suspects. In March 1994, four of the terrorists—Nidal Ayyad, Mohammed Salameh, Ahmad Ajaj, and Mahmud Abouhalima—are convicted, and each is sentenced to 240 years in prison without parole. In October 1995, Sheikh Rahman and nine of his followers are convicted of plotting the bombings and planning other acts of terror in New York. In January 1996, Rahman is sentenced to life without parole plus sixty-five years, and the others are given terms from twenty-five years to life.

APRIL 14, 1993—IRAQI INTELLIGENCE AGENTS ATTEMPT THE ASSASSINATION OF PRESIDENT GEORGE H. W. BUSH:

The Iraqi Intelligence Service attempts to assassinate former president Bush as he visits Kuwait to celebrate the coalition victory and the removal of Saddam Hussein two years earlier. Kuwaiti security forces uncover the plot to load 175 pounds of explosives into a Toyota Land Cruiser and detonate them in proximity to President Bush; the security forces immediately round up seventeen suspects associated with the plot.

OCTOBER 3 to 4, 1993—"BLACK HAWK DOWN":

The Battle for Mogadishu occurs, thanks to the miscalculation of President Bill Clinton. President George H. W. Bush originally deployed 28,000 U.S. troops to Mogadishu, Somalia, as part of a humanitarian mission to feed drought-stricken Somalis. But when President Clinton inherited the mission, he immediately reduced troop levels to only 4,500. In a demonstration of ignorance and tragic miscalculation, he also dramatically expanded the scope of the mission, moving from humanitarian aid to nation-building and targeting Somali warlord Mohammad Farah Aidid. In the days leading up to the Battle for Mogadishu, U.S. Army General William Garrison, commander of the U.S. troops, formally requests much-needed armored vehicles, tanks, and AC-130 Spectre gunships. The Clinton administration, through Secretary of Defense Les Aspin, denies the request. On October 3, members of the U.S. Task Force Ranger are ambushed as they raid the Olympic Hotel in Mogadishu, where a meeting of warlord Aidid's lieutenants is under way. The Somali fighters, who have been trained by al Qaeda and bin Laden, shoot down two Black Hawk helicopters and drag the

American dead in the streets through wildly cheering mobs. Eighteen elite U.S. soldiers are killed and eighty-four wounded. Democratic congressman John Murtha urges Clinton to begin an immediate and complete pullout of U.S. troops from the region. Clinton takes the advice and orders the withdrawal only four days after the battle. Osama bin Laden learns a valuable lesson that day. He will later say that America's withdrawal was what convinced him that America could be attacked with impunity: "Our boys no longer viewed America as a superpower. So, when they left Afghanistan [after defeating the Soviet Union], they went to Somalia and prepared themselves carefully for a long war. They had thought that the Americans were like the Russians, so they trained and prepared. They were stunned when they discovered how low was the morale of the American soldier. . . . They realized that the American soldier was just a paper tiger. After a few blows, it forgot all about those titles and rushed out of Somalia in shame and disgrace, dragging the bodies of its soldiers."

DECEMBER 8, 1994—OPERATION BOJINKA BEGINS IN THE PHILIPPINES:

Al Qaeda member Ramzi Yousef joins his uncle Khalid Sheikh Mohammed, Wali Khan Amin Shah, and Abdul Hakim Ali Hashim Murad in Manila to begin Operation Bojinka, the precursor to the 9/11 attacks. The planned operation has three phases: (1) the assassination of Pope John Paul II; (2) the bombings of multiple commercial airliners as they head to the United States; and (3) piloting and crashing commercial airliners into U.S. targets, namely, CIA headquarters, the Pentagon, the World Trade Center, the Sears Tower in Chicago, the Transamerica Tower in San Francisco, and a nuclear power plant. The money for the operation comes to the terrorists in Manila from Osama bin Laden through his brother-in-law Mohammed Jamal Khalifa. The assassination of the pope is designed to be a diversion for the second phase. To prepare for the last phase, Murad has trained as a pilot in North Carolina, and several other al Qaeda operatives now attend flight schools in the

United Sates. On the night of January 6, 1995, a fire begins inside the terrorists' apartment as Yousef and Murad inadvertently cross bombmaking chemicals. Responding to the complaints of residents, the Philippine police stumble onto a treasure trove of terrorist evidence.

Just two weeks prior to its implementation, Operation Bojinka is busted. Murad confesses and is extradited to the United States, where he is sentenced to life imprisonment. Shah is arrested in Malaysia and extradited to the United States, where he also is sentenced to life imprisonment. Khalifa, bin Laden's brother-in-law and al Qaeda's moneyman, is arrested in Mountain View, California, as he prepares to fly to Manila; he is arrested for his involvement in the 1993 World Trade Center bombing. In March 1995, Philippine authorities forward the information about the foiled Bojinka plot to the U.S. government, including specific details that Khalifa was the funding source for the terrorist operation. The FBI argues to detain Khalifa for questioning, but the Clinton administration sides with the State Department and deports Khalifa to Jordan, where he is acquitted on murder charges unrelated to the attack in the United States and is allowed to flee to Saudi Arabia. In April 1995, the Clinton administration receives specific evidence of terror plans to hijack airliners and use them as flying weapons in New York and Washington, D.C. Nothing is done. Only a year later the president will personally turn down an offer from the Sudanese government for Osama bin Laden's arrest and extradition to the United States.

FEBRUARY 7, 1995—RAMZI YOUSEF IS CAPTURED IN PAKISTAN:

Operation Bojinka planner Yousef is apprehended while staying at a hotel in Islamabad, Pakistan, by members of the U.S. Diplomatic Security Service. After extradition to the United States, he will be convicted and sentenced to life imprisonment plus 240 years for his involvement in the 1993 World Trade Center bombing. Khalid Sheikh Mohammed will successfully escape Manila and rejoin al Qaeda in Afghanistan, becoming the architect for future operations.

He will propose turning Yousef's Operation Bojinka into a new attack on a grander scale. Mohammed's plot will be executed on September 11, 2001. Yousef will watch his plan unfold on cable TV from his cell in Colorado's "Supermax" penitentiary.

MARCH 8, 1995—AL QAEDA-AFFILIATED TERRORISTS MURDER U.S. DIPLOMATS IN PAKISTAN:

Three armed gunmen in a stolen taxi step from their vehicle and begin firing on a U.S. Embassy van in Karachi, Pakistan. U.S. diplomats Jacqueline Keys Van Landingham and Gary C. Durell are killed, and Mark McCloy is wounded. The attack comes as retaliation for the capture of Ramzi Yousef a month earlier and is carried out by the al Qaeda–affiliated Abu Sayyaf Group.

NOVEMBER 13, 1995—BIN LADEN-CONNECTED TERRORISTS BOMB THE U.S. MILITARY TRAINING COMPLEX IN RIYADH, SAUDI ARABIA:

A powerful car bomb rips through an American military training complex in Riyadh, killing seven people, including five Americans, and wounding sixty others. Officials quickly arrest four Saudi nationals and will behead them in June 1996, in an effort to stem potential unrest and preserve relations with the United States. The terrorists involved are all veterans of the mujahedeen in Afghanistan and boast of their relationship to Osama bin Laden.

1996—THE TALIBAN CONQUERS JALALABAD AND KABUL AND TAKES CONTROL OF AFGHANISTAN

MAY 1996—SUDAN EXPELS BIN LADEN, WHO RETURNS TO AFGHANISTAN:

Sudan expels bin Laden because of international pressure from the United States and Saudi Arabia, and for his involvement in a failed assassination attempt on Egyptian president Hosni Mubarak in June 1995. President Bill Clinton turns down the offer from the Sudanese government to bring bin Laden to the United States, which allows the terror chief to return to Afghanistan and reestablish al Qaeda and jihadist training camps.

JUNE 25, 1996—HEZBOLLAH BOMBS THE KHOBAR TOWERS AT DHAHRAN AIR BASE, SAUDI ARABIA:

At about 10:00 p.m., a fuel truck loaded with 20,000 pounds of explosives detonates just outside the fence of the U.S. military complex in Dhahran, Saudi Arabia, killing nineteen Americans and wounding more than 500. The blast creates a crater eighty-five feet by thirty-five feet. On June 21, 2001, a federal grand jury in Alexandria, Virginia, will indict thirteen members of the pro-Iran Saudi Hezbollah for the attack. The entire operation was planned, funded, and coordinated by Iran's security services on orders from the highest levels of the Iranian government. In 2004, the 9/11 Commission will note the possibility that Osama bin Laden was involved as well.

AUGUST 23, 1996—OSAMA BIN LADEN ISSUES THE FIRST OF TWO DECLARATIONS OF WAR:

Bin Laden issues his first fatwa, published in *Al-Quds Al-Arabi*, a London-based newspaper. The fatwa is titled "Declaration of War against the Americans Occupying the Land of the Two Holy Places."

FEBRUARY 23, 1997—A PALESTINIAN GUNMAN OPENS FIRE ON TOURISTS ATOP NEW YORK CITY'S EMPIRE STATE BUILDING:

Ali Hassan Abu Kamal, a Palestinian teacher, kills a young Dutch tourist and wounds six other people before turning the gun on himself. A handwritten note on his body claims that the attack was in retaliation against the "enemies of Palestine."

NOVEMBER 12, 1997—ISLAMIC TERRORISTS MURDER FOUR AMERICAN OIL COMPANY EMPLOYEES IN KARACHI, PAKISTAN:

Thirty-six hours after Mir Aimal Kasi is pronounced guilty of the murder of two CIA employees at the front gate of CIA headquarters in 1993, two gunmen assassinate four Americans and their driver in Karachi. The Islamic Revolutionary Council and the Aimal Khufia Action Committee are responsible.

NOVEMBER 17, 1997—THE LUXOR, EGYPT TOURIST MASSACRE:

Islamist terrorists from the group Jihad Talaat al-Fath, meaning "War of the Vanguard of the Conquest," attack an archaeological site in Luxor killing sixty-two people, most of them Western tourists.

FEBRUARY 23, 1998—BIN LADEN AND AYMAN AL-ZAWAHIRI REUNITE AND DECLARE WAR ON THE UNITED STATES:

Bin Laden and Zawahiri of the Egyptian Islamic Jihad reunite in Afghanistan. Zawahiri has just recently returned to Afghanistan from Baghdad, where he met with Saddam Hussein and other Iraqi leaders on February 3, 1998. According to *U.S. News & World Report,* Saddam provided $300,000 in funding for al Qaeda and Zawahiri. Three weeks later, bin Laden and Zawahiri declare war on the United States, saying, "We—with God's help—call on every Muslim who believes in God and wishes to be rewarded to comply with God's order to kill the Americans and plunder their money wherever and whenever they find it. We also call on Muslim ulema, leaders, youths, and soldiers to launch the raid on Satan's U.S. troops and the devil's supporters allying with them, and to displace those who are behind them so that they may learn a lesson. The ruling to kill the Americans and their allies—civilians and military—is an individual duty for every Muslim who can do it in any country in which it is possible to do it."

AUGUST 7, 1998—AL QAEDA BOMBS THE U.S. EMBASSIES IN NAIROBI, KENYA, AND DAR ES SALAAM, TANZANIA:

A small pickup truck packed with explosives is driven to the delivery entrance of the U.S. Embassy in Nairobi and detonated. The blast destroys the left and rear of the embassy and the adjacent business building. At the same time, a vehicle containing a large explosives cache approaches the main gate of the U.S. Embassy in Dar es Salaam and explodes. The east wing of the concrete block building is destroyed, and debris rains on streets and houses for a mile in every direction. The two near-simultaneous attacks kill 224 and wound more than 5,000. Within days, Pakistan announces the arrest of Palestinian Mohammed Saddiq Odeh, who admits his role in the blasts and that he was recruited and financed by Osama bin Laden. Odeh describes al Qaeda as a terror network of 5,000 with intent to attack American interests abroad. He also details a litany of attacks on the United States, including the ambush in Somalia. He confirms al Qaeda's involvement in the attacks against the American military in Riyadh and Dhahran in 1995 and 1996. Federal officials publicly charge bin Laden's al Qaeda with the Kenya bombing in a complaint made public on August 28. In November, a federal grand jury returns an indictment against bin Laden and his top military commander, Muhammed Atef, also believed to be hiding in Afghanistan. In December 1998, an unnamed bin Laden aide—identified only as "Confidential Source-1"—confesses that he participated in a plot to attack American military facilities around the world, implicating the Saudi millionaire and his disciples in the embassy explosions in Africa, according to reports.

DECEMBER 1998—IRAQI INTELLIGENCE PLOTS TO BOMB RADIO FREE EUROPE IN PRAGUE, CZECH REPUBLIC:

Jabir Salim, the Iraqi Consul in the Czech Republic and the head of its intelligence operations, oversees a plot to bomb Radio Free Europe. The bombers plan to use a truck bomb loaded with explosives to collapse the headquarters. Salim has received $150,000 in two payments from Saddam's government to purchase untraceable explosives and recruit terrorists. Later that month, however, Salim defects and furnishes details of the plot to Western intelligence services.

DECEMBER 28, 1998—YEMENI TERRORISTS KIDNAP AND MURDER WESTERN TOURISTS:

Sixteen Western tourists—twelve Britons, two U.S. citizens, and two Australians—are kidnapped outside of Aden, Yemen, by the radical jihadist Aden Abyan Islamic Army. Four of the hostages are killed the next day during a raid by Yemeni security forces.

NOVEMBER 12, 1999—ROCKET ATTACKS TARGET U.S. INSTALLATIONS IN ISLAMABAD, PAKISTAN:

Six rockets are fired from improvised launchers in three vehicles at American and United Nations offices in Islamabad. The rockets are all fired within minutes of one another. The attacks are aimed at the U.S. Embassy in the Diplomatic Enclave, the UN headquarters inside the Saudi Pak Tower, and the American Center. Rockets also land on a parked vehicle outside the UN World Food Program.

AUGUST 12, 2000—ISLAMISTS KIDNAP AMERICANS IN UZBEKISTAN:

Four American mountain climbers are kidnapped by members of the Islamic Movement of Uzbekistan. They are able to escape six days later.

OCTOBER 12, 2000—TERRORISTS BOMB THE USS COLE IN THE PORT OF ADEN, YEMEN:

Two men guide a tender boat alongside the USS *Cole,* a U.S. Navy Aegis destroyer docked in the port of Aden, and detonate explosives, blowing a hole twenty feet high and forty feet wide in the hull of the ship. Seventeen sailors aboard the *Cole* are killed, and thirty-nine are injured.

DECEMBER 30, 2000—THE U.S. EMBASSY IN MANILA SURVIVES MULTIPLE BOMBINGS:

Members of Jemaah Islamiyah, the South Asian terrorist operation for al Qaeda, explode five bombs in Manila, killing twenty-two people. One of the bombs detonates across the street from the U.S. Embassy.

SEPTEMBER 11, 2001—TERROR ATTACKS ON U.S. HOMELAND

DECEMBER 22, 2001—"SHOE BOMBER" RICHARD REID CAUGHT ATTEMPTING TO BLOW UP AMERICAN AIRLINES FLIGHT 63

JANUARY 23, 2002—KIDNAPPING AND MURDER OF DANIEL PEARL:

Wall Street Journal reporter Daniel Pearl is kidnapped by al Qaeda operatives in Pakistan on his way to interview a terrorist leader and subsequently held for demands. He is beheaded and a video of the murder is broadcast by radical Islamists. Al Qaeda's military planned the murder, and 9/11 mastermind Khalid Sheikh Mohammed will later confess in a military hearing held at Guantanamo Bay in 2007 that he had personally beheaded Pearl.

JUNE 14, 2002—BOMBING OF THE U.S. CONSULATE IN KARACHI, PAKISTAN:

A truck containing a fertilizer bomb is detonated outside the U.S. Consulate and the Marriott Hotel in Karachi, Pakistan, killing eleven and injuring fifty-one. Al Qaeda is suspected.

AUGUST 14, 2002—TERRORIST ABU NIDAL MURDERED IN BAGHDAD, IRAQ:

The terror kingpin responsible for killing or injuring more than 900 people over two decades is killed by Saddam Hussein's agents. Nidal reportedly dies of multiple gunshot wounds in his apartment in Baghdad. Palestinian sources say Abu Nidal was assassinated on the orders of Hussein after refusing to train al Qaeda fighters based in Iraq. Iraqi officials claim he committed suicide.

OCTOBER 6, 2002—FRENCH OIL TANKER BOMBING:

Al Qaeda floats a small dinghy loaded with explosives into the side of the French tanker *Limburg*, killing one and injuring twelve. Ninety thousand barrels of crude oil leak into the Gulf of Aden. Al Qaeda claims responsibility for the attack, and Abd al-Rahim al-Nashiri, who also planned the USS *Cole* attack, is thought to have been the mastermind.

OCTOBER 12, 2002—NIGHTCLUB BOMBINGS IN BALI:

Car bombs detonated outside the Sari Club Disco and Paddy's Bar in Bali, Indonesia, kill 202 people. Most of the dead are Australian tourists. Seven Americans are also killed. Al Qaeda claims responsibility. Iman Smudra, who trained in Afghanistan in al Qaeda camps, is sentenced to death.

OCTOBER 28, 2002—U.S. DIPLOMAT ASSASSINATED IN JORDAN:

Laurence Foley, the Executive Officer for the U.S. Agency for International Development, is assassinated in Amman, Jordan, as he enters his car to drive to the U.S. Embassy. Salem Sa'ed bin Suwied and Yasser Fathi Ibraheem are the assailants who kill Foley at the direction of al Qaeda in Iraq leader Abu Musab al-Zarqawi. He is also responsible for the 2005 bombing of three hotels in Amman, Jordan. Al-Zarqawi will later be tracked down by U.S. troops and killed when two U.S. Air Force F-16 jets drop two 500-pound laser guided bombs on his safehouse in Iraq.

MARCH 1, 2003—AL QAEDA LEADER KHALID SHEIKH MOHAMMED CAPTURED IN KARACHI, PAKISTAN:

The mastermind behind the 9/11 attacks, as well the Richard Reid shoe bombing attempt, the Bali Nightclub bombings, and the 1993 bombing of the World Trade Center in New York, is captured in his hotel room in Pakistan.

OCTOBER 15, 2003—U.S. DIPLOMATIC CONVOY
BOMBED IN THE GAZA STRIP:

A roadside bomb goes off beneath a convoy carrying U.S. diplomats in Gaza, killing three American members of a security detail and injuring another. The American diplomats were on their way to interview Palestinian students for the awarding of the prestigious Fulbright scholarships to study in the United States.

MARCH 11, 2004—TRAIN BOMBINGS IN MADRID, SPAIN:

Three days before Spanish elections, terrorists launch a coordinated attack on Madrid's commuter train system during morning rush hour, killing 191 people and wounding almost 1,800. Spanish courts determine that a terror group inspired by al Qaeda is responsible for the attacks.

NOVEMBER 11, 2004—PALESTINIAN LEADER YASSIR ARAFAT DIES

DECEMBER 7, 2004—THE U.S. CONSULATE IN JEDDAH,
SAUDI ARABIA ATTACKED:

Terrorists storm the U.S. Consulate in Jeddah, Saudi Arabia, killing five consulate employees.

APRIL 19, 2005—U.S. NAVAL VESSELS ATTACKED IN AQABA, JORDAN:

In the most significant attack against U.S. Naval vessels since the USS *Cole* in 2000, terrorists shoot three rockets at an amphibious assault ship docked in the Port of Aqaba, Jordan, killing one Jordanian sailor.

JULY 7, 2005—LONDON TRANSIT SYSTEM BOMBINGS:

In attacks, also known as 7/7, suicide bombers launch a series of coordinated attacks on the London Underground train system and on one double-decker bus and three London Underground trains, killing 52 people and injuring over 700. The bombings coincide with the G8 Conference being held in London. The terrorists, all of whom are killed in the attacks, were inspired by the American Muslim Cleric Anwar al-Awlaki.

JULY 21, 2005—A SECOND ATTACK ON LONDON'S TRANSIT SYSTEM:

A follow-on attempt is made by terrorists again attempting to target London's Underground train system, but only minor injuries occur. Four bombs were designed to cause as much damage as the 7/7 attacks, but the explosives fail to detonate.

NOVEMBER 9, 2005:—HOTEL BOMBINGS IN AMMAN, JORDAN:

A series of coordinated bomb attacks are launched on three western-affiliated hotels in Amman, Jordan, killing 60 people and injuring 115 others. The attacks are said to have come from Iraq at the direction of al Qaeda in Iraq leader Abu Musab al-Zarqawi.

NOVEMBER 26, 2008—TERROR IN MUMBAI, INDIA:

A series of ten coordinated shooting and bombing attacks are launched across Mumbai, India, killing 173 people and wounding 308. Islamic terrorists from Pakistan are the attackers.

JUNE 1, 2009—GUNMAN ATTACKS TWO U.S. ARMY RECRUITERS IN LITTLE ROCK, AR:

Abdulhakim Mujahid Muhammad, a converted Muslim, shot and killed Private William Long and seriously injured Private Quinton Ezeagwula both U.S. Army recruiters as they stood in front of their office in Little Rock, Arkansas.

NOVEMBER 5, 2009—U.S. ARMY MAJOR HASAN ATTACKS FORT HOOD, TX:

Major Nidal Malik Hasan, a psychiatrist in the U.S. Army, shouting "Allahu Akbar!" ("God is Great!") shoots and kills thirteen and wounds thirty in the Soldier Readiness Center at Fort Hood, Texas. Previously, Hasan was known to frequent the mosque of the America-born terrorist Imam Anwar al-Awlaki in Silver Spring, Maryland.

DECEMBER 25, 2009—BOMBING ATTEMPT ON
NORTHWEST AIRLINES FLIGHT 253:

Umar Farouk Abdulmutallab unsuccessfully attempts to detonate a explosive device onboard Northwest Airlines flight 253 as it descended for landing into Detroit, MI. If successful, the attack would have killed up to 289 people. It is suspected that Abdulmutallab received his weapons training in Yemen from al Qaeda and is a devoted follower of terror Imam Anwar al-Awlaki.

MAY 1, 2010—BOMBING ATTEMPT AT TIMES SQUARE:

Pakistani-born Faisal Shahzad attempts to detonate a car bomb at the bustling Times Square in New York City. Two street vendors notify the police when they see Shahzad's SUV smoking and parked with its hazards on. Shahzad is a follower of Imam Anwar al-Awlaki and had received his munitions training from the Pakistani Taliban. The self-proclaimed "Muslim soldier," when asked why he would attempt such an attack, explained to the judge "It's a war."

ARE YOU SAFER?

Reproduced with permission of the Center for Security Policy.
For updates please visit www.centerforsecuritypolicy.org.

JANUARY 2009

21 JANUARY 2009

White House website announces willingness to talk to Iran "without preconditions"

Source: Borger, Julian, "Barack Obama: Administration willing to talk to Iran 'without preconditions'," The Guardian, *21 January 2009.*

The day after President Obama's inauguration, the White House website posted a statement saying that the Obama administration was willing to talk to Iran "without preconditions" and that it intended to work towards the abolition of nuclear weapons. By declaring itself committed to a foreign policy of appeasement and disarmament, the Obama White House essentially unilaterally disarmed itself before the entire world on its first day in office. Given the realities of an Iranian regime zealously dedicated to achieving a deliverable nuclear weapon, wiping Israel off the face of the map, exporting revolution and terror abroad, and brutally suppressing all domestic dissent, such a posture is exceptionally dangerous to US national security and that of our friends and allies.

21 JANUARY 2009

Obama invites president of Islamic Society of North America (ISNA) to speak at inaugural prayer service

Source: The Investigative Project on Terrorism. "ISNA's Mattson to Speak at Inaugural Prayer Service," IPT News, 20 January 2009.

ISNA was an unindicted co-conspirator in the Holy Land Foundation terrorism financing trial, and was founded by the Muslim Brotherhood, a Shariah-promoting organization that has the self-described goal of "destroying American civilization from within." Embracing ISNA sends a dangerous signal to Shariah-supporting jihadists that the United States does not recognize the threat posed by jihadist doctrine.

22 JANUARY 2009

DNI-Designate Adm. Dennis Blair issues conciliatory statement on Iran

Source: Mikkelsen, Randall, "Obama spy choice sees opportunity on Iran, Muslims," Reuters, 22 January 2009.

Two days after the inauguration of the Obama administration, Director of National Intelligence-designate Adm. Dennis Blair asserted that US intelligence agencies should seek ways to work with Muslim countries such as Iran. While admitting that there exist "anti-American leaders, policies and actions in Iran," he said that intelligence agencies can also help US policymakers to identify and understand "other leaders and political forces" in order to find common ground "in both our interests." Coming from the US's top appointed intelligence official, a statement like this at the very outset of the new US administration served to let the Tehran regime know that the hallmark of the new team would be dialogue and a willingness to turn a blind eye to Iran's defiance of U.N. Security Council Resolutions regarding its nuclear weapons program, its support for Islamic jihadi terrorists abroad, and abysmal human rights record at home. Further, Blair's understanding of the national security responsibilities of the US Intelligence Community towards this country's adversaries would appear to be deeply flawed.

22 JANUARY 2009

Terrorist holding facilities closed

Source: Executive Order 13491 Ensuring Lawful Interrogations Sec. 4(a). Prohibition of Certain Detention Facilities

Immediately upon taking office, Obama ordered that the CIA shall close "any detention facilities that it currently operates and shall not operate any such detention facility in the future." On the one hand, CIA personnel are being asked to risk their lives on the frontlines against terrorists; on the other, they cannot set up the basic infrastructure they need to succeed. It is predictable that time-urgent intelligence will be lost because captured terrorists cannot be held in US controlled facilities in the field.

22 JANUARY 2009

White House task force to micromanage detainee interrogations

Source: Executive Order 13491 Ensuring Lawful Interrogations Sec. 5(a) Establishment of Special Interagency Task Force

Immediately upon taking office, Obama set up an interagency task force to oversee and review detainee interrogations and transfers, removing lead responsibility for such interrogations from wartime intelligence operations and turning it over to the law enforcement/ criminal prosecution-oriented FBI. More bureaucratic layers and more Washington second-guessing mean a less agile, more risk-averse war effort to go after terrorists and the time urgent intelligence America needs to stop them and protect lives.

22 JANUARY 2009

Terrorist detainees ordered to be tried in civilian courts

Source: Executive Order 13492, Review and Disposition of Individuals Detained at the Guantanamo Bay Naval Base and Closure of Detention Facilities Sec, 4 (c) (3) Determination of Prosecution.

Immediately upon taking office, Obama directed that GITMO detainees shall be released, transferred or tried in civilian courts—another case of act first, think later. Now terrorists can count on the same protections given US citizens under the constitution—the very system of government they seek to destroy—including the right against self-incrimination. Captured terrorists are our best source of intelligence—except when they are told they have the right not to talk.

27 JANUARY 2009

President Obama gives first formal TV interview to Al-Arabiya and offers 'hand of friendship' to Iran

Source: "Obama reaches out to Muslim world," BBC, 27 January 2009.

One week into his new administration, President Obama gave his first formal television interview to the Saudi-funded, Arabic language Al-Arabiya network. In it, he offered the hand of friendship to Iran if it "unclenched its fist." Aside from the symbolism of this choice of outlets, Obama's over-eager outreach signaled a US posture of supplication vis-à-vis thuggish theocrats whose regime remains according to the Department of State the preeminent state-sponsor of terror in the world. Such a proffer was immediately taken by the Iranian regime and other Muslim/Arab audiences as an unambiguous indication of American weakness. In such circles, far from encouraging moderation and conciliation, weakness spawns aggression and belligerence.

29 JANUARY 2009

President Obama Drafts a letter to Iranian President Ahmadinejad

Source: MacAskill, Ewen and Robert Tait, "Revealed: the letter Obama team hope will heal Iran rift," Guardian, *29 January 2009.*

The British press reported in late January 2009 that the Obama State Department was working on a letter from Obama to the Iranian regime intended to unfreeze relations and open the way for bilateral talks. The letter, oddly never acknowledged by the Obama White House, reportedly was intended as a reply to Iranian president Ahmadinejad's letter of congratulations, sent after Obama's November 2008 election win. The Obama administration's insistence upon demonstrating pacific intentions towards the Tehran regime through a gentlemanly exchange of diplomatically-worded missives projected a deadly image of weakness at the outset of its tenure. That image will cripple US foreign policy with a regime and in a part of the world where only strength is respected.

JANUARY–DECEMBER 2009

The Administration refuses to detain the vast majority of illegal workers they find

Sources: Alden, Edward. "Obama Quietly Changes US Immigration Policy," New American Media, December 28, 2009; Mayer, Matt A.,"US Border Security: Realities and Challenges for the Obama Administration," The Heritage Foundation, June 17, 2009.

The Administration has also drastically revised immigration policy, by halting workplace raids, stripping local law enforcement of its ability to pursue illegals, closing down detention facilities, and allowing "political asylum" applicants to live freely in the United States.

JANUARY 2009–JANUARY 2010

Obama Administration appoints supporters of rapprochement with Tehran to top US foreign policy positions

Source: Lopez, Clare, "Supporters of 'dialogue' with the Iranian Mullahs Keep the US from 'meddling' on behalf of freedom," Center for Security Policy, 22 June 2009. See also: Ward, Jon, "It's official: controversial Chas Freeman to NIC," The Washington Times, 26 February 2009.

The current, dangerous policy of conciliation and rapprochement towards the terrorist regime in Tehran was advanced by key appointments to the Obama administration. Prominent among these were individuals who have long records of advocating appeasement, diplomacy and engagement with the mullahs, while opposing condemnation of the regime, coercive diplomacy, or military force even as a final resort. Among these appointees were: Dr. Susan Rice

(U.N. Ambassador); Dr. Vali Nasr (senior advisor to President Obama's Special Envoy for Afghanistan and Pakistan, Ambassador Richard Holbrooke); Dennis Ross (senior Iran advisor at the National Security Council); and Ray Takeyh (Assistant to the US Special Advisor for the Gulf and Southwest Asia). Another was nominated to be chairman of the National Intelligence Council but withdrew his name in the face of a storm of criticism, former Ambassador to Saudi Arabia, Charles W. Freeman, Jr.

FEBRUARY 2009

4 FEBRUARY 2009

US Treasury designates the Free Life Party of Kurdistan (PJAK) a terrorist organization

Source: US Department of the Treasury, Office of Foreign Assets Control, "Recent OFAC Actions," 4 February 2009.

The US Treasury designated the Free Life Party of Kurdistan (PJAK) a terrorist organization under Executive Order 13224. Pursuant to this action, the US froze the group's assets and prohibited American citizens from doing business with it. This action was designed to be a conciliatory gesture to the Turkish government, which views the PJAK as an element of the Turkish terrorist organization, the PKK. By designating as a terrorist organization a group whose primary focus is the rights of Kurds inside Iran, however, the US government sent a signal to all opponents of the mullahs' regime that the Obama administration prioritizes efforts to establish a relationship with the Tehran regime above all else.

8 FEBRUARY 2009

Vice President Biden announces that the US desires to "reset" relations with Russia at the Munich International Security Council
Source: "'Reset' Sought on Relations With Russia, Biden Says," The Washington Post, *8 February 2009.*

The statement that the new administration was determined to "reset" US-Russian relations implied that all or most previous Kremlin positions were, in fact, valid and made it harder for the US to defend its legitimate security interests in relations with Russia. It also increased the threat to Russia's neighbors, particularly Georgia. For example, there is strong evidence that the decision to invade Georgia in April 2008 was taken after NATO failed to offer a Membership Action Plan to Georgia and Ukraine during its annual summit in Bucharest. Russia did not achieve its strategic objectives in the subsequent invasion of Georgia in August of that year. Saakashvili is still in power and Georgia still serves as a supply corridor for energy for the West. Many Russian leaders want to finish the job and may see in the "reset" new opportunities to do so.

20 FEBRUARY 2009

Clinton downgrades human rights in relations with Beijing

Source: Hillary Clinton, "Working Toward Change in Perceptions of US Engagement Around the World," US Department of State, February 20, 2009.

Secretary of State Hillary Rodham Clinton said human rights can't interfere with other issues to be discussed with Beijing. Chinese leaders were reported to have been ecstatic when she said these words as they signaled Washington's perceptions of its own weakness. In fact, Beijing adopted a markedly more aggressive attitude toward the United States since then.

26 FEBRUARY 2009

Tax hike to put "mom and pop" oil producers out of business

Source: Hebert, H. Josef, "Obama: New tax on oil drilling," Associated Press/North Dakota News, February 26, 2009; National Stripper Well Association. Press Statement on Obama Administration's Extraction Tax Policies, 12 August 2009.

Obama sought new taxes on new drilling in his 2010 budget that could put small "mom and pop" producers out of business, according to the group representing "stripper wells"—those yielding only about 15 barrels daily of harder to extract oil, but which add up to over a million barrels per day. This one measure, taken ironically in the name of "energy independence," could reduce domestic oil output by 15.4 percent and gas output by about 9 percent almost overnight by penalizing small producers at home who produce about as much oil as we import from our friends the Saudis. "The decreased production that will result from the proposed tax increases will have a catastrophic effect upon the American consumer since less domestic oil means higher prices," said Dewey Bartlett, Jr., chairman of the National Stripper Well Association. "The OPEC leadership will have almost exclusive control over the world-wide pricing of crude oil as well as all products refined from crude oil such as gasoline, jet fuel and diesel fuel.

26 FEBRUARY 2009

White House announces plans to slash the US Defense Budget

Source: Congressional Budget Office, Office of Management and Budget, "A New Era of Responsibility: Renewing America's Promise," 26 February 2009, Table S-8; and Office of Management and Budget, Budget of the United States Government, FY 2010, Historical Tables, Table 5.1.

The Obama Administration releases a 10-year budget plan which proposes a declining defense budget, beginning at 3.81 percent of gross domestic product in 2010 and dropping to a startling 3.01 percent in 2019. Flat or declining defense budgets will undermine the US military's ability to meet its commitments.

26 FEBRUARY 2009

Locking up land, increasing energy insecurity

Sources: "Bush Oil-Shale Leases Canceled by Salazar," The Washington Post, 26 February 2009; "Energy Experts Agree: CLEAR Act (H.R. 3534) Will Delay American Wind, Solar, Uranium, Oil and Natural Gas Production," House Natural Resources Committee Republican Press Office, 18 September 2009.

While proclaiming a drive for "energy independence," President Obama's administration canceled deals for domestic oil and gas exploration that had been approved by the Bush administration, and sealed off much of the rest of the country from hydrocarbon exploration and production. This entailed excluding hundreds of thousands of acres from land-lease deals for domestic energy E&P (e.g., Utah, Colorado), shortening lease-times and slow-walking the extant Bush plan for a billion more acres (US Outer Continental Shelf). The cumulative effect was to leave the United States more dependent on foreign energy sources by making it harder to find and exploit American oil and natural gas reserves.

FEBRUARY 2009

Loss of key financial talent to foreign competitors threatens economic security

Sources: "Bankers Face Sweeping Curbs on Pay," The Wall Street Journal, 18 September 2009; "FDIC to bonus-loving banks: Pay up!" CNN Money, 12 January 2010; and "Hedge funds may benefit from bank bonus clampdown," Reuters, 16 December 2009.

Government-mandated limits on compensation and bonuses, including those dictated by the "pay czar," regulatory limits and excessive taxation on banker pay (including executives, traders, and loan officers) have created a climate that promotes an exodus of top talent to less-regulated areas, including foreign hedge funds. From the lens of an economic warfare perspective, this is tantamount to sending the best warriors to the opposition. A loss of this talent threatens US capital market superiority, which has provided superior economic growth and supported the national security.

FEBRUARY 2009

Obama signs $787 billion stimulus into law; excessive budget deficits put US Dollar and economy in jeopardy

Sources: "Deficit Projected to Soar with New Programs," The Washington Post, 26 August 2009; "Obama's Tripling of the National Debt," The Heritage Foundation, 28 August 2009; "Stimulus? There's No Stimulus Here," The Wall Street Journal, 11 January 2010; "China bidding dollar goodbye? Harvard economist says currency dying 'slow death,'" WorldNetDaily, 23 October 2009; "Dollar Reaches Breaking Point as Banks Shift," Bloomberg, 12 October 2009.

Massive stimulus programs with primary effect of wealth transfer rather than productive investment have ballooned the government debt in both the near- and longer-term. This debt will require historic government borrowing predominantly from foreign sources, providing tremendous leverage by China and other creditor nations and placing the dollar at risk of mass devaluation and loss of reserve currency status. Such trends compromise the US economy and hinders future governmental ability to fund national defense, essentially mimicking several factors that led to collapse of the Soviet Union.

MARCH 2009

13 MARCH 2009

Congress introduces Open Fuel Standard Act, but both the executive and legislative branch fail to move it forward in 2009.

Source: THOMAS Library of Congress Database. House Version (HR 1476) and Senate Version (S.835).

The Open Fuel Standard Act (OFS) requires that most cars made or sold in the United States be "flex fuel vehicles"—that is, automobiles capable of operating on gasoline, ethanol (from any source) or methanol (from any source) or any combination of the three. Providing fuel choice at the pump will reduce the strategic value of oil, making countries that sponsor or enable terrorism less capable of using oil revenues to bankroll terror or threatening to bring the global economy to a halt. This commonsensical and urgently needed means of providing the consumer with "fuel choice" and of undermining the OPEC cartel could have been enacted by now but has not been due to a lack of leadership from the President and his allies on Capitol Hill.

13 MARCH 2009

No longer "enemy combatants," terrorist supporters have new legal protections against being detained

Source: In Re: Guantanamo Bay Litigation, Respondents' Memorandum Regarding the Government's Detention Authority Relative to Detainees Held at Guantanamo Bay, US District Court District of Columbia Misc. No. 08-442 (TFH), March 13, 2009.

Under new standards promulgated by the Obama administration, individuals who supported al Qaeda or the Taliban are detainable only if the support was "substantial" and the term "enemy combatant" is struck from the official lexicon in favor of "unlawful enemy belligerents." House Intelligence Committee ranking member Pete Hoekstra says this means that, "If we knew that Mohammed Atta had planned to board a plane tomorrow and we had intelligence that he intended to fly it into the World Trade Center, we could not hold him unless he provided 'substantial' support to other terrorists," In other words, "intention and intelligence become irrelevant."

17 MARCH 2009

President waives export control to allow transfer of high-tech items to China

Source: President Barack Obama, "Message to the Congress from the President concerning exports to China," The White House, March 17, 2009.

The President certified that the transfer of certain inherently dual-use items would not "measurably improve the missile or space launch capabilities" of China. Unfortunately, Beijing sees space primarily in military terms. In view of the substantial advances in the Chinese space program (notably, its anti-satellite and other space-control capabilities), the United States should not export any technology or equipment that can help China improve its ability to dominate space in the absence of congressional approval.

21 MARCH 2009

Obama 'Nowruz' greetings convey weakness to regime and alienate Iranian people

Source: Aryamand, Mani, "Khamenei Slams Obama Nowruz Message," Marze Por Gohar Party, 27 March 2009.

After President Obama sent official greetings to "the Islamic Republic of Iran" on the occasion of the traditional Persian New Year ('Nowruz'), Iran's Supreme Leader Khamenei responded by slamming the US president, whom he said had "insulted the Islamic Republic of Iran from the first day." The Obama administration apparently inadvertently marked the occasion of an ancient, pre-Islamic celebration of spring that is scorned by Iran's revolutionary clerics. Further, by referring to "the Islamic Republic of Iran," Obama managed to insult the Iranian people as well, who cherish their Nowruz observances as a tradition that pre-dates the Arab Islamic conquest by more than a thousand years.

23 MARCH 2009

Obama nominates transnationlist Harold Koh to be State Department Legal Adviser

Source: The White House Press Office, "President Obama Announces more key Administration Posts," 23 March 2009.

Harold Koh, President Obama's choice for State Department Legal Adviser, subscribes to "transnationalism"—the view that American jurisprudence should be "informed by" (read, subordinated to) international legal regimes and "norms" and that courts, not Congress, should take the lead in "internalizing" international law into domestic law so as to better develop a "global legal system." Koh's views are demonstrated through his support for such sovereignty-sapping global legal arrangements as the International Criminal Court and the Law of the Sea Treaty, his belief that UN authorization is required prior to any US use of force, and other notions that serve to erode American constitutional governance and exceptional-ism.

25 MARCH 2009

Treasury Secretary Geithner says the US "open" to a global currency

Source: Roger C. Altman and Timothy F. Geithner, "A Conversation with Timothy F. Geithner," Council on Foreign Relations. March 25, 2009.

In so doing, he encouraged the Chinese, the Russians, Persian Gulf states and others who seek substantially to diminish the power of the United States in international markets and commerce. Beijing has proposed the adoption of a global currency to replace the American dollar. Such a new currency could also limit Washington's ability to manage the American economy. Efforts to supplant the dollar as the world's preeminent reserve currency should be discouraged, not abetted by the US government.

APRIL 2009

6 APRIL 2009

Terminating acquisition of America's most advanced military aircraft and shutting down its only hot production line for "fifth generation" fighters

Source: Defense Industry Daily, "Gates Lays Out Key FY 2010 Budget Recommendations," April 6, 2009.

The Obama administration capped F-22 Raptor procurement at 187 aircraft, despite Air Force Chief of Staff General Norton Schwartz's assessment that only 243 F-22s would place the Air Force at moderate risk during future conflicts. The Air Force has said that an inventory of just 183 Raptors would entail "moderate to high" risk.

6 APRIL 2009

Obama gives speech in Turkey, apologizing for America, even as Turkey embraces Iran, Syria

Source: Remarks of President Obama in Address to the Turkish Parliament (April 6, 2009)

At a time when President Obama should have been voicing deep concern over Turkey's growing entente with Iran and Syria—both anti-democratic sponsors of global terrorism—he traveled to Istanbul to give a speech before the so-called "Muslim world" which amounted to an apology for past American policies and behavior. Such "outreach" only served to embolden the Turkish leadership to intensify its rapprochement with its longtime adversaries, Iran and Syria, and reinforces the impression of Western submission to Islam that can only intensify the jihadist ambitions of the ideology authoritative Islam calls "Shariah."

16 APRIL 2009

Justice Department legal opinions on terrorist interrogations disclosed and overruled by the Obama Administration

Source: Office of the Legal Counsel (OLC) at the Department of Justice Website. See OLC Opinions Disclosed by the Obama Administration 16 April 2009

Obama released detailed information on specific "enhanced" interrogation techniques, enabling enemies to exploit the revelations for propaganda value and rendering those techniques useless. In the wake of such disclosures of extremely sensitive information, foreign intelligence partners have become more reluctant to trust American counterparts with their secrets; cooperation is already shutting down in some areas. And we are left with the question no one wants to ask. What if the United States captures a terrorist with perishable knowledge of a pending attack: Will the new, tempered interrogation guidelines be good enough to elicit such information in time?

17 APRIL 2009

Obama gives apologetic speech on Latin America

Source: Vucci, Evan, "Obama Pledges 'Equal Partnership' in the Americas," USA Today *and Associated Press, 17 April 2009.*

In a speech in Trinidad and Tobago, Obama continued what some have called his "international apology tour." He declared that "[The United States has] at times been disengaged, and at times we sought to dictate our terms. But I pledge to you that we seek an equal partnership. There is no senior partner and junior partner in our relations; there is simply engagement based on mutual respect and common interests and shared values ... The United States will be willing to acknowledge past errors where those errors have been made." Obama's message was seized upon by America's regional enemies like Venezuelan autocrat Hugo Chavez and discouraged its relatively few remaining friends in the hemisphere.

17 APRIL 2009

Obama lifts restrictions on travel to Cuba

Source: Stolberg, Sheryl Gay and Alexei Barrionuevo, "Obama Says the US will Pursue Thaw with Cuba," The New York Times, *April 17, 2009.*

President Obama acceded to pressure from the left-leaning Secretary General of the Organization of American States to ease the historic isolation by the OAS of the Castro Brothers' Cuba. Mr. Obama also unilaterally lifted restrictions on Cuban-Americans traveling to Cuba. Such US concessions were not tied to reciprocal movement on democratic liberalization by the Castro regime or, for that matter by other despots in the hemisphere like Chavez in Venezuela or Daniel Ortega in Nicaragua.

19 APRIL 2009

Pentagon backs down in face of Chinese belligerence

Source: Roughead, Adm. Gary, "Press Conference of the US Chief of Naval Operations," Embassy of the United States in the People's Republic of China, April 19, 2009.

Soon after the Chinese harassed unarmed US Navy ships in international waters in the South China Sea (one of which probably constituted an act of war), the Navy proposed to "advance our military-to-military relationship and the context of a broader and comprehensive US-China relationship." The Navy should have publicly warned the Chinese instead of trying to provide more technology and operational know-how to Beijing. The Navy, however, was following the President Obama's lead in essentially soft-pedaling criticism of the Chinese for their aggressive conduct, an attitude he exhibited when he met with China's foreign minister on March 12.

MAY 2009

7 MAY 2009

White House requests no specific finding for border fence required by the Secure Fence Act of 2006

Source: "Obama's Budget Proposal Cuts Border Fence Funds," The Dallas Morning News, May 7, 2009.

Despite declaring border security and the violence along the southwest border to be an important issue, in its FY 2010 budget request, the Obama administration requested no funding specifically for the border barrier required by Congress in the Secure Fence Act of 2006. Homeland Security and FBI officials have testified on several occasions that suspected terrorists are among the large number of immigrants who have crossed into the United States illegally from Mexico.

12 MAY 2009

US Envoy in Tehran just before journalist set free

Sources: "Senior Obama advisor comes to Iran: Report," Iran Press TV, 13 May 2009; McCarthy, Andrew, "Obama Frees Iranian Terror Masters," National Review, *11 July 2009.*

Amid reports that US Iranian-born envoy Vali Nasr was in Tehran, the American journalist Roxana Saberi was set free in a surprising conclusion to five months imprisonment on trumped up espionage charges. Two months later, in mid-July 2009, the Obama administration released five Islamic Revolutionary Guard Corps (IRGC) Qods Force commanders who had been caught in Irbil, Iraq coordinating terrorist attacks that killed hundreds of US troops. It is difficult to avoid the conclusion that the latters' release was forthcoming at least in part to secure Saberi's freedom. The willingness thus exhibited to accede to direct Iranian involvement in the deaths of American soldiers communicated to the Iranian regime that such behavior would, under President Obama, be cost-free.

14 MAY 2009

House Speaker Nancy Pelosi accused CIA briefers of lying to her and other lawmakers about the use of enhanced interrogation techniques, such as waterboarding

Source: Klein, Ron and Human Khan, "House Speaker Nancy Pelosi: CIA Lied to Me," ABC World News with Diane Sawyer, 14 May 2009.

Pelosi had no proof to support this outlandish charge and was properly called out on it by both CIA Director (and former Representative) Leon Panetta and Republicans in Congress. In short order, the Speaker's allies were scrambling to find anything that would make CIA look bad. In so doing, they have played into the hands of America's adversaries who want nothing more than to discredit CIA. Politicians pay no political cost for attacking CIA, but the collateral effect is to expose secrets that make our adversaries' work easier. Not surprisingly, morale in the intelligence community has never been worse, which means new opportunities for enemy spy services out to recruit Americans to work for them.

21 MAY 2009

President Signs US-UAE Civilian Nuclear Cooperation Agreement

Source: Philip Walter Wellman, "US Signs Nuclear Deal with UAE," Voice of America News, December 18, 2009.

This deal is intended to clear the way for the United Arab Emirates to gain access to sensitive, inherently dual-use US nuclear technology. Never mind that the UAE is a state that transships more advanced goods to Iran than any other nation. The agreement ostensibly was conditioned on the UAE not trying to make its own nuclear fuel (a process that brings states within weeks or months of getting the bomb). It is being sold as the model for pushing more such nuclear accords in the Middle East. But the deal also allows the UAE to ignore that key requirement if the US strikes deals with other Middle Eastern states that has no such caveat. Also, the White House has failed to get other nuclear reactor-supplying states (notably, France) to impose similar conditions on their sales to the Middle East, opening the door further to Middle Eastern proliferation. Ironically, instead of the US securing reactor sales to the UAE, the Emirates awarded the contract late in 2009 to South Korea.

MAY 2009

Iranian Supreme Leader Khamenei publicly spurns Obama letter

Source: MacAskill, Ewen, "Obama sent letter to Khamenei before the election, report says," Guardian, 24 June 2009

Sometime in May 2009, President Obama personalized his effort to "engage" the mullahs of Tehran by sending a private letter to the Iranian Supreme Leader. In it, he offered the prospect for cooperation in regional and bilateral relations and a resolution of the dispute over Iran's nuclear weapons program. Khamenei publicly and contemptuously spurned this initiative during a belligerent Friday prayers sermon one week after Iran's disputed June 12 presidential elections.

MAY 2009

Cutting core defense capabilities

Sources: Gingrich, Newt, "Maintaining America's Safety to Build Our Prosperity and Freedom," Heritage Lecture #1128, August 6, 2009; Talent, Jim and Mackenzie Eaglen, "Obama's 2010 Defense Budget: Top Five Worst Choices for National Security," Heritage Web Memo #2486, June 15, 2009.

President Obama submitted a defense budget request to Congress for fiscal year 2010 that will dramatically reshape America's military by cutting funding for key weapons acquisition programs, notably, the F-22 air superiority fighter, C-17 transport aircraft and missile defenses (for more on the last of these, see below). When Congress ultimately gave the Administration substantially what it wanted, America's armed forces were denied capabilities that the troops require and that our citizens assume they will be afforded. Specific areas that are being impacted include, but are hardly limited to: strategic defense; control of the seas; air superiority; space control; projecting power to distant regions; and information dominance throughout cyberspace.

MAY 2009

Slashing missile defense funding and capabilities

Source: Department of Defense Fiscal Year 2010 Budget Request Summary Justification, p. 3–34.

The Obama Administration's FY 2010 defense budget request reduces total missile defense funding by $1.62 billion—nearly a 15 percent decline from the FY 2009 appropriations level. A robust US missile defense posture provides greater international stability and more successful non-proliferation and nuclear disarmament initiatives. Cutting US missile defenses is undermining American allies and emboldening such foes as Iran and North Korea.

JUNE 2009

2 JUNE 2009

Government handling of GM bankruptcy transfers auto industry capability to China

Sources: "GM Collapses into Government's Arms," The Wall Street Journal, *June 2, 2009; "2009/2010 Auto Industry Analysis: GM's Transition to China," eMotion Reports, December 2009.*

The method with which the government has collapsed General Motors included a rush to sell off or close potentially strategic technology and manufacturing capabilities, including the Opel, Saab, Saturn, Pontiac, and Hummer lines. One of the prime beneficiaries of these fire-sales has been Communist China. Beijing has enhanced its indigenous capabilities to compete with US car producers and secured some level of de facto Chinese control over a vital US company that has long enjoyed a significant position within that industry. Industry analysts regard these steps as but part of the endgame in China's takeover of the US auto industry.

12 JUNE 2009

US observes passively as Iranian Security Forces brutally attack unarmed civilians protesting fraudulent elections

Source: "Obama Offers Rhetorical Support to Iran Protestors— Is It Enough?" Fox News, 28 December 2009.

When the Iranian population erupted in fury following the June 2009 announcement that President Mahmoud Ahmadinejad had emerged victorious in elections widely seen as fraudulent, President Obama reacted belatedly and timidly. When he did address the Tehran regime's repression of the "Green Revolution," Mr. Obama spoke only of "bearing witness" to the violent and bloody events unfolding on the streets of Iranian cities. His remarks were was cynically calibrated to ensure no offense was given to the ruling clerics whose vicious black-clad Bassij forces were clubbing, gassing, knifing, and shooting their countrymen across Iran. In the subsequent months, as the demonstrations continued notwithstanding brutal repression intended to suppress those struggling against the tyranny that brutalizes them and threatens us, the Obama administration reluctantly expressed the bare minimum of rhetorical support for the Iranian freedom fighters—a posture that exposed its continuing, albeit unrequited, dedication to dialogue with the regime.

15 JUNE 2009

Obama fights to repeal REAL-ID

Source: Kephart, Janice L. and Jena Baker McNeill, "The PASS ID Act: Rolling Back Security Standards for Driver's Licenses," The Heritage Foundation, June 28, 2009.

This administration made clear its ambition to repeal the REAL ID Act, legislation designed to make it vastly more difficult for illegal aliens, including terrorists, to obtain drivers' licenses. The Administration supports instead the PASS ID, which weakens the REAL ID requirement that the issuance of identification documents used to obtain a driver's license must be verified. Eighteen of the 19 9/11 terrorists obtained more than 60 state driver's licenses between them, even though some of the jihadists were in the United States illegally. They used such IDs to board the planes with which they murdered nearly 3,000 Americans.

23 JUNE 2009

Obama returns Ambassador to Syria

Source: Wilson, Scott, "US To Return Ambassador to Syria after 4-Year Absence," The Washington Post, 23 June 2009

Syria is one of several countries listed by the State Department as a state sponsor of terrorism. Its support for Hezbollah and other terrorist organizations, as well as its relationship with Iran, are well known. Damascus has also played a leading role in destabilizing post-liberation Iraq and facilitating attacks on American forces there. Sending an ambassador back to Syria under these circumstances further emboldened that country's support for terrorism against the United States and Israel, and also had the effect of undermining Lebanon's democrats.

26 JUNE 2009
House of Representatives passes Cap-and-Trade legislation
Source: John Carey, "House Passes Carbon Cap-and-Trade Bill," Bloomberg Businessweek Money & Politics, *26 June 2009.*

The House of Representatives passed "cap-and-trade" legislation that would place caps on carbon dioxide emissions, which some believe cause global climate change. If signed into law, cap-and-trade will substantially raise the cost of energy production and industrial operations in the United States, and will force consumers to pay the price in an already shaky economy.

29 JUNE 2009
Obama calls removal of Honduran President a "coup"
Source: Arshad Mohammed and David Alexander, "Obama Says Coup in Honduras is Illegal," Reuters, 29 June 2009.

When pro-Chavez Honduras President Mel Zelaya was deposed by order of the Honduran congress and supreme court, the Obama administration adopted the position of Hugo Chavez and his friends in the OAS, calling the removal a "coup d'etat" and demanding the restoration of Zelaya to power. In addition, the administration blocked $30 million in aid to the impoverished country and revoked US visas of top Honduras officials in the interim government. Initially, Mr. Obama's State Department indicated that it would not recognize the scheduled November 29, 2009 elections. Such support for a Chavista-style take-over of a allied democracy was a serious blow to America's standing as a bulwark for freedom and debilitating to its few remaining democratically elected friends in governments in the hemisphere.

JUNE 2009

Obama Administration first invites, then disinvites, Iranian diplomats to July 4 celebrations

Source: Kessler, Glenn, "Iran Envoys Disinvited from July 4 Festivities," The Washington Post, *25 June 2009.*

In late June 2009, the Obama administration announced the withdrawal of previously offered invitations to Iranian diplomats to attend US 4th of July celebrations at its diplomatic posts abroad. Even as graphic scenes of the Iranian regime's brutality flooded the Internet, and despite the fact that the US and Iran have not had diplomatic relations for three decades, Obama's Secretary of State Hillary Clinton had nevertheless authorized the invitations as a way of reaching out to the clerical regime. After no Iranians RSVP'd to the invitations, though, the president apparently got the message and took them back. The embarrassing incident demonstrated a risible ineptitude on the part of the US administration and held it up to international ridicule.

JUNE 2009

CIA director Panetta kills program to explore options for assassinating Osama bin Laden

Source: Warrick, Joby, "CIA Assassin Program Was Nearing New Phase; Panetta Pulled Plug After Training Was Proposed," The Washington Post, *July 13, 2009; Panetta, Leon, "Congress and the CIA: Time to Move On,"* The Washington Post, *August 2, 2009.*

Looking to throw a sop to House Speaker Nancy Pelosi in the hope of mollifying her and ending her jihad against the CIA, Obama's CIA director agreed with some fanfare to terminate an old program aimed at developing options for killing Osama bin Laden. This program never came up with an operational plan, let alone carried one out, mooting the need to notify Congress of the existence of such an activity. Whether or not the program met the legal threshold for reporting (it did not) is not the real issue. The real issue is: Are we safer if the CIA isn't even permitted to think about options for killing bin Laden?

JULY 2009

7 JULY 2009

During Moscow summit meeting, President Obama declines to raise the issue of human rights, except in very general terms

Sources: Hechtkopf, Kevin, "Text: Obama's Speech in Russia," CBS News, *7 July 2009; Landler, Mark, "Clinton Defends Human Rights Approach,"* The New York Times, *14 December 2009.*

Determined to "reset" relations with Russia, President Obama declined in his talks with Russian leaders and with representatives of Russian civil society to cite specific cases of human rights abuse. His deference to his hosts was not reciprocated by the Kremlin, either with respect to appreciably improved bilateral ties or greater respect for dissidents and other opponents. This episode simply reinforces past experience: the murders of journalists and human rights defenders in Russia can only be addressed effectively with the help of external pressure. At the same time, the state of human rights in Russia has strategic implications. A population that lacks democratic rights and is subject to constant anti-Western propaganda can easily be mo- bilized against the United States.

8 JULY 2009

Administration resends 'No-Match' immigration regulation

Sources: Office of the Press Secretary, "DHS: Secretary Napolitano Strengthens Employment Verification with Administration's Commitment to E-Verify," Department of Homeland Security, July 8 2009; Miller, Charles M., "No-Match Rescission Leaves Matter in Limbo," Immigration Employment, 19 October 2009.

This administration rescinded the "No-Match" rule that laid out procedures for employers to follow if they received a "No-Match" letter from the Social Security Administration (SSA) about an employee. According to journalist Charles Miller, the regulation (72 Fed. Reg. 4561145624 promulgated on Aug. 15, 2007)), "had changed the legal obligations of an employer when receiving a no-match letter from the SSA or a notice of suspect documents letter from ICE. The rule had amended the definition of constructive knowledge to include receipt by an employer of a no-match letter from SSA or a notice from the Department of Homeland Security, with a potential finding that the employer had constructive knowledge that it was employing an alien not authorized to work in the United States." As a result of the Obama change, many employers will have no choice but to continue to employ individuals they know are illegal.

10 JULY 2009

Obama Gives Iran a September deadline on nuclear program
Source: Dinan, Stephen, "Obama gives Iran deadline on nuclear program," The Washington Times, 10 July 2009.

Speaking in Italy in mid-July 2009, President Obama told Iran that it had until the G-20 summit to be held in Pittsburgh, Pennsylvania on 24-25 September to show good faith efforts to halt its nuclear weapons program. This was but the latest in a succession of so-called 'deadlines' issued by this and previous US administrations to the Iranian regime. Regrettably, the president's statement failed to impress either Tehran or the international community. The former ignored it, the latter imposed no appreciable penalties for the mullah's behavior. In the process, US credibility in the international sphere was eroded further.

27 JULY 2009

Politicizing Congressional oversight and subjecting CIA officers to political witch hunts
Source: US House of Representatives Select Committee on Intelligence, press release, "Chairman Reyes Statement on Committee Investigation," July 17, 2009.

In another effort to provide political cover for Speaker Pelosi in her self-declared war against the CIA, House Democrats launched an investigation into the aforementioned "program" aimed at neutralizing Osama bin Laden—one studied but never operationalized in any way by the CIA. No one should be surprised that CIA is becoming less agile and more risk-averse under threat of continuing politicization and debilitating investigations. It took decades for the CIA to recover from the investigations of the 1970s—years that the Russians and others used to advantage in undermining pro-Western governments, supporting insurgencies and implanting spies.

28 JULY 2009

US fails to protest when Iraqi forces attack Iranian opposition group

Source: Abouzeid, Rania, "At Tehran's Bidding? Iraq Cracks Down on a Controversial Camp," Time, 29 July 2009.

On July 28, armed Iraqi troops launched a brutal assault against the unarmed inhabitants of Camp Ashraf, a northern Iraqi base for the Iranian opposition group, the Mujahedeen-e Khalq (MEK). Placed under US security guarantees in 2004 according to provisions of the 4th Geneva Convention, the defenseless group that day suffered six dead and hundreds of wounded in attacks that involved water cannon, pepper spray, nail-studded clubs, and gunfire. The failure of nearby US troops to intervene sent a signal to Tehran that its increasingly cozy relationship with Baghdad would not be opposed by an American administration eager to exit Iraq and open dialogue with the mullahs.

AUGUST 2009

6 AUGUST 2009

Secretary of State Clinton voices "regret" that US is "not yet" a Member of the International Criminal Court

Source: MacAskill, Ewen, "US may join international war crimes Court, Clinton Hints," The Guardian, 6 August 2009.

By declaring her "regret" that the United States is "not yet" a member of the International Criminal Court, Secretary Hillary Clinton is signaling the Obama administration's support for membership—a longstanding goal of transnationalists like her Legal Advisor, Harold Koh. Membership in the ICC would legitimize an international organization that has already shown no regard for national sovereignty, including through its investigations of the United States and Israel (both non-parties) for alleged "war crimes" in Afghanistan and Gaza, respectively.

13 AUGUST 2009

President Obama announces review of US export controls system for dual-use and defense trade items

Sources: The White House Office of the Press Secretary, "Statement of the Press Secretary on Exchange Controls overhaul"; Gary Locke, "Remarks at Bureau of Industry and Security Update Conference on Export Controls," US Department of Commerce, 1 October 2009.

The review aims to "update" a system "rooted in the Cold War era of over 50 years ago ... to address the threats we face today and the changing economic and technological landscape." Yet, it is driven largely by unfounded claims that today's export controls "unnecessarily undercut our companies' global competitiveness." Strongly supported by developers and manufacturers of inherently dual-use products and technologies with long records of supplying dangerous products and technologies to America's adversaries, the review could well loosen controls further and jeopardize national security in return for minimal economic growth and, if any, highly ephemeral job creation.

24 AUGUST 2009

Investigation into conduct of CIA interrogations

Source: Holder, Eric, "Statement of Attorney General Eric Holder Regarding a Preliminary Review into the Interrogation of Certain Detainees," US Department of Justice, 24 August 2009.

Attorney General Holder Jr. announced that he would after all investigate CIA officers for their conduct of terrorist interrogations even though President Obama promised this would not happen and despite the fact that such techniques—which were employed in good faith pursuant to guidelines laid down by the Justice Department—obtained time-sensitive intelligence on terrorist plans. Now, American intelligence officers have to question every order they are given, wondering whether, even if the order is lawful, they may be punished anyway if the political climate changes. Inevitably, the risk-takers will be suppressed or leave, and the rest will hesitate for fear of jeopardizing their careers. As a result, new operations that might save lives are being delayed or not pursued, subjected to ever-more lawyers and layers of review.

SEPTEMBER 2009

1 SEPTEMBER 2009

Secretary of Defense Gates denies request by House Intelligence Committee Ranking Member to lead Michigan delegation to Gitmo

Source: Gates, Robert, "Letter to Representative Hoekstra," Office of the Secretary of Defense, 1 September 2009.

When Standish, Michigan was under serious consideration as a destination for terrorist detainees Mr. Obama is determined to transfer from Guantanamo, Rep. Peter Hoekstra (R-Michigan), the

Ranking Member on the House Intelligence Committee, requested that certain information about the Gitmo detainees be de-classified, and that he be allowed to lead a delegation of state/local officials to Gitmo. Secretary Gates turned down this request, and stated that the administration would engage state/local officials only after the administration had decided where to send Gitmo detainees. By denying this request, the administration was deciding not to inform the affected state and community about the potential consequences of housing Gitmo detainees.

17 SEPTEMBER 2009

Obama Administration abandons Poland and Czech missile defense

Source: Joyner, James, "Obama Abandons Poland and Czech Missile Defense," Atlantic Council, 17 September 2009. Accessed online, 10 January 2010, at http://www.acus.org/new_atlanticist/obama-abandons-poland-and-czech-missile-defense.

President Obama announced the cancellation of the long-range missile defense system that was to be based in Poland and the Czech Republic pursuant to an agreement painstakingly crafted by his predecessor, President George W. Bush and the respective allied governments. In dropping plans to base interceptor missiles in Poland and a radar system in the Czech Republic, Mr. Obama capitulated to Russian protests against the system, apparently in hopes that Moscow would support US calls for stricter sanctions against Iran over its nuclear weapons program and to lubricate negotiation of a new Strategic Arms Reduction Treaty (START). The Kremlin was made aware of the decision well in advance; apparently Warsaw and Prague were not. The integrated missile and radar system had been intended to defend against a potential Iranian missile launch. By scrapping it, Obama displayed contempt for America's international commitments, a callous disregard for two of the US's closest allies, an alarming tendency to buckle in the face of Russian bullying, and finally, a misplaced confidence that the Iranian missile threat is not imminent.

24 SEPTEMBER 2009

Obama declares his intent to move forward on ratification of Comprehensive Test Ban Treaty (CTBT)

Source: Senator John Kyl, "Why We need to Test Nuclear Weapons," Opinion Piece in The Wall Street Journal, *20 October 2009.*

Obama announced at the United Nations that he would press forward with seeking ratification of the CTBT. If ratified, the CTBT would prevent the United States from conducting tests of its nuclear weapons capabilities at a time when the nuclear arsenal and infra-structure are badly in need of modernization. The resulting lack of faith in the reliability and effectiveness of the American nuclear deterrent would encourage other nations—both adversaries and allies—to pursue their own nuclear weapons programs.

25 SEPTEMBER 2009

The CIA's Center on Climate Change and National Security

Sources: Press office of the Central Intelligence Agency, "CIA Opens Center on Climate Change and National Security," 25 September 2009; Broad, William J., "CIA Is Sharing Data with Scientists," The New York Times, *4 January 2010.*

With much fanfare, the CIA launched the Center on Climate Change and National Security, supposedly to study "the national security impact of phenomena such as desertification, rising sea levels, population shifts and heightened competition for natural resources." Interestingly, on Jan. 4, 2010, less than two weeks after the CIA failed to prevent the attempted Christmas Day terror attack on a US airliner, the New York Times reported that the CIA is using its intelligence resources and satellites to monitor ice in the Arctic. So, rather than using all of its resources and expertise to protect

Americans from the very real and present dangers (which include, the immediate threat of Islamic terrorism, proliferation of nuclear and other weapons of mass destruction, North Korea, China, Russia, etc.), the CIA is diverting taxpayer money to speculative assessments of the hypothetical (if not entirely imaginary) and certainly years-off consequences of putative climate change. Similar diversions of limited resources are reportedly underway in the Pentagon and military services where an "infrastructure" for responding to climate change is now being established.

25 SEPTEMBER 2009

President Obama reveals existence of secret underground Iranian enrichment plant

Source: "Iran's Nuclear Program," The New York Times, *10 January 2010.*

At the G-20 Summit meeting in Pittsburgh, flanked by UK Prime Minister Gordon Brown and French President Nicholas Sarkozy, President Obama revealed what Western intelligence agencies had known and treated as a closely held secret for a number of years: the existence of an underground uranium enrichment facility beneath a well-guarded mountain near the Iranian holy city of Qom. As a practical matter, its small size meant that it could only be used for one purpose: supporting a nuclear weapons program. The next day, the five members of the UN Security Council held talks with Iranian officials during which a tentative agreement was reached for Iran to export most of its enriched uranium for processing abroad. The previous deadline of 25 September was quickly forgotten and a new year-end deadline was set for completion of that accord. By the end of October 2009, however, Iran told the UN's chief inspector that it was rejecting the deal. Certainly by this point, it was beyond obvious that the Iranians were simply jerking the Obama administration around. The evidence was now indisputable that Tehran was flagrantly violating the provisions of the Nuclear Non-Proliferation Treaty, and was confident that the mullahocracy would be allowed to get away with it. The Obama administration's inability to muster the fortitude to call Iran to account and impose consequences for Tehran's serial abrogation of its commitments and responsibilities have grievously undercut US global credibility and prompted many in the region who have relied on our protection to seek separate peaces with the Iranians or to acquire their own nuclear capabilities.

26 SEPTEMBER 2009

Obama Administration announces it is cutting the number of Border Patrol agents at the US-Mexico border beginning in October 2009

Source: Terence P. Jeffrey, "Administration Will Cut Border Patrol Deployed on US-Mexico Border," CNSNews, September 26, 2009.

"Even though the Border Patrol now reports that almost 1,300 miles of the US-Mexico border is not under effective control, and the Department of Justice says that vast stretches of the border are 'easily breached,' and the Government Accountability Office has revealed that three persons 'linked to terrorism' and 530 aliens from 'special interest countries' were intercepted at Border Patrol checkpoints last year, the administration is nonetheless now planning to decrease the number of Border Patrol agents deployed on the US-Mexico border."

29 SEPTEMBER 2009

White House transfers to the Commerce Department authority to approve sales to China of missile and space technology

Source: President Barack Obama, "Memorandum to the Secretary of Commerce concerning delegations of certifications," The White House, September 29, 2009.

The Commerce Department has the responsibility within the US government for promoting exports. Putting it in charge of sensitive missile and space-related dual-use technology export decisions is a classic case of the fox guarding the chicken coop. This move will surely result in further relaxation of export controls and will, in all probability, result in transfers that enhance Chinese military capabilities, especially those relating to missiles. Those controls were enacted after the scandals in the 1990s involving transfers of sensitive space technology to China by Loral and Hughes Electronics Corporation that markedly increased Beijing's ability to threaten the United States and others with its nuclear forces.

30 SEPTEMBER 2009

Obama denies Venezuela's Chavez is national security threat
Source: Oppenheimer, Andres, "Obama's confidence-building moves good—to a Point," The Miami Herald, *3 October 2009.*

This Administration remained unmoved as Iran and Venezuela announced a nuclear cooperation pact. Dan Restrepo, head of the Latin American desk for the National Security Council pointed out in an interview to a Miami newspaper that "[The president] does not see Venezuela as a challenge to US national security. There is no Cold War [nor] Hot War. Those things belong to the past. We have to look at the present and see how we can work constructively with those countries that are interested in working with us. It may be that not all of them want to do so, but the vast majority of the people and countries in Latin America are interested in doing so." When asked about his thought on Iran-Venezuela nuclear cooperation Restrepo pointed out: "Look, we hope that all countries in the Americas respect international rules, and their international responsibilities regarding nuclear energy." Such statements, against the backdrop of US indifference to the steady progress of the Iranian nuclear weapons program can only be interpreted in Caracas as a green light for its own ambitions in that area.

OCTOBER 2009

15 OCTOBER 2009

Obama fails to address China's currency manipulations

Sources: Palmer, Doug and Jackie Frank, "Obama, Clinton back Senate trade bill on China currency," Reuters, 1 May 2008; Office of International Affairs, "Report to Congress on International Economic and Exchange Rate Policies," US Department of Treasury, 15 April 2009; Office of International Affairs, "Report to Congress on International Economic and Exchange Rate Policies," US Department of Treasury, 15 October 2009.

On May 1, 2008, as a presidential candidate, Barack Obama rightly denounced China's currency manipulation as an "unacceptable," subsidy-like policy that has devastated American industry. That day, then- Senator Obama also became a cosponsor of strong legislation to combat currency manipulation. Beijing's exchange-rate protectionism has also fueled China's multi-hundred billion dollars-worth of annual trade profits with the United States, and therefore greatly increased the financing available for Beijing's dangerous military buildup. But in his administration's first two congressionally required reports on foreign currency policies, Obama absolved China of these charges. As a result, during his tenure as President, Mr. Obama has enabled China's merchandise trade surplus with the United States to reach more than $191 billion, and continue to feed China's military buildup.

19 OCTOBER 2009

White House floats Iranian nuclear fuel swap offer

Source: Hiedeh, Farmani, "Iran will enrich uranium to 20%: Ahmadinejad," AFP, December 2.

The White House announced that it was willing to give Iran all of the 20-percent enriched uranium fabricated nuclear fuel it might need to run its research reactor near Tehran in exchange for 1,200 kilograms of low (3.5 percent) enriched uranium (LEU) gas that Iran had produced at its plant at Natanz. 1,200 kilograms of LEU is roughly the amount Iran would need to re-enrich to higher levels to make its first nuclear bomb. Iran initially rejected the deal, but continues to exploit the United States' willingness to make the offer to justify Iran enriching its uranium to 20 percent, which would bring Iran dramatically closer to having the weapons-grade uranium it needs for its bomb.

27 OCTOBER 2009

Defense Secretary Gates invites General Xu Caihou to the Pentagon

Source: Garamone, Jim, "US Relations with the People's Republic of China: Gates Asks Xu to Help Stop 'On-Again, Off-Again' Cycle," American Forces Press Services, October 27, 2009.

In a bid to establish better military-to-military ties with the Chinese military, Secretary Gates invited General Xu to tour various American military installations, such as Fort Benning, Offut Air Force Base, Nellis Air Force Base, North Island Naval Air Station, and the headquarters of the US Pacific Command. The Chinese have rarely reciprocated and even more rarely with invitations to comparably sensitive facilities. Consequently, such so-called "exchanges" amount to one-way transfers of information to China's People's Liberation Army and signal a form of kow-towing that only emboldens Chinese ambitions to assert an ever-more dominant position, both regionally and globally.

NOVEMBER 2009

5 NOVEMBER 2009

Obama endorses "media shield" legislation

Source: National Press Photographers Association, "White House Endorses Federal Shield Law for Journalists," 5 November 2009.

The "media shield" bill prohibits a federal court from forcing a journalist to disclose the identity of a confidential source—even in a situation where national security information has been leaked—unless the government is able to overcome various, significant hurdles. In addition, the bill allows judges to determine whether the national interest is better served by disclosing the source's identity or not, a responsibility properly placed pursuant to the Constitution in the executive. By creating a presumption that journalists will not be forced to identify sources, the bill serves to incentivize the leaking of national security information and protect the leaker of such information from ever being discovered, let alone punished.

5 NOVEMBER 2009

Senate votes to allow 9/11 masterminds to be tried in federal court in New York City

Source: James Rosen, "Graham Bill on 9/11 trials defeated," McClatchy Newspapers, 6 November 2009.

The Senate defeated a measure that would have required the 9/11 masterminds to be tried before military commissions only. The defeat of this measure cleared the way for Obama's decision to try the perpetrators in civilian court, where legal procedures serve to weaken the government's case against them and could possibly lead to their release.

6 NOVEMBER 2009

White House signals America's dependence on China

Source: Bush, Richard and Jeffrey Bader, "Obama Goes to Asia: Understanding the President's Trip," The Brookings Institution, November 6, 2009

The National Security Council's Jeffrey Bader said in a policy statement delivered at the Brookings Institution that China's cooperation on "the great issues of the day" is essential. The Chinese probably read Bader's words as further confirmation that the United States is effectively conceding Beijing's right to exercise a veto in such matters as the Iranian and North Korean nuclear weapons programs. In effect, Bader, on the eve of President Obama's trip to Asia, signaled the administration's perception that it needs China more than China needs the United States.

8 NOVEMBER 2009

Army Chief of Staff, in response to Fort Hood shooting, states that loss of diversity in Army would be "worse" than shooting itself

Source: Tabassum, Zakaria, "General Casey: diversity shouldn't be casualty of Fort Hood," Reuters, November 8, 2009.

General George Casey, the US Army's most senior officer, stated in response to the Fort Hood Shooting carried out by Major Malik Nidal Hassan: "Our diversity, not only in our Army, but in our country, is a strength. And as horrific as this tragedy was, if our diversity becomes a casualty, I think that's worse." This statement demonstrates a failure to understand the nature of the jihadist threat from within the ranks at the Army and to prioritize it appropriately over considerations of political correctness.

9 NOVEMBER 2009

US issued a 'rebuke' as Iran charges three American hikers with espionage

Source: Healy, Jack and Nazila Fathi, "Iran Accuses US Hikers of Espionage," New York Times, 9 November 2009.

In early November 2009, Iran announced espionage charges against three American hikers arrested in the summer of 2009 who had innocently strayed over the Iranian border. The White House and Secretary of State Clinton issued calls for their release, but in the wake of the Saberi case earlier in the year, speculation centered on the possibility that Tehran intended to use the latest US hostages as bargaining chips in nuclear weapons program discussions. Having once capitulated to Iranian demands for the release of a citizen, a weakened Obama administration can expect to face ever-expanding ransom costs in the future, as well as repeat hostage-taking.

12 NOVEMBER 2009

Public dispute between Director of National Intelligence and CIA Director over who manages intelligence relationships abroad

Source: Classified memo by National Security Advisor Jim Jones reported inter alia at "Settling an intelligence turf war," The Washington Post, November 17, 2009.

In warring memos, the DNI and the Director of the CIA each asserted the right to manage America's relationships with its intelligence partners. Those partners were already confused about who is in charge within the US; now they are confused about who is in charge abroad, further undermining confidence in working with the US and supplying opportunities for adversaries who want to sow mistrust. The White House tried to settle the dispute by memo issued November 12, but foreign services still wonder who they should talk to, or who they should listen to. And the turf wars continue.

13 NOVEMBER 2009

9/11 detainees—including Khalid Sheik Mohammad—to be tried in civilian court

Source: "Holder defends decision to try accused 9/11 terrorists in New York," CNN, 18 November 2009.

By order of Attorney General Holder, the key 9/11 suspects in US custody are being treated like "common criminals" with a right to greater constitutional protections than they would receive in a military trial while the interests of national security take a back seat. Other current and future detainees see their day in court coming, which means (along with the interrogation investigations) that CIA will be embroiled in more public litigation than ever before. Under civilian court procedures, court filings, the "discovery" process and open court proceedings will invariably result in secrets being lost, to the detriment of US security.

17 NOVEMBER 2009

White House announces technical collaboration for China's ARJ21 commuter jet

Source: Pasztor, Andy and Norihiko Shirouzu, "Chinese Jet Gets Boost from Obama," The Wall Street Journal, November 17, 2009.

The White House announced it would help China develop a commercial plane and push for its safety certification. At the very least, the administration should not take steps that compromise the safety of the American flying public. At a broader level, Washington should not help the Chinese aviation industry, which will soon compete with America's and inevitably has implications for Beijing's military programs, as well.

18 NOVEMBER 2009

Obama calls Israeli construction in East Jerusalem "dangerous"

Source: "Obama Calls Israeli Settlement Building in East Jerusalem 'Dangerous,'" Fox News Online, 18 January 2009.

President Obama's declaration that Israeli construction of 900 apartments to an existing community in East Jerusalem is "dangerous" for peace efforts represents a lack of understanding of the real reason for the lack of a peace agreement: the fundamental rejection of the Palestinians and their supporters of Israel's right to exist as a sovereign Jewish state. The use of the word "dangerous" in reference to Israeli construction also serves to rationalize Palestinian violence against Israelis. The act of rationalizing Palestinian violence at the expense of Israeli sovereignty undermines the security of our most important ally in the region.

19 NOVEMBER 2009

Department of Homeland Security agrees to audit NSEERS program for tracking potential terrorists

Source: Press Statement, "Office of Inspector General at DHS to Audit NSEERS at the Request of ADC and Other Major Organizations," Arab-American Anti-Discrimination Committee, 18 January 2009

At the request of interest groups such as the Arab-American Anti-Discrimination Committee (ADC) and the Council on American-Islamic Relations (CAIR), the Department of Homeland Security agreed to audit the National Security Entry-Exit Registration System (NSEERS), a program implemented after 9/11 to enhance monitoring of visa overstays by individuals from countries where terrorism and jihad are prevalent. Agreeing to audit NSEERS constitutes accepting the notion that political correctness, and deflecting accusations of "profiling" or "Islamophobia," are more important than terror prevention. If the audit leads to the termination of the program, as these interest groups have requested, such termination will create a major vulnerability in monitoring potential terrorists inside the United States.

DECEMBER 2009

2 DECEMBER 2009

Obama announces Afghanistan surge and prompt withdrawal

Source: Stolberg , Sheryl Gay and Helene Cooper, "Obama Adds Troops, but Maps Exit Plan," The New York Times, *December 1, 2009.*

President Obama announced that he will dispatch 30,000 more US troops to Afghanistan within the next six months and begin withdrawing troops shortly after they are all in place, starting in June 2011. Inherently, the surge will expose US troops to higher levels of risk. That risk has been intensified, however, by Mr. Obama's decision to reject General McChrystal's "low risk" strategy, which reportedly called for 60,000 to 80,000 more troops, and even his "medium risk" strategy, which reportedly called for 40,000. There is also concern that the announcement of such a hasty deadline for withdrawal will embolden US enemies and lead them to believe that they can outlast the US mission.

4 DECEMBER 2009

Administration continues to negotiate a treaty to replace expired START I treaty

Source: Reed, Jason, "Obama, Russia work on soon-to-expire arms treaty," Reuters/USA Today, *4 December 2009.*

The Obama administration is working hard to negotiate a treaty that the US does not need and which, by appearing to confirm Russia's superpower illusions, will make Russia more aggressive rather than less. Russia is unable to maintain its nuclear arsenal and will be compelled to retire a large group of launchers irrespective of whether or not there is a new agreement. Russian military leaders have stated publicly that not a single Russian launcher with remaining service life will be withdrawn under a new treaty. The American cuts, however, will be real. The purpose of the treaty is not to strengthen US security but to reduce our strategic forces to a level that would make it possible for Russia to preserve strategic parity. It goes almost without saying that this should not be a strategic goal of the US

4 DECEMBER 2009

End of US on-site inspection activities in Russia

Source: Statement by Ian Kelly, State Department Spokesman at the Daily Press Briefing, Washington, DC, December 4, 2009

One of the most highly valued intelligence sources on Russian missile modernization came from the US presence at the missile assembly site at Votkinsk, Russia, which began in 1988 and continued until December of last year. While negotiations are now underway to replace the START arms control agreement with a new US-Russia accord, the Obama administration decided not to seek an interim agreement that would allow Americans to remain on site. As a result, the intelligence community will be less able to provide insights into Russian nuclear modernization, which—while part of a shrinking of the Kremlin's strategic forces—continues, to be robust. This stands in sharp contrast with the American deterrent which is, as a practical matter, not being modernized at all.

8 DECEMBER 2009

President sends Ambassador Bosworth for direct talks with North Korea

Source: Powell, Bill, "US Tries Direct Talks with North Korea," Time, *December 8, 2009*

In a reversal of previous US policy only to talk with North Korean officials in the context of 6-Party denuclearization talks with China, Russia, Japan, and South Korea, the Obama administration sent Ambassador Bosworth to Pyongyang for direct one-on-one negotiations with North Korean officials. Subsequently, the North Koreans refused to rejoin the 6-party talks to determine how to disarm North Korea's nuclear arsenal until the US drops all sanctions against North Korea. The United States has thus been outmaneuvered yet again by one of the most repressive, dangerous and poorest regimes on the planet.

15 DECEMBER 2009

President announces intent to transfer Guantanamo detainees to prison in Thomson, IL

Source: Parsons, Christi, "US to buy prison for Guantanamo Bay detainees," The San Francisco Chronicle, 15 December, 2009.

As part of his plan to close Guantanamo, President Obama decides to transfer a large segment of the remaining detainee population to a prison in Thomson, Illinois. This will increase the likelihood of a terrorist attack on targets of interest in Illinois, as well as the likelihood that terrorist detainees will be given greater rights both within the prison (enabling them to radicalize other prisoners) and in a courtroom, which will risk the dissemination of sensitive intelligence information—and possibly the release of detainees.

16 DECEMBER 2009

INTERPOL authorized to operate within the US immune from search and seizure

Source: Executive Order 13524, Amending Executive Order 12425 Designating Interpol as a Public International Organization Entitled To Enjoy Certain Privileges, Exemptions, and Immunities, The White House, 16 December 2009.

By Obama's order, the "property and assets of [INTERPOL], wherever located and by whomsoever held, shall be immune from search, unless such immunity be expressly waived, and from confiscation." Among other concerns, the risk is that INTERPOL personnel, facilities and activities may be exploited for foreign intelligence operations within the United States, with the physical and logistics infrastructure of a police force—a potential new nightmare for US counterintelligence and the FBI.

16 DECEMBER 2009

New asylum detention policy: foreigners who arrive at a port of entry and are found to have a credible fear will automatically be considered for release into the US

Source: Associated Press, "Feds revising asylum detention policies," MSNBC, December 16, 2009.

This administration reversed the longstanding policy to detain aliens who show up at ports-of-entry without proper documentation and request asylum. This will return US ports-of-entry to a situation where thousands of individuals who posses counterfeit documentation—or none at all—request asylum, are simply allowed to enter the United States and then abscond when they are supposed to report for their asylum determination hearing. The detention policy originally was put into place in part because the asylum system had become a known tool for terrorists seeking entry into the country. Under the new policy, terrorists can once again take advantage of our failure to learn the lessons of the past.

19 DECEMBER 2009

Top Obama Aide signals slippage on December 31 deadline for Iranian nuclear weapons program

Source: Malcolm, Andrew, "Obama aide Axelrod fudges Dec. 31 deadline for Iran on nuclear weapons," The Los Angeles Times, 20 December 2009.

Appearing on the 19 December 2009 Sunday morning talk show, ABC's This Week, Obama administration advisor David Axelrod let it be known that the US had no intention of holding Iran to the 31 December deadline for Iran to respond to the Western plan for it to ship its nuclear fuel abroad for reprocessing. As with myriad earlier "deadlines," this one too was allowed to pass by with absolutely no consequences. The serial failure of the Obama administration to hold Iran to account for repeatedly disregarding an apparently endless procession of meaningless deadlines exposes the US as an enfeebled paper tiger whose word means nothing.

29 DECEMBER 2009

National declassification order

Source: Executive Order 13526, Classified National Security Information and Accompanying Presidential Memorandum, The White House, 29 December 2009.

Obama ordered the federal government to change longstanding practices for protecting the nation's secrets, including a requirement that every record be released eventually. This order will result in the release of more than 400 million pages of Cold War-era records, exposing a wealth of secret data on US-Soviet relations, including the Soviet invasion of Afghanistan, the fall of the Berlin Wall, diplomacy and espionage that the Russians and other adversaries have been trying to steal for decades. To make the protection of secrets even more difficult, Obama also reversed a decision by President George W. Bush that had allowed the intelligence community to block the release of a specific document.

JANUARY 2010

1 JANUARY 2010

Latest Obama deadline for Iran's nuclear program passes without incident

Source: Tobin, Jonathan, "Obama's Iran deadline gets thrown down the memory hole," Commentary Magazine, 8 January 2010.

A full week after the latest US deadline for an Iranian response on its nuclear weapons program had expired, Secretary of State Clinton explained that the Obama administration really doesn't like the word "deadline" very much. "We've avoided using the term 'deadline' ourselves," said Secretary Clinton. "That's not a term that we have used, because we want to keep the door to dialogue open." At this point, the US has lost all credibility with Iran, its friends and allies, and most importantly, with its adversaries around the world. The damage done by the Obama administration to US national security is grave and worsening because the entire world now knows that calling America's bluff brings no consequences. The country is entering an extremely dangerous period in terms of its ability to exert influence, project power, or even defend the nation.

3 JANUARY 2010

New TSA Procedures Demonstrate Obama's Retrospective Approach to National Security

Source: "TSA Tightens Security for International Travel"—January 3, 2010, Fox News

All individuals flying into the United States from designated, "countries of interest" will be subject to enhanced screening techniques, such as body scans and pat-downs, the Transportation Security Administration announced. The State Department lists Cuba, Iran, Sudan and Syria as state sponsors of terrorism. The "other countries" whose passengers will face enhanced screening include Nigeria, Yemen and Pakistan. Though this may be a necessary step as an individual policy, the Obama Administration's reliance on this enhancement as a comprehensive approach to aviation security is problematic. As the Heritage Foundation notes: "Requiring one hundred percent inspections on travelers from 14 'terrorist' countries is a kind of feel good, but useless idea. Terrorists route their attacks through the international air hubs that are not the most suspicious. Nor is geography an indicator of security. Remember 9/11 was launched from a domestic airport. The Christmas Day attack could have been launched from a domestic flight too. Why are we preparing to thwart the last attack instead of the next one?"

4 JANUARY 2010

CIA and Pentagon Said to be Assessing Global Warming

Source: "C.I.A. is Sharing Data with Climate Scientists," The New York Times, *January 4, 2010.*

As directed by the Obama Administration, scientists and spies from the CIA and Pentagon are collaborating on the national security implications of climate change, a program shut down by the Bush Administration. This collaboration will involve the use of the federal government's intelligence assets "—including spy satellites and other classified sensors—to assess the hidden complexities of environmental change." President Obama has acknowledged the intelligence failures associated with the attempted Christmas Day bombing of a US bound flight from Nigeria. Rather than addressing these failures to prevent future acts of terrorism, the president has instead directed valuable CIA resources to study glaciers, polar bears, and penguins. This argument can be seen more in depth, here.

5 JANUARY 2010

Entrusting national security secrets to an individual with a proven blatant disregard for the Nation's security

Sources: Snider, L. Britt and Daniel S. Seikaly, "Improper Handling of Classified Information by John M. Deutch," Office of the Inspector General, 18 February 2000; "DOD Announces New Defense Science Board Membership," Office of the Assistant Secretary of Defense for Public Affairs, 5 January, 2010; Report Of Investigation Allegations Of Breaches Of Security: Dr. John M. Deutch, Former Deputy Secretary Of Defense And Former Under Secretary Of Defense For Acquisition And Technology. Department Of Defense Office Of The Inspector General, 28 August, 2000; DDCI Actions Relating to Deutch Investigation, statement by CIA Spokesman Bill Harlow on DDCI Actions Relating to Deutch Investigation, 25 May 2000.

John Deutch, who left office in disgrace after it was learned that he had compromised a treasure trove of the nation's most highly sensitive secrets, was named as a member of the Obama Pentagon's Defense Science Board. Separate IG investigations found that throughout the years he served as Deputy Secretary of Defense and Director of the CIA during the Clinton administration, Deutch routinely copied files marked "top secret" and beyond to his Internet-accessible home computers; he would have a criminal record but for the fact that Clinton pardoned him just before leaving office. While the Obama administration has said it is serious about leakers, who can be expected to take seriously their responsibility to safeguard national security secrets if they give Deutch access to highly classified intelligence and defense weapons programs?

7 JANUARY 2010

Obama responds to "Christmas Day bomber" by blaming intelligence but not fixing the problem

Source: "Memorandum from the President to National Security Council. Subject: Attempted Terrorist Attack on December 25, 2009: Intelligence, Screening, and Watchlisting System Corrective Actions," The White House, January 7, 1010.

After action reviews show the intelligence about Umar Farouk Abdulmutallab was collected and it was disseminated. The problem isn't a failure to "share" or even to "connect the dots;" it is a failure to think and take action. We need an effective warning system from early indications through operations, where the significance of information is recognized and timely communicated to people with clear responsibility and capability for taking action. But that compelling requirement will never be met so long as the Administration treats terrorist activities as crimes instead of war.

13 JANUARY 2010

Obama-appointed Commission on Fort Hood shootings releases report that fails to mention Islamic extremism

Source: Department of Defense Independent Review, "Protecting the Force: Lessons from Fort Hood," Department of Defense, January 13, 2010.

The report does not mention jihad, Shariah, or any other indication that the shooting massacre at Fort Hood was motivated by jihadist doctrine and belief. The lack of recognition of what motivated this shooting, and others like it, makes it highly unlikely that our government will be able to prevent another such tragedy.

20 JANUARY 2010

China No Longer a Top Intelligence Priority

Source: "China removed as a top priority for spies: Intelligence chiefs object," The Washington Times, January 20, 2010.

The White House National Security Council recently directed US spy agencies to lower the priority placed on intelligence collection for China from "Priority 1" status, to "Priority 2" status, despite opposition to the policy change from Director of National Intelligence Dennis Blair and CIA Director Leon Panetta, fearing it would hamper efforts to obtain secrets about Beijing's military and its cyber-attacks, espionage, technology theft, and economic spying. Officials have expressed concern, noting that lowering intelligence priority for China is a subtle but significant change that will affect intelligence activities, including a reduction in spending on intelligence operations on China. Michelle Van Cleave, former national counterintelligence executive, concurs, stating, "I am very troubled by how little US intelligence really knows about the Chinese, in part because they have been so successful against us. Our national leadership should be pushing to close this intelligence gap, because if they don't, they will risk making serious miscalculations in dealing with China."

20 JANUARY 2010

White House directs intelligence agencies to lower China as intelligence-collection target

Source: Gertz, Bill, "China Removed as Top Priority for Spies," The Washington Times, *January 20, 2010.*

This direction to American intelligence agencies may have been the result of China's lobbying of the White House. In view of China's extensive and covert efforts to obtain information from American defense and civilian sources, this directive will increase vulnerability to Chinese espionage. The recent revelation of cyber-attacks against Google and other American businesses highlights the indefensibility of this decision.

21 JANUARY 2010

Gates/DOD announce plans to give Drone Technology to Pakistan

Source: The Economic Times, *21 January 2010*

"Pakistan's demand for provision of drone technology has been accepted by the US and we are working together with Pakistan Army in this connection. We are considering the provision of planes for intelligence surveillance and unmanned planes to Pakistan. Discussions are under way with the Pakistan military leadership on technical matters in this regard." said US Defense Secretary Robert Gates on a visit to Pakistan. However, political analysts have deemed this to be evidence of further deteriorating Indo-US relations, which have been strained by the new administration's courting of China. It would be very reasonable for the Indian government to fear that drone technology could be used in a conflict with India. There is also some evidence to suggest that Pakistan is reluctant to suppress Islamist groups because Pakistan foresees allying itself with these groups in the case of another active India-Pakistan conflict.

30 JANUARY 2010

Secretary of the Navy Downplays China as Threat to American Navy

Source: Pearlman, Jonathan, "China's Military No Threat: US," The Age, *30 January, 2010.*

During a visit to Australia, Secretary of the Navy Ray Mabus stated that he did not believe China's military program posed a long-term threat to American Navy supremacy in the Pacific, despite official Australian government assessments to the contrary. However, China's force modernization program has grown at a double-digit rate for the past decade. According to the former Commander-in-Chief of the US Pacific Fleet: "China is a real and growing threat to US naval forces in Asia, to US allies and friends such as Taiwan and to freedom of navigation in the maritime and outer-space realms."

31 JANUARY 2010

Obama Working to Speed Up Arms Deals with Saudi Arabia

Source: "US steps up arms sales to Persian Gulf allies," The Washington Post, *January 31, 2010.*

The Obama administration is working to expand and speed up arms sales to Saudi Arabia as a measure to deter a future attack by Iran. The administration is selling arms that would allow the Saudis to triple the size of a 10,000-man protection force meant to defend infrastructure from a possible Iranian strike. It is worth noting that despite increased joint military exercises between the two countries, as well as other Arab countries such as the U.A.E., the administration has yet to publicly acknowledge that Iran's action in the area is the greatest threat to regional security and has nothing to do with the Israel-Palestinian conflict. Iranian aggression towards Saudi Arabia is clearly not a reaction to Saudi Arabia's Israel policy, as the country does not have official ties.

FEBRUARY 2010

1 FEBRUARY 2010

Quadrennial Defense and Homeland Security Reviews Fail to Mention Nature of Enemy as "Islamist"

Sources: "Quadrennial Defense Review Report," United States Department of Defense, February 2010; "Quadrennial Homeland Security Review Report," United States Department of Homeland Security, February 2010; Waterman, Shaun, "Terrorist reviews avoid word 'Islamist,'" Washington Times, 12 February 2010.

The Quadrennial Defense and Homeland Security Reviews—intended to articulate the Obama administration's defense and homeland security strategies for the next four years—does not mention "Islam" or any derivatives of Islam when describing the enemy. Our enemies continue to frame their tactics, strategy and objectives through the lens of Islamic teachings—our government cannot hope to defeat them without acknowledging this fact.

9 FEBRUARY 2010

White House Counter-terrorism Advisor Accuses Critics of "Fear-Mongering"

Source: Brennan, John, "We Need No Lectures," USA Today, 9 February 2010.

In the wake of the Obama administration's decision to Mirandize failed Christmas Day bomber Omar Faruk Abdelmutallab just fifty minutes after interrogation by the FBI, several Members of Congress criticized the administration for its handling of the incident, specifically because the decision to treat Adbelmutallab as a criminal defendant enabled him to remain silent and deprived authorities of valuable intelligence. White House counter-terrorism advisor John Brennan wrote in response that such critics were engaged in "fear-mongering" and that "terrorists are not 100 feet tall." These statements demonstrate Brennan's failure to understand the risks associated with treating terrorist operatives as criminals rather than wartime combatants.

11 FEBRUARY 2010

Vice President Biden Says Major 9-11-type Terrorist Attack "Unlikely"

Source: Interview with Larry King, "Biden: Major terror attack on US unlikely," CNN, 11 February 2010.

During an interview with CNN's Larry King, Vice President Biden stated: "The idea of there being a massive attack in the United States like 9/11 is unlikely, in my opinion." If this administration views such a large-scale terrorist attack inside the United States as "unlikely", it will not allocate the proper resources to detect and prevent such a plot.

13 FEBRUARY 2010

White House Counterterrorism Advisor Downplays Significance of Guantanamo Recidivism Rate

Source: Tapper, Jake, "Counterterrorism Czar Brennan Draws Fire for Comments on Gitmo Recidivism," ABC News, 14 February 2010.

While commenting on Pentagon figures indicating that twenty percent of detainees released from Guantanamo Bay have returned to some level of terrorist activity, White House Counterterrorism Advisor John Brennan said: "People sometimes use that figure, 20 percent, say 'Oh my goodness, one out of five detainees returned to some type of extremist activity ... You know, the American penal system, the recidivism rate is up to something about 50 percent or so, as far as return to crime. Twenty percent isn't that bad." Brennan's comments reflect the administration's overall policy to treat terrorism as simply another form of crime. Recidivism rates from the civilian penal system cannot be compared to Guantanamo recidivism rates because terrorism is a unique threat to American national security, quite apart from the threat posed by any common criminal.

14 FEBRUARY 2010

Brennan Vernacular Shifts Against Israel

Source: The White House February 13, 2009.

At New York University, the Assistant to the President for Homeland Security and Counterterrorism, John Brennan, spoke at an event entitled "A Dialogue on our National Security". The event was sponsored by the school's Islamic and the Islamic Law Student's Association. Brennan, an Arabist, referred to Jerusalem, the capital of Israel since 1967, as its Arabic name "Al Quds" in a February speech, sponsored by the White House, which represents a major shift in the generally accepted vernacular of American government officials. Referring to the capital of the Jewish State by its Arabic name in affect establishes an opening to delegitimize the Jewish-Hebrew claim to Jerusalem within the American political dialogue. The change in the lexicon of the new administration, away from its traditionally moderate tone should not come as a surprise, as Secretary Clinton referred to the Falkland Islands as "Las Malvinas," last March. Experts believe that this change is a reflection of the administration's beliefs in cultural relativism and their lack of belief in a Western ideal.

MARCH 2010

2 MARCH 2010

Obama Officials Called Falkland Islands "Las Malvinas" at Clinton Meeting with Argentina's Kirchner

Source: "Clinton meeting with Kirchner adds to British unease over Falklands," Times Online, *March 2, 2010.*

In a meeting in Buenos Aires between Secretary Clinton and Argentine President Cristina Fernandez de Kirchner, US Officials used the Spanish name "Las Malvinas" for the British Falkland Islands, which the British consider part of their sovereign territory. The British won a decisive victory that led to the surrender of Argentina in 1982, but Argentina has increasingly taken to revisiting the conflict because the Islands may rest above a large oil reserve. Roughly 90% of the population of the Falklands consider themselves British, and the largest non-British minority of 6.5% of the population are most likely to identify as Chilean, not Argentinean. The British have interpreted the use of the term "Las Malvinas" by Obama administration officials as a challenge to "The Special Relationship" and a break from the traditional American lexicon. Additionally, they are interpreting this change as inferred support for Argentina in the conflict. The question arises if the Obama administration is on a path of intentionally using semantics to alienate its allies in order appear more "fair" on conflicts that should have been put to rest decades ago.

6 MARCH 2010

Obama's UN Delegation Fails to Prevent Security Council State-ment Condemning Israel

Source: "US repudiates U.N. council remarks on Mideast clash," Reuters, March 6, 2010.

Yesterday, Washington failed to block a U.N. Security Council statement condemning Israel. These statements require consensus, and historically the US delegation has blocked statements concern-ing Israel. Gabon's U.N. Ambassador Issoze-Ngondet, who is serv-ing as Security Council President for the month of March, read the statement: "The members of the Security Council expressed their concern at the current tense situation in the occupied Palestinian territories, including east Jerusalem," Issoze-Ngondet said. East Jerusalem contains the holiest location in the entire Jewish faith and was annexed by Israel over 40 years ago. A US representative to the U.N. anonymously declared that the adoption of the statement was caused by "confusion," Yet this type of confusion never occurred during the previous administrations of Presidents Bush or Clinton. Reports to the contrary suggest that the failure to block this state-ment was intentional, and that the US delegation did not attempt to raise any objections to the final version of the text. If the US delegation has indeed allowed statements to be adopted by mistake, that signifies incompetence. If it is not due to "confusion" then the administration is undermining decades of American policy towards Israel.

13 MARCH 2010

Clinton chastises Israel over announcement of construction in East Jerusalem

Source: Kessler, Glenn, "Clinton rebukes Israel over East Jerusalem plans, cites damage to bilateral ties," Washington Post, 13 March, 2010.

In response to Israel's announcement, during a visit by Vice President Biden, that Israel was proceeding with construction in East Jerusalem, Secretary Clinton called Israeli Prime Minister Netanyahu to demand that Israel take immediate steps to show its commitment to the peace process, declaring the announcement had "undermined trust and confidence in the peace process and in America's interests." This reaction sent US-Israel relations to their lowest point in thirty-five years. The Obama administration could have expressed disagreement with Israel's announcement without this level of public castigation. More importantly, this reaction demonstrates the extent to which the Obama administration mistakenly believes that Israeli urban planning, rather than Palestinian terrorism and anti-Semitism, undermines the peace process.

15 MARCH 2010

DOJ Investigation into Gitmo May Endanger US Intel Officers' Lives

Source: "Justice, CIA clash over probe of interrogator IDs," The Washington Times, March 15, 2010.

A current probe by Attorney General Holder and the DOJ into accounts of "torture" of top al-Qaida terrorists at Guantanamo Bay has put a number of CIA Intelligence Officers life at risk. There are reports that counsel for the terrorists snapped photographs of

covert CIA officers and presented these photographs to the terrorist detainees. The campaign in favor of these investigations is lead
by ACLU supporters within the DOJ and the investigation has been
ongoing. However, the report that the terrorist's lawyers possess
pictures of covert American officers working has given new urgency
to the consideration of this investigation. Simply put, the investigation has already proved a major security threat to American officers and their civilian family members.

16 MARCH 2010

Attorney General insists bin Laden will be killed, making
Miranda warnings irrelevant, while Gen. McChrystal says mission
is to capture bin Laden alive

*Sources: Gerstein, Josh, "Eric Holder: Osama bin Laden won't
be brought in alive," Politico, 16 March 2010; Lubold, Gordon,
"US wants Osama bin Laden alive, US commander in Afghanistan
says,"* Christian Science Monitor, *17 March 2010.*

During testimony before Congress, Attorney General Eric Holder
was asked whether al Qaeda leader Osama bin Laden would have
to be read his Miranda rights if captured, given that several 9/11
planners were still scheduled to be tried in civilian court in New
York. Holder responded that bin Laden "will never appear in an
American courtroom … he will be killed by us, or he will be killed
by his own people so he's not captured by us. We know that." The
next day, the US commander in Afghanistan, Gen. Stanley
McChrystal, indicated that the goal of US forces remains to capture
bin Laden alive. The contradiction further illustrates the problems
with Holder's law enforcement-centered approach to terrorism.
Holder again tried to avoid the obvious implications of trying 9/11
masterminds in federal court—that they will have to be given constitutional protections to which any criminal defendant is entitled—
by saying bin Laden would not be captured alive. The fact that bin
Laden will be captured alive if possible shows that Holder's
approach is a highly problematic one.

19 MARCH 2010

Foreign Aerospace Company EADS Considering Tanker Bid; Would Have Access to US Technologies

Source: "EADS Mulls New Tanker Bid," Associated Press, March 19, 2010.

Foreign owned aerospace and defense company EADS said it is considering a new bid for a $35 billion Pentagon contract for midair refueling tankers The Defense Department "indicated it would welcome a proposal from EADS North America as prime contractor for the KC-X tanker competition" Tim Keating, Senior Vice President of Boeing's Washington operations, has pointed out that if the France-based Airbus, wins the tanker competition, the European governments that own the company could direct it to withhold supplies of parts in the event of a policy dispute with the US. Additionally, EADS would be granted access to sensitive communications technology, the first time a foreign contractor would be privileged to such developments. Previously, foreign companies were only allowed to be subcontractors due to these exact security risks. This development sets a precedent allowing all foreign subcontractors or prime contractors access to US communications technology, posing a major risk to US security.

25 MARCH 2010

US backs away from tougher components of Iran sanctions proposal

Source: Crawford, David, Richard Bourdreaux, Joe Lauria and Jay Solomon, "US Softens Sanction Plan Against Iran," The Wall Street Journal, March 25, 2010.

In an attempt to win support from China and Russia for United Nations sanctions against Iran for its pursuit of a nuclear weapons program, the Obama administration watered down its original draft Security Council resolution, lessening the economic penalties Iran would face for its defiance. In seeking unanimity on the Security Council, the administration left open the strong possibility that the resulting sanctions would be insufficient to dissuade Iran from the pursuit of its nuclear program. Additionally, the administration's actions demonstrate a failure to appreciate the financial interest that Russia and China have in minimizing sanctions against Iran.

APRIL 2010

6 APRIL 2010

Nuclear Posture Review Takes Nuclear Option Off Table
Source: "Statement by President Barack Obama on the Release of Nuclear Posture Review," Defense News, April 6, 2010.

In Barack Obama's statement regarding the DOD's Nuclear Posture Review, President Obama said, "The United States is declaring that we will not use or threaten to use nuclear weapons against non-nuclear weapons states that are party to the Nuclear Non-Proliferation Treaty," indicating that the nuclear option is no longer available even as a response to a biological or chemical attack. Additionally the Nuclear Posture Review indicates that the US will not develop any new nuclear warheads and will instead favor refurbishing older models. Rep. Michael Turner of Ohio, the ranking Republican on the House Armed Services Strategic Forces Subcommittee said, "I am deeply concerned by some of the decisions made in the Nuclear Posture Review and the message this administration is sending to Iran, North Korea and non-state actors who may seek to harm the United States or our allies. By unilaterally taking a nuclear response off the table, we are decreasing our options without getting anything in return and diminishing our ability to defend our nation from attack."

7 APRIL 2010

Terms "Islam," "Jihad" Banned from National Security Strategy

Source: Associated Press, "Obama Bans Islam, Jihad from National Security Strategy Document," Fox News, April 7, 2010.

Advisers to President Obama have indicated that they will remove references to "Islam" and "jihad" from the National Security Strategy, a major document that helps guide the US national security doctrine. Press reports indicate that the document under the previous administration read: "The Struggle against militant Islamic radicalism is the great ideological conflict of the early years of the 21st century." This constitutes a major failure of the Obama Administration to acknowledge the nature of the enemy we face and what motivates him to attack the United States, and arguably rises to the level of deliberate disinformation as to the religious motivations of terrorists and their sympathizers. The deliberate downplaying of the ideological motivations of those who seek to harm the United States guarantees that this Administration will be unprepared to combat these forces effectively.

8 APRIL 2010

Obama signs ill-advised "New START" arms control treaty with Russia

Source: Baker, Peter and Dan Bilefsky, "Russia and US Sign Nuclear Arms Reduction Pact," New York Times, April 8, 2010.

President Obama signed, along with Russian Presdient Medvedev, an arms control treaty known as the New Strategic Arms Limitation Treaty, or "New START". The treaty reduces the number of deployed nuclear warheads allowed by each country to 1,550, and places other limits on the use of nuclear weapons by each country. However, the treaty contains a number of serious flaws, including:

(1) a "counting rule" that states that one heavy bomber will count as a single deployed warhead, even if the bomber can carry several warheads; and (2) major restrictions on US missile defense; among others. The treaty also fails to address tactical nuclear weapons (where Russia enjoys a major strategic advantage) and fails to address the real nuclear proliferation problems—Iran and North Korea. The treaty is better understood as a component of President Obama's vision of a "world without nuclear weapons"— this is especially so given that there is no serious effort underway to modernize America's nuclear enterprise.

8 APRIL 2010

New Gates-Obama Plan to Gut Military Announced

Source: "Obama and Gates Gut the Military," The Wall Street Journal, *April 8, 2010.*

On Monday, Secretary Gates announce a plan to reduce defense spending—in effect, however, these cuts will gut the military. The cuts include the F-22, which is used to defend reconnaissance planes in important intelligence gathering flyovers. The military already had to scrap plans for drone flyovers during the Russian-Georgian conflict because F-22s were not provided. Additionally, these budget cuts will likely continue a course in which Naval ships are retired at a pace faster than new ones are being built, ensuring the Navy's goal of 313 ships is not met. Gates' statements suggest that these cuts are being made specifically to balance cost against safety: ""[E]very defense dollar spent to over-insure against a remote or diminishing risk … is a dollar not available to take care of our people, reset the force, win the wars we are in." However, what is clear from 9-11 is that the most remote risks are often the scenarios that, if they were to occur, would have the greatest negative impact. It is exactly these scenarios for which the US has to be prepared, no matter the cost.

13 APRIL 2010

US- Russia Sign Deal to "Dispose" Plutonium
Source: Reuters, April 13, 2010.

On Tuesday, US Secretary of State Hillary Clinton and Russian Foreign Minister Sergei Lavrov signed an agreement to "destroy" 34 metric tons of plutonium by burning it in nuclear reactors. The US will be contributing roughly $400 million dollars to the Russ ian efforts. However, many skeptics are worried about the validity of the program, because the nuclear reactors used by the Russians are also capable of reprocessing the fuel back into weapons grade plutonium. Additionally, some experts also worry that the transportation of plutonium and the downgraded nuclear product known as "MOX" (a fuel useful in civilian-use reactors) is vulnerable to theft.

14 APRIL 2010

Attorney General Holder defends decision not to release names of DOJ attorneys who previously defended Gitmo detainees; cites interest in protecting "these kids"

Source: York, Byron, "Holder Defends DOJ 'kids' Who Represented Gitmo Detainees," Washington Examiner, April 14, 2010.

During testimony before the Senate Judiciary Committee, Attorney General Eric Holder defended his decision not to disclose to the committee the names of Justice Department senior attorneys who had previously represented Guantanamo Bay detainees, saying: "There has been has been an attempt to take the names of people who represented Guantanamo detainees and to drag their reputations through the mud ... I'm not going to allow these kids—I'm not going to be part of that effort." As National Review's Andy McCarthy notes, the "kids" to which Holder refers include several senior Justice Department attorneys in their forties. They include

(1) Justice Department Civil Division Chief Tony West, who defended "American Taliban" John Walker Lindh; (2) Deputy Solicitor General Neal Katyal, who voluntarily represented Salim

Hamdan, Osama bin Laden's former bodyguard; and (3) Jennifer Daskal, a former Human Rights Watch attorney who exposed a top-secret CIA program to detain high-value al Qaeda terrorists in prisons overseas. Attorney General Holder fails to recognize that the American public is entitled to know about political appointees who, prior to joining the administration, voluntarily represented terrorists and acted to jeopardize national security.

18 APRIL 2010
Gates Warns That US Has No Long-Range Policy to Deal with Iran

Sources: Sanger, David E. and Thom Shanker, "Gates Says US Lacks a Policy to Thwart Iran," New York Times, *April 18, 2010; Mostafavi, Ramin, "Iran to start work on new enrichment plant,"* Washington Post, *April 19, 2010.*

In a secret three-page memo issued to the White House, the Secretary of Defense, Robert Gates, warned that the United States does not have an effective long-range policy for dealing with Iran's steady progress toward nuclear capability, according to government officials familiar with the document. However, White House officials dispute this, claiming that for the past 15 months they have been creating extensive plans to address possible outcomes of Iran's nuclear program. Having only recently signed the START II Treaty and issued the Nuclear Posture Review, this is another signal to Iran that the Obama administration will not and cannot take action against Iranian nuclear facilities. Today, Mojtaba Samareh-Hashemi, a senior adviser to President Mahmoud Ahmadinejad, confirmed Iran is going ahead with the construction of a new nuclear site. He is quoted as saying, "The president has confirmed the designated location of a new nuclear site and on his order the building process will begin.

18 APRIL 2010

Obama Nominates Anti-Military Elena Kagan to Supreme Court

Source: "Foes may target Kagan's stance on military recruitment at Harvard," The Washington Post, *April 18, 2010.*

After the announcement of Supreme Court Justice Stevens' retirement, President Obama announced the nomination of former Dean of Harvard Law School, Elena Kagan. Kagan, who has no experience on the bench, was at the heart of a major controversy when she attempted to ban the recruitment of Harvard law students by the US Military to become JAG officers. Ultimately, the matter went all the way to the Supreme Court, which sided with the military by holding that the Solomon Amendment, barring federal funds for schools that refused to allow military recruitment on campus, was constitutional. Kagan's overly strong language in the matter, calling military hiring practices, "moral injustice of the first order," is in striking contrast to the Supreme Court's ultimate ruling 8-0 against the law schools. This demonstrated hostility towards the military should be thoroughly considered as the Senate determines whether she is fit to serve on the Court.

21 APRIL 2010

Obama's Undersecretary of Defense Publicly Takes Military Strike on Iran "Off the Table"

Source: Kennedy, Alex, "Pentagon undersecretary: Iran strike ruled out," Military Times, *April 21, 2010.*

Michelle Flournoy, Undersecretary of Defense for Policy, stated with respect to Iran's pursuit of nuclear weapons: "[US] Military force is an option of last resort ... it's off the table in the near term." This public declaration removed much needed strategic ambiguity on this issue, leaving Iran to pursue its weapons programs without fear of military consequences. If the statement is an accurate reflection of policy, then the Obama administration is effectively allowing Iran to "go nuclear"; if the statement is not an accurate reflection of policy, it nonetheless will embolden Iran further to pursue its nuclear weapons program.

26 APRIL 2010

National Security Advisor makes joke that depicted a member of the Taliban getting tricked by a Jewish merchant looking to make a sale

Source: "National Security Adviser Apologizes for Joke About Jewish Merchant," Fox News, April 26, 2010.

At a recent address for the 25th anniversary of the Washington Institute for Near East Policy, National Security Advisor James Jones made a joke about a Jewish Merchant refusing to sell a member of the Taliban some water and instead offering to sell him a tie. He began the address by saying he wanted to "set the stage" by telling a "story that I think is true" from a recent incident in southern Afghanistan before going on to make the joke. The address was meant to be focused on America's commitment to a strong relationship with Israel, and a joke like this from a high-ranking member of the security apparatus will have done nothing to help the situation.

27 APRIL 2010

Obama administration refuses to release documents on Fort Hood shootings to Senate Committee

Sources: Keith Johnson, "Senators Seek Documents on Fort Hood Suspect," Wall Street Journal, April 20, 2010; Anne Flaherty, "Senate committee subpoenas Fort Hood documents," Associated Press, April 19, 2010; "Administration Sets Up Potential Clash With Senate Over Fort Hood Documents," Fox News, April 27, 2010.

The Obama administration will only release some, not all, of the necessary documents to the Senate Homeland Security and Governmental Affairs Committee with regard to their inquiries into the Fort Hood shooting by Major Nidal Hasan. The committee issued a statement on the matter: "DOD and DOJ have produced a limited set of documents in response to the subpoenas, which we appreciate. However, they still refuse to provide access to their agents who reportedly reviewed Major Hasan's communications with radical extremist cleric Anwar al-Awlaki and to transcripts of prosecution interviews with Hasan's associates and superiors, which DOD already provided to its internal review. DOD and DOJ's failure to comply with the subpoenas is an affront to Congress's Constitutional obligation to conduct independent oversight of the Executive Branch, a right all the more critical in order to ensure that our government operates effectively to counter the threat of terrorism." (See Senate Committee on Homeland Security and Government Affairs, "Administration fails to comply with Ft. Hood subpoenas; Senators receive additional but not all documents and none of the witnesses required", press release, 27 April 2010) The Departments of Justice and Defense say that the release of these documents would possibly compromise the prosecution of Major Hasan.

Secretary Gates highlighted this position recently when he said, "We have no interest in hiding anything, but what's most important is that prosecution."

29 APRIL 2010

US Delegation Does not Object to U.N. Electing Iran to Commission on Women's Rights

Source: Joseph Abrahams, "U.N. Elects Iran to Commission on Women's Rights," Fox News, April 29, 2010.

The United Nations has handed Iran a four-year seat on the Commission on the Status of Women even though the stoning and lashing of women is codified in Iranian law. Recently a senior cleric, Hojatoleslam Kazem Sedighi, suggested that women were to blame for earthquakes and was quoted as saying, "Many women who do not dress modestly ... lead young men astray, corrupt their chastity and spread adultery in society, which (consequently) increases

earthquakes". It was decided that Iran would be "elected by accla-
mation," meaning that no open vote by members was required or
requested by member states, including the United States. In failing
to even attempt to prevent such an outcome, the Obama administration demonstrated little regard for women's rights or human
rights, particularly in the Muslim world.

29 APRIL 2010

Obama Administration Wants to Sue Arizona Over Immigration
Legislation

*Source: "Justice Department considers suing Arizona to block
immigration law,"* The Washington Post, *April 29, 2010.*

Officials in the Obama administration are considering suing Arizona over its new immigration law in order to block the legislation
from taking effect. The Arizona law criminalizes illegal immigration by defining it as trespassing and empowers police to question
anyone they have a "reasonable suspicion" is an illegal immigrant
if the individual is stopped for some other legitimate reason. President Obama and Attorney General Eric Holder have been fervent
critics of the new law. The Obama Administration contends the law
has potential to lead to racial profiling. However, the legislation
specifically states that police may not "solely consider race, color
or national origin" in questioning people about their immigration
status. One lawyer who contends that the new law is constitutional
says, "Arizona passed this law because the federal government abdi-
cated its enforcement responsibilities on immigration." It seems the
Obama Administration would rather protect the civil liberties of
illegal aliens than enforce laws drafted by and aimed to protect US
citizens.

30 APRIL 2010

DOD Announces Obesity as Major Security Threat

Source: "The latest national security threat: obesity," The Washington Post, *April 30, 2010.*

According to the Department of Defense, as of 2005, 9 million young adults in between the ages of 17 and 24 were rejected from military service because they were deemed too overweight to serve. The Department of Defense is concerned that because of the skyrocketing rates of obesity in children, which more often than not carries on into their adult years, the US military will have difficulty in reaching their recruiting numbers in years to come. Government officials and First Lady Michelle Obama have called for "fixing" school lunch programs and encouraging more fitness programs in response, however some believe these calls are misguided. Perhaps a more sensible effort would to be to expand Junior ROTC programs in high schools.

MAY 2010

3 MAY 2010

Gates says Need of Marine Corps and Amphibious Assault Capabilities in Doubt

Source: "Gates wary of Marines' amphibious vehicle spending," Reuters, May 3, 2010.

On Monday, while speaking about new defense spending, Secretary of Defense Robert Gates in effect questioned the need for the Marine Corps when he criticized their planned spending on amphibious landing vehicles. The secretary said that it is neither "necessary or sensible" to utilize amphibious landings in future conflicts, "especially as advances in anti-ship systems keep pushing the potential launch point further from shore." Amphibious warfare is the specialty of the Marines, and saying that amphibious fighting in the future will be unnecessary is a major strategic shift for the US

Military. In fact, Marine Corps Commandant General James Conway has gone on the record staying that the Expeditionary Fighting Vehicle (EFV) would be necessary in the case of a conflict that requires traditional warfare.

4 MAY 2010

US Publicly Reveals the Size of Nuclear Arsenal

Sources: Jay Solomon, "US Declares Size of Nuclear Arsenal," Wall Street Journal, *May 4, 2010; Mary Beth Sheridan, "Obama administration discloses size of US nuclear arsenal,"* The Washington Post, *May 4, 2010.*

During the review conference for the Nuclear Non-Proliferation Treaty at the United Nations, the Obama administration released the number of nuclear warheads currently in the US arsenal, which until now has been a closely-guarded secret. Secretary of State Hilary Clinton went so far as to say that releasing these figures would bolster our national security: "We think it is in our national security interest to be as transparent as we can about the nuclear program of the United States." In a misguided attempt to "set an example" for the rest of the world, the Obama administration removed much-needed strategic ambiguity about the nature of the US nuclear arsenal.

8 MAY 2010

Secretary of Defense Gates Calls for Sweeping Cuts to the Defense Budget

Source: "Gates Seeks Pentagon Overhaul," Defense News, *May 8, 2010.*

Defense Secretary Robert Gates said the US military spends too much and must live within a tighter budget. Speaking at the Eisenhower Library on May 8, Gates said the Defense Department must trim "around $10 billion" for 2012, and up to $15 billion per year after that. These cuts he argues, "are the only way" the military can afford its planned force structure. Secretary Gates' plan, though

economically admirable, is dangerous. These proposals cut spending on new weapons programs designed for future conflicts, and
focuses limited DOD resources on current counterinsurgency
efforts. Already, Gates has capped the production of the most capable fighter jet in world, the F-22, at 187 planes, though the Air
Force said 243 was the minimum number it needed to be successful. Cuts in missile defense and efforts to modernize the naval fleet
will also have potentially serious ramifications in the future.

10 MAY 2010

John Brennan: "We're not lucky we're good." That's why the
Christmas Day and Times Square attempts failed

*Source: Brennan Out Of Touch: "We're Not Lucky, We're
Good,"* Fox News Sunday, *May 10, 2010.*

When asked whether the failed Times Square attack was a success for Homeland Security, John Brennan, Barack Obama's Assistant for Homeland Security and Counterterrorism, stated on Fox
News Sunday that "we have a very strong track record and that's
why we have redundant capabilities in place. We're not lucky—
we're good." This comment suggests that the Obama administration believes the attempt was foiled by law enforcement agencies
rather than by the incompetence of the would-be bomber.

14 MAY 2010

Attorney General reluctant to admit that "radical Islam" was
behind Times Square and Christmas Day bombing attempts

*Sources: Stephen Dinan, "Holder balks at blaming 'radical
Islam' for terror attempts,"* Washington Times, *May 14, 2010;
Andy McCarthy, "AG Eric Holder Refuses to Say 'Radical Islam'
Is a Cause of Terrorism Committed by Muslims,"* National Review
Online, *May 13, 2010.*

Eric Holder, Attorney General of the United States, refused to say
that the root cause of the attempted bombings in Times Square and
on Christmas Day was radical Islam, stating instead that "there are

a variety of reasons why people do these things. Some of them are potentially religious." This represents a continuation of the Obama administration's new rule which requires that word such as 'jihad' do not appear in policy documents in an attempt not to upset the Muslim world.

14 MAY 2010

US joins UN group dedicated to bridging divide between the West and the Islamic World

Source: Patrick Goodenough, "US Joins U.N. Initiative Whose Stated Goal Is to Bridge Islam-West Divide," CNS News, May 14, 2010.

The United States has joined a grouping in the United Nations called the "Alliance of Civilizations" which aims to build bridges between the West and Islam. However, a report by this group states that terrorism "committed by radical groups on the fringes of Muslim societies," was caused primarily by Western policies and repression in the Islamic world, not Islamist ideology. This is another organization that the United States has joined which shows weakness towards tackling Islamic extremism.

18 MAY 2010

Assistant Secretary of State for Human Rights Apologizes to China for Arizona Immigration Law

Source: "Obama State Dept. Tells Communist China: AZ Immigration Law is 'Troubling Trend' of 'Discrimination' in US," CNSNews, May 18, 2010.

Engaging in human rights dialogue with officials from the People's Republic of China last week, Assistant Secretary of State for Human Rights and Labor Michael Posner brought up Arizona's new immigration enforcement law, telling the Chinese that the law was an example of a "troubling trend" in the United States and an indication of "discrimination or potential discrimination" in American society. For some reason, Posner felt the need to apologize to the Communist China for the passage of the Immigration legislation in Arizona. Posner's comments set off a series of criticisms directed at the Obama White House for continuing to feel the need to apologize for America on the world stage. Arizona Senators Kyl and McCain wrote a letter to Posner calling his comments, "particularly offensive" and demanded that he formally apologize . The New York Post also took a shot at Posner asserting, "China is one of the most flagrant violators of human rights on the planet, and for the Obama administration even to hint that America is on the same plane is despicable."

18 MAY 2010

Attorney General Holder Refuses to Allow Legally Required Congressional Oversight of Intelligence Activities

Source: "Holder Tightens Grip on Intelligence Agencies," Real Clear Politics, May 18, 2010; Attorney General Eric Holder has not exactly championed candidate Obama's pledge for transparency in government. The Attorney General has taken oversight of our intelligence agencies upon himself, requiring them to get Justice Department permission to release classified information to the House and Senate Intelligence Committees, according to Senate sources.

Sen. Christopher Bond (R-Mo), Ranking Republican on the Senate Select Committee on Intelligence, and three Senate staffers working for other members have recently asked the Director of National Intelligence for information on the interrogation of the failed Times Square bomber, Faisal Shazad. All four were told the information would not be provided until the disclosure of that information was approved by the Justice Department. Traditionally and legally speaking, the Attorney General has no role in intelligence oversight. But Eric Holder has seemingly seized control of intelligence oversight from congress, with the support of the President, essentially achieving what all intelligence professionals fear: the politicization of intelligence.

21 MAY 2010

ICE Commissioner Refuses to Enforce Arizona Immigration Law
Source: "Top Official Says Feds May Not Process Illegals Referred From Arizona," Fox News, May 21, 2010.

John Morton, the Assistant Secretary of Homeland Security for Immigration and Customs Enforcement (ICE), stated that ICE will not automatically process illegal aliens referred to it by Arizona authorities. The new law requires law enforcement officials to check suspects for immigration status if those suspects have been stopped for some other legitimate reason, and the officials come to suspect they are in the US illegally. Morton argues that the best way to reduce illegal immigration is through a comprehensive federal approach and not a patchwork of state laws. No matter if Secretary Morton feels the Arizona law is good government, or not, his duty is to enforce the law. Congressman Steve King (R-IA) echoed this same sentiment: "Mr. Morton should realize that in his role at Immigration and Customs Enforcement, he is entrusted with the responsibility to ensure the enforcement of the laws that are on the books. Nothing grants Mr. Morton the ability to ignore the application of the United States' immigration laws simply because he has personal objections to them … If Mr. Morton wants to be in a position in which his preferred policy objectives can be given the force of law, perhaps he should run for Congress so that he may have a hand in drafting legislation. Until such time, he should remember that the American people expect him either to fully enforce the nation's immigration laws as written or to make way for those who will."

23 MAY 2010

A New World Order—Obama's Commencement Speech at West Point

Source: "At West Point, Obama offers a new security strategy," The Washington Post, *May 23, 2010.*

President Obama, despite admitting "...the shortfalls" of the international system, said while delivering the Commencement Speech to the graduating class at West Point that the United States would move ahead on a policy of "national renewal and global leadership." The president vowed to press for a new international order "that can resolve the challenges of our times" and help the United States defeat al-Qaeda and other threats to freedom. According to the president, this new world order could accomplish goals of combating violent extremism and prevent the proliferation of nuclear weapons. This new found reliance on the international system demonstrates the Obama Administration's desire to distance itself from the foreign policy initiatives of George W. Bush, and relies on global institutions and America's role in promoting democratic values to protect American national security interests, rather than fighting terrorism and other threats head-on with the Doctrine of Preemptive War.

24 MAY 2010

Department of Defense Publicly Announces Plans for Clandestine Military Operations in the Middle East Before they are Launched

Source: "US is Said to Expand Secret Military Acts in Mideast Region," The New York Times, *May 24, 2010.*

The US has ordered a broad expansion of clandestine military activity in an effort to disrupt militant groups or counter threats in Iran, Saudi Arabia, Somalia and other countries in the region. This new order authorizes sending American Special Operations troops to both friendly and hostile nations in the Middle East, Central Asia and the Horn of Africa to gather intelligence and build ties with local forces. The order also calls for secretive reconnaissance missions that may aid possible military strikes in Iran if the day arrives. By announcing our plans to conduct clandestine operations the operations themselves have now been jeopardized and will lack effectiveness because the enemy knows we are coming. How can secret, clandestine operations stay secret if the Administration announces where these actions will take place and who will be conducting them on the front page of the New York Times?

24 MAY 2010

Brennan Praises Foreign Terrorist Organization Hezbollah

Source: "Brennan: US Should Foster 'Moderate Elements' of the Terrorist Group Hezbollah," CNS News, May 24, 2010.

John Brennan called Hezbollah a "very interesting organization" in remarks at the Washington-based Nixon Center. He also said the United States needs to "build up the more moderate elements" of Hezbollah, which the State Department has designated as a Foreign Terrorist Organization (FTO). Brennan reflected on Hezbollah's history with admiration, crediting the group as a developing political force. "Hezbollah started out as purely a terrorist organization back in the early '80s and has evolved significantly over time," Brennan said. "And now it has members of parliament, in the cabinet; there are lawyers, doctors, others who are part of the Hezbollah organization." Brennan added that, "there (are) certainly the elements of Hezbollah that are truly a concern to us—what they're doing. And what we need to do is to find ways to diminish their influence within the organization and to try to build up the more moderate elements." Brennan's recognition of a terrorist organization as legitimate and his outright willingness to build them up is nothing short of a dereliction of duty. His post as Counterterrorism Advisor to the President would seemingly require him to promote strategies to combat terrorism. Mr. Brennan has apparently chosen to promote groups such as Hezbollah instead.

25 MAY 2010

Officials Move to Repeal "Don't Ask Don't Tell"

Source: "Congress press Ahead with Vote to Repeal 'Don't Ask Don't Tell,'" Fox News, May 25, 2010.

In an effort to change the military's "Don't Ask, Don't Tell" policy, Congress is set to vote as early as this week on a proposal to repeal the rule barring gays from serving openly in the military, before the Pentagon completes its review of how to implement the policy and its effect. The Obama administration has continued to back the plan, despite serious concerns about doing so voiced by the Chiefs of the service branches. Those opposing the repeal of the policy include: Marine Corps Commandant Gen. James Conway, Army Chief of Staff Gen. George Casey, Navy Chief of Staff Adm. Gary Roughead, and Air Force Chief of Staff Gen. Norton Schwartz. The letter co-signed by each of these Chiefs cited concerns about the repeal's effectiveness, implementation, and readiness of the military as a whole to function with openly gay service members. The rush to repeal a policy that, "works," as Gen. Conway stated, is dangerous for the cohesion and morale of our fighting forces.

26 MAY 2010

Obama to Send 1,200 National Guardsmen to the Arizona Border, Shortchanging the State's Request for 6,000

Source: "Obama's Border Plan Looks Similar to Bush's," Associated Press, May 26, 2010.

Yesterday, President Obama announced his plan to send 1,200 National Guard troops to the US-Mexico border in order to reduce the ever increasing violence. This is an unexpected move, to say the least, considering Homeland Security Secretary Janet Napolitano stated on the same day that the border is the most secure it has ever been, as well as news that the Department of Justice is moving forward with its efforts to file a lawsuit challenging Arizona's immigration legislation. Despite a more robust request by Arizona

Senator John McCain for 6,000 National Guard troops, the President chose instead to send only a fraction of those troops, and limited their abilities to a support function, conducting intelligence, surveillance, and reconnaissance missions. Some law enforcement officials along the border said they worry that Obama will repeat the mistake make by President Bush when he sent 6,000 troops to the border in 2006. Limiting the troops to support roles, rather than letting them make arrests and confront smugglers, will ultimately render those troops less effective. Officials also believe the scale of the force—one-fifth of the size of the one sent by Bush—is too small to make a difference along the length of the 2,000-mile border. 1,200 soldiers might make a difference, but only if concentrated in a smaller portion of the border.

26 MAY 2010

Mexico Displays Increasing Influence on US Immigration Policy
Source: "US troops won't be used to stop illegal immigration: US," Breitbart, May 26, 2010.

After announcing the deployment of 1200 National Guard troops to the southern border, the State Department issued a statement that the troops will not be used to stem illegal immigration from Mexico. The statement followed a diplomatic conversation with Mexican officials, who urged the US to not enforce the border. Instead the troops will be used to stop the transport of drugs across the border, ignoring the fact that cartel workers are more often than not "illegal" aliens. After soaring past Mexico economically and militarily for the past 200 years, Secretary of State Hillary Clinton is allowing US sovereignty be challenged by our neighbors to the south. Allowing a foreign government to dictate the flow of their citizens into our country sends a clear message that the boundaries to the geographic US are at risk.

26 MAY 2010

Arizona Gets Minimal Assistance from National Guard, Texas Is Ignored

Source: "Arizona Gets Border Soldiers; None for Texas," NBC News- Dallas/Fort Worth, May 26, 2010.

After mounting political pressure to help secure the Arizona border, President Obama has agreed to send 1,200 National Guard troops to Arizona's border with Mexico. But, Texas issued that same request almost a year and a half ago. The Texas request for assistance has seen less press coverage and has been virtually ignored by the Obama Administration. Gov. Rick Perry has sent letters to President Obama, Defense Secretary Robert Gates and Department of Homeland Security Secretary Janet Napolitano requesting National Guard troops for the Texas-Mexico border. Almost a year and a half after the first letter was sent, Gov. Perry still hasn't received an answer. As enforcement is stepped up in Arizona with new legislation, the refusal to secure Texas' border seems problematic. One is left to wonder what will keep those attempting to enter the US illegally from entering in Southwest Texas, as Texas is admittedly doing an inadequate job of immigration enforcement.

27 MAY 2010

Obama: Let Me Clarify, National Guard Troops in Arizona are Not for Illegal Immigration

Source: "National Guard Won't Be on Front Lines in Arizona," Fox News, May 27, 2010.

The 1,200 National Guard troops President Obama is dispatching to the US-Mexico border will provide intelligence, reconnaissance and other support functions, but one thing they won't be doing is helping the Border Patrol and local law enforcement nab illegal immigrants and smugglers flowing into Arizona. Speaking at a press conference on Thursday, the president said the troops will not be in a primary role combating illegal immigration, but will be offering support roles, for drug and human trafficking interdiction.

This follows the State Department's announcement on Wednesday that the border troop surge was, "not about immigration," but rather about the unregulated flow of drugs and guns. The President continues to be at odds with Arizona officials, seemingly separating the flow of humans, drugs, and guns from illegal immigration. The Administration's directive to send troops to the border appears to be more political rather than practical, as the troops' ability to truly be effective has been handcuffed and downgraded to a support role.

27 MAY 2010

Counter-terrorism Adviser Brennan Says Jihadists are Not America's Enemy

Source: "Counter-terrorism Adviser Defends Jihad as 'Legitimate Tenet of Islam," Fox News, May 27, 2010.

Wednesday, John Brennan called jihad a "legitimate tenet of Islam," and then argued that Islamic extremists are victims of "political, economic and social forces." Additionally he argued that those who have attacked the US and described their own cause as religious should still not be described in "religious terms." Brennan's full statement is "Nor do we describe our enemy as 'jihadists' or 'Islamists' because jihad is a holy struggle, a legitimate tenet of Islam, meaning to purify oneself or one's community, and there is nothing holy or legitimate or Islamic about murdering innocent men, women and children." Unfortunately the definition that Brennan has seemingly adapted on behalf of the administration refuses to define what jihadists and fundamental Islamists define as innocent—which doesn't include anyone deemed an 'infidel.' Brennan, an Arabist, also referred to Jerusalem by its Arabic name "Al Quds" in a February speech, sponsored by the White House, which represents a major shift in the generally accepted vernacular of American government officials.

27 MAY 2010

Obama Administration's New National Security Strategy to Focus on Homegrown Threats; Says Terror is a Tactic not an Enemy

Source: "Obama to Focus on Homegrown Extremists in New Security Strategy," UK Telegraph*, May 27, 2010.*

President Obama's new National Security Strategy will stress that US military superiority must be matched by muscular diplomacy and all the tools of statecraft. For the first time, the government strategy document is likely to focus attention on the threat posed by homegrown, radical extremists. "The president's national security strategy explicitly recognizes the threat to the United States posed by individuals radicalized here at home," Mr Brennan said Wednesday at the Center for Strategic and International Studies. "The president's strategy is absolutely clear about the threat we face. Our enemy is not terrorism because terrorism is but a tactic." The assertion that our enemy is not terrorism motivated by jihadist ideology is a new, and frankly, dangerous assertion by the Obama Administration. If America's enemy is not terrorism or jihadists, as Brennan asserts, who or what is?

27 MAY 2010

DHS Intelligence Memo says More Attempted Attacks Against US than Ever Before

Source: "Document Says the Number of Attempted Attacks on US is At All-Time High," CNN, May 27, 2010.

Just weeks after the failed car bombing of New York's Times Square, the Department of Homeland Security says "the number and pace of attempted attacks against the United States over the past nine months have surpassed the number of attempts during any other previous one-year period." That assessment, contained in an unclassified DHS intelligence memo prepared for various law enforcement groups, does not bode well for the Obama Administration's counterterrorism efforts. The memo also says terror groups are expected to try attacks inside the United States with "increased frequency," and continues to notify officials that, "we have to operate under the premise that other operatives are in the country and could advance plotting with little or no warning." A day after the President rolled out his new national security strategy, which calls for tough diplomacy over pre-emptive military and law enforcement strength, this news is another demonstration of the Obama Administration's failed approach to counterterrorism.

31 MAY 2010

While Obama Waits for Sanctions and Talks, Iran Gets Closer to Nuclear Armament

Source: "U.N. Says Iran Has Fuel for 2 Nuclear Weapons," The New York Times, *May 31, 2010.*

International nuclear inspectors declared that Iran has now produced a stockpile of nuclear fuel that experts say would be enough, with further enrichment, to make two nuclear weapons. When Iran tentatively agreed eight months ago to ship some of its nuclear material out of the country, the White House said the deal would temporarily deprive Iran of enough fuel to make even a single weapon. These talks continued for months with Iran refusing to commit to the agreement. Now, with the Obama Administration's focus on health care reform rather than the Iranian threat, the figures contained in the inspectors' report on Monday indicated that even if Iran now shipped the agreed-upon amount of nuclear material out of the country, it would retain enough for a single weapon, undercutting the American rationale for the deal.

JUNE 2010

1 JUNE 2010

US Ambassador to the UN Skips Emergency Meeting on Israeli Raid of a Gaza Flotilla

Source: *"Critics Questions Rice's Low-Profile Approach at the UN," Fox News, June 1, 2010.*

The US ambassador to the United Nations, Susan Rice, chose to stay in Washington on Memorial Day as an emergency meeting was convened over the Israeli raid on a Gaza aid flotilla. In her place, Deputy US Representative Alejandro Wolff was present at the emergency session. A U.N. official said Rice was fully engaged the entire time, "managing the situation and in constant communication." But Richard Grennell, a former UN Spokesman, criticized the US ambassador, calling her absence part of a pattern of passivity, and "troublesome" "It's just unbelievable that Susan Rice didn't go out there," Grennell said. "She had plenty of time to get to New York....She clearly wants to be the popular ambassador and has demonstrated that she's unwilling to take on the controversial issues." Ambassador Rice's neglect of the emergency meeting is just the latest event in a series of Obama Administration events and policies that distance the US from full-fledged support of Israel. The Administration continues to make concessions to the world in US-Israeli relations to improve its image in the Middle East.

1 JUNE 2010

Obama Makes Clear His Willingness to Abandon Israel

Source: *"Obama Abandons Israel to UN Feeding Frenzy," Fox News, June, 1, 2010.*

The UN Security Council Presidential Statement on the Gaza flotilla incident involving Israeli soldiers, describes the incident in a manner similar to the outline designed by its Arab and OIC sponsors. All the civilians who participated in the flotilla are cast as humanitarians—including the armed thugs caught on video-tape brutally attacking Israeli soldiers. The Presidential Statement was agreed upon unanimously—with American approval. The Obama team is sailing into new waters, refusing to take a stand for Israel and caving to political pressure from Middle Eastern States. The resolution, which is supported by the Obama Administration, makes no mention of Iran's dedication to Israel's annihilation, no mention of the smuggling of arms into Gaza, and no mention of the use of those weapons against Israel and its people. Apparently, the Security Council suggests that there is no justification for Israel's interest in the ship's cargo or its legal blockade of an enemy, Hamas, with which it is at war. The Obama Administration may have made more productive use with its time if it had brought the Council's focus back to dealing with international peace and security items constantly delayed or ignored, like an Iranian bomb or the torpe-doing of a South Korean naval ship by North Korea. For some rea-son, the Obama team insists on separating ties with Israel while Iran has amassed enough enriched uranium to produce two nuclear war-heads, according a to recent UN assessment.

4 JUNE 2010

DOJ Ill-prepared for Potential WMD Attack on US

Source: "'Justice Department isn't ready for WMD attack, report says" Los Angeles Times, *June 1, 2010.*

A new report issued by the Justice Department's Inspector Gen-eral says "the department is not prepared to fulfill its role' in coor-dinating federal law enforcement activities in the event of an attack utilizing a weapon of mass destruction." In the event of a nuclear, biological, or chemical attack, the responsibility for coordinating federal law enforcement activities and ensuring public safety and security is that of the Justice Department. The Inspector General's report concluded that, "the department is not prepared to fulfill its role." This is the latest in a series of reports criticizing the government for inadequate planning for WMD attacks. In January, a bipartisan commission gave the Obama Administration and Congress an "F" for its preparation for a biological attack. With the President announcing that obtaining nuclear weapons has become a priority for terrorist and other extremist groups, this revelation is particularly disturbing and demonstrates the Administration's lack of focus on job number one: national security.

11 JUNE 2010
Obama White House Seeks to Ease US Sanctions Against Iran
Source: "White House works to ease Iran proposal in congress," Los Angeles Times, *June 11, 2010.*

After the recent set of sanctions placed on Iran by the UN, the US Congress is hard at work on their own set of sanctions. The Obama administration, however, is now pushing in the opposite direction against Congress fearing the sanctions may go too far. The new legislation would punish companies that sell refined petroleum products to Iran or help the country's oil industry. These actions have strong congressional support. However, the administration fears that the legislation also could damage relations with Europe, Russia and China, all of whom cooperated with US efforts on the U.N. sanctions. To avoid that possibility, the administration wants authority to waive US punishment against companies from countries that have cooperated on Iran. Rep. Brad Sherman (D-CA) says, "The administration doesn't carry out the laws that are on the books, and they want the new law to be as weak and loophole-ridden as possible." This is a particularly concerning revelation. The Obama administration has been extremely ineffective in dealing the Iranian desire for nuclear capabilities. On the same day that Iranian President claimed that Israel is, "doomed," word of Obama's lack of desire to pressure Iran and enforce sanctions jeopardizes national security, essentially appeasing the Iranian government and buying more time for it to continue work on its nuclear program.

11 JUNE 2010

Obama Supports UN Investigation on Israel

Source: The Weekly Standard, *June 11, 2010.*

Rebelling against 62 years of American foreign policy precedent, the Obama administration as decided to support a UN investigation into Israel's defensive actions that resulted in the boarding by IDF officers of one of the ships participating in the terrorist sponsored "Flotilla." An Obama official reportedly said that, "We are open to different ways of ensuring the credibility of this Israeli-led investigation, including international participation, and have been in intensive talks with our Israeli partners in the past few days on how to move forward," said the official. "We know of no resolution that will be debated at the UN on the flotilla investigation next week." However, the Obama administration has signified that a "kosher panel" led by the US and Israel would not be satisfactory the international community, most likely because it would not include enough of Israel's sworn enemies and therefore appear bias. So far, the planned investigation will only investigate Israel's actions on the ship, and will not investigate the actions of the United States' belligerent NATO ally, Turkey, or the "activists" connections with terrorist organizations. Additionally the administration is ignoring the precedent that an investigation will create, that may in the future allow for investigations against United States military personnel.

15 JUNE 2010

Obama Compares BP Oil Spill to 9/11

Source: "BP Oil Spill: Fury as Obama Compares BP Oil Spill to Twin Towers Attack," UK Daily Mail, *June 15, 2010.*

While discussing the BP oil disaster that has become a national issue, President Obama compared the spill to the terrorist attacks of 9/11 stating that just as September 11th profoundly shaped, "our view of our vulnerabilities and our foreign policy", the oil disaster would shape thinking on the environment and energy in the same way. Obama continued by saying there have been, "echoes" between the Gulf of Mexico disaster and the Al Qaeda suicide attacks which killed 3,000. Jack Lynch, the father of a fireman who died, said: 'To compare an environmental accident, if that's what you call it, to a premeditated terrorist attack is ridiculous.' Relations between London and Washington have been increasingly distant because of Obama's anti-British rhetoric over the oil spill. Some have argued that the President's comparison of the oil spill to 9/11 was a deliberate attempt to take another shot at the British. Outrage regarding Obama's lack of friendliness with America's closest ally came to a head when the President had to call British Prime Minister Cameron to reassure him of his support. This is another dangerous development in the national security mindset of the Obama Administration. Not only have they alienated our closest ally, but the equation of an accidental oil spill to the murderous, premeditated terrorist attacks on American soil further demonstrates his lack of understanding and priority on national security issues.

NATIONAL SECURITY STRATEGY

May 2010

"If you know the enemy and know yourself, you need not fear the
result of a hundred battles. If you know yourself but not the enemy,
for every victory gained you will also suffer a defeat. If you know neither
the enemy nor yourself, you will succumb in every battle."

— Sun Tzu

The first rule of war is to know your enemy. If you don't, you
have no possibility for success. You can't defeat what you
can't identify. It is clear that Barack Obama does not, or
cannot bring himself to identify the enemy he faces as America's
commander in chief.

What follows is the United States' National Security Strategy, the
central document outlining America's strategic vision, which is
telling both in what it says and in what it does not. As you read,
you'll notice nowhere in this document are the words "Islamic
extremism," "Islamist," or "jihad" mentioned. Our enemy, stretch-
ing from the tunnels in Afghanistan to the United States Army post

at Fort Hood in Texas, has no aversion to calling itself what it is. Major Nidal Malik Hasan, the Fort Hood jihadist, carried around a business card identifying him as a Soldier of Allah. Faisal Shahzad, the failed Times Square bomber, pleaded guilty as charged, telling the court that he was a "mujahid," a "Muslim soldier." But what our enemies freely acknowledge, we are not allowed to say; and that in itself is a victory for our enemy. The radical Islamists have already succeeded in convincing the Obama administration to deny the truth and to enforce censorship on the men and women charged with identifying, analyzing, and fighting our enemies.

As Sun Tzu said, "If you know neither the enemy nor yourself, you will succumb in every battle." Unfortunately, that lack of knowledge is now official United States national security policy.

NATIONAL SECURITY STRATEGY

May 2010

THE WHITE HOUSE
WASHINGTON

Time and again in our Nation's history, Americans have risen to meet — and to shape — moments of transition. This must be one of those moments. We live in a time of sweeping change. The success of free nations, open markets, and social progress in recent decades has accelerated globalization on an unprecedented scale. This has opened the doors of opportunity around the globe, extended democracy to hundreds of millions of people, and made peace possible among the major powers. Yet globalization has also intensified the dangers we face — from international terrorism and the spread of deadly technologies, to economic upheaval and a changing climate.

For nearly a decade, our Nation has been at war with a far-reaching network of violence and hatred. Even as we end one war in Iraq, our military has been called upon to renew our focus on Afghanistan as part of a commitment to disrupt, dismantle, and defeat al-Qa'ida and its affiliates. This is part of a broad, multinational effort that is right and just, and we will be unwavering in our commitment to the security of our people, allies, and partners. Moreover, as we face multiple threats — from nations, nonstate actors, and failed states — we will maintain the military superiority that has secured our country, and underpinned global security, for decades.

Yet as we fight the wars in front of us, we must see the horizon beyond them — a world in which America is stronger, more secure, and is able to overcome our challenges while appealing to the aspirations of people around the world. To get there, we must pursue a strategy of national renewal and global leadership — a strategy that rebuilds the foundation of American strength and influence.

Our strategy starts by recognizing that our strength and influence abroad begins with the steps we take at home. We must grow our economy and reduce our deficit. We must educate our children to compete in an age where knowledge is capital, and the marketplace is global. We must develop the clean energy that can power new industry, unbind us from foreign oil, and preserve our planet. We must pursue science and research that enables discovery, and unlocks wonders as unforeseen to us today as the surface of the moon and the microchip were a century ago. Simply put, we must see American innovation as a foundation of American power.

We must also build and integrate the capabilities that can advance our interests, and the interests we share with other countries and peoples. Our Armed Forces will always be a cornerstone of our security, but they must be complemented. Our security also depends upon diplomats who can act in every corner of the world, from grand capitals to dangerous outposts; development experts who can strengthen governance and support human dignity; and intelligence and law enforcement that can unravel plots, strengthen justice systems, and work seamlessly with other countries.

The burdens of a young century cannot fall on American shoulders alone — indeed, our adversaries would like to see America sap our strength by overextending our power. In the past, we have had the foresight to act judiciously and to avoid acting alone. We were part of the most powerful wartime coalition in human history through World War II, and stitched together a community of free nations and institutions to endure a Cold War. We are clear-eyed about the challenge of mobilizing collective action, and the shortfalls of our international system. But America has not succeeded by stepping outside the currents of international cooperation. We have succeeded by steering those currents in the direction of liberty and justice — so that nations thrive by meeting their responsibilities and face consequences when they don't.

To do so, we will be steadfast in strengthening those old alliances that have served us so well, while modernizing them to meet the challenges of a new century. As influence extends to more countries and capitals, we will build new and deeper partnerships in every region, and strengthen international standards and institutions. This engagement is no end in itself. The international order we seek is one that can resolve the challenges of our times — countering violent extremism and insurgency; stopping the spread of nuclear weapons and securing nuclear materials; combating a changing climate and sustaining global growth; helping countries feed themselves and care for their sick; resolving and preventing conflict, while also healing its wounds.

In all that we do, we will advocate for and advance the basic rights upon which our Nation was founded, and which peoples of every race and region have made their own. We promote these values by living them, including our commitment to the rule of law. We will strengthen international norms that protect these rights, and create space and support for those who resist repression. Our commitment to human dignity includes support for development, which is why we will fight poverty and corruption. And we reject the notion that lasting security and prosperity can be found by turning away from universal rights — democracy does not merely represent our better angels, it stands in opposition to aggression and injustice, and our support for universal rights is both fundamental to American leadership and a source of our strength in the world.

As a Nation made up of people from every race, region, faith, and culture, America will persist in promoting peace among different peoples and believes that democracy and individual empowerment need not come at the expense of cherished identities. Indeed, no nation should be better positioned to lead in an era of globalization than America — the Nation that helped bring globalization about, whose institutions are designed to prepare individuals to succeed in a competitive world, and whose people trace their roots to every country on the face of the Earth.

As a citizen, Senator, and President, I have always believed that America's greatest asset is its people — from the awe I felt as a child watching a space capsule pulled out of the Pacific, to the strength I drew from workers rebuilding their lives in Illinois, to the respect that I have for the generation of Americans who serve our country today. That is why I also believe that we must foster even deeper connections among Americans and peoples around the globe. Our long-term security will come not from our ability to instill fear in other peoples, but through our capacity to speak to their hopes. And that work will best be done through the power of the decency and dignity of the American people — our troops and diplomats, but also our private sector, nongovernmental organizations, and citizens. All of us have a role to play.

From the birth of our liberty, America has had a faith in the future — a belief that where we're going is better than where we've been, even when the path ahead is uncertain. To fulfill that promise, generations of Americans have built upon the foundation of our forefathers — finding opportunity, fighting injustice, and forging a more perfect Union. We have also created webs of commerce, supported an international architecture of laws and institutions, and spilled American blood in foreign lands — not to build an empire, but to shape a world in which more individuals and nations could determine their own destiny, and live with the peace and dignity that they deserve.

In 2010, America is hardened by wars, and inspired by the servicemen and women who fight them. We are disciplined by a devastating economic crisis, and determined to see that its legacy is a new foundation for prosperity; and we are bound by a creed that has guided us at home, and served as a beacon to the world. America's greatness is not assured — each generation's place in history is a question unanswered. But even as we are tested by new challenges, the question of our future is not one that will be answered for us, it is one that will be answered by us. And in a young century whose trajectory is uncertain, America is ready to lead once more.

I. Overview of National Security Strategy

At the dawn of the 21st century, the United States of America faces a broad and complex array of challenges to our national security. Just as America helped to determine the course of the 20th century, we must now build the sources of American strength and influence, and shape an international order capable of overcoming the challenges of the 21st century.

The World as It Is, A Strategy for the World We Seek

To succeed, we must face the world as it is. The two decades since the end of the Cold War have been marked by both the promise and perils of change. The circle of peaceful democracies has expanded; the specter of nuclear war has lifted; major powers are at peace; the global economy has grown; commerce has stitched the fate of nations together; and more individuals can determine their own destiny. Yet these advances have been accompanied by persistent problems. Wars over ideology have given way to wars over religious, ethnic, and tribal identity; nuclear dangers have proliferated; inequality and economic instability have intensified; damage to our environment, food insecurity, and dangers to public health are increasingly shared; and the same tools that empower individuals to build enable them to destroy.

The dark side of this globalized world came to the forefront for the American people on September 11, 2001. The immediate threat demonstrated by the deadliest attacks ever launched upon American soil demanded strong and durable approaches to defend our homeland. In the years since, we have launched a war against al-Qa'ida and its affiliates, decided to fight a war in Iraq, and confronted a sweeping economic crisis. More broadly, though, we have wrestled with how to advance American interests in a world that has changed—a world in which the international architecture of the 20th century is buckling under the weight of new threats, the global economy has accelerated the competition facing our people and businesses, and the universal aspiration for freedom and dignity contends with new obstacles.

Our country possesses the attributes that have supported our leadership for decades—sturdy alliances, an unmatched military, the world's largest economy, a strong and evolving democracy, and a dynamic citizenry. Going forward, there should be no doubt: the United States of America will continue to underwrite global security—through our commitments to allies, partners, and institutions; our focus on defeating al-Qa'ida and its affiliates in Afghanistan, Pakistan, and around the globe; and our determination to deter aggression and prevent the proliferation of the world's most dangerous weapons. As we do, we must recognize that no one nation—no matter how powerful—can meet global challenges alone. As we did after World War II, America must prepare for the future, while forging cooperative approaches among nations that can yield results.

Our national security strategy is, therefore, focused on renewing American leadership so that we can more effectively advance our interests in the 21st century. We will do so by building upon the sources of our strength at home, while shaping an international order that can meet the challenges of our time. This strategy recognizes the fundamental connection between our national security, our national competitiveness, resilience, and moral example. And it reaffirms America's commitment to pursue our interests through an international system in which all nations have certain rights and responsibilities. This will allow America to leverage our engagement abroad on behalf of a world in which individuals enjoy more freedom and opportunity, and nations have incentives to act responsibly, while facing consequences when they do not.

Renewing American Leadership—
Building at Home, Shaping Abroad

Our approach begins with a commitment to build a stronger foundation for American leadership, because what takes place within our borders will determine our strength and influence beyond them. This truth is only heightened in a world of greater interconnection—a world in which our prosperity is inextricably linked to global prosperity, our security can be directly challenged by developments across an ocean, and our actions are scrutinized as never before.

At the center of our efforts is a commitment to renew our economy, which serves as the wellspring of American power. The American people are now emerging from the most devastating recession that we have faced since the Great Depression. As we continue to act to ensure that our recovery is broad and sustained, we are also laying the foundation for the long term growth of our economy and competitiveness of our citizens. The investments that we have made in recovery are a part of a broader effort that will contribute to our strength: by providing a quality education for our children; enhancing science and innovation; transforming our energy economy to power new jobs and industries; lowering the cost of health care for our people and businesses; and reducing the Federal deficit.

Each of these steps will sustain America's ability to lead in a world where economic power and individual opportunity are more diffuse. These efforts are also tied to our commitment to secure a more resilient nation. Our recovery includes rebuilding an infrastructure that will be more secure and reliable in the face of terrorist threats and natural disasters. Our focus on education and science can ensure that the breakthroughs of tomorrow take place in the United States. Our development of new sources of energy will reduce our dependence on foreign oil. Our commitment to deficit reduction will discipline us to make hard choices, and to avoid overreach. These steps complement our efforts to integrate homeland security with national security; including seamless coordination among Federal, state, and local governments to prevent, protect against, and respond to threats and natural disasters.

Finally, the work to build a stronger foundation for our leadership within our borders recognizes that the most effective way for the United States of America to promote our values is to live them. America's commitment to democracy, human rights, and the rule of law are essential sources of our strength and influence in the world. They too must be cultivated by our rejection of actions like torture that are not in line with our values, by our commitment to pursue justice consistent with our Constitution, and by our steady determination to extend the promise of America to all of our citizens. America has always been a beacon to the peoples of the world when we ensure that the light of America's example burns bright.

Building this stronger foundation will support America's efforts to shape an international system that can meet the challenges of our time. In the aftermath of World War II, it was the United States that helped take the lead in constructing a new international architecture to keep the peace and advance prosperity—from NATO and the United Nations, to treaties that govern the laws and weapons of war; from the World Bank and International Monetary Fund, to an expanding web of trade agreements. This architecture, despite its flaws, averted world war, enabled economic growth, and advanced human rights, while facilitating effective burden sharing among the United States, our allies, and partners.

Today, we need to be clear-eyed about the strengths and shortcomings of international institutions that were developed to deal with the challenges of an earlier time and the shortage of political will that has at times stymied the enforcement of international norms. Yet it would be destructive to both American national security and global security if the United States used the emergence of new challenges and the shortcomings of the international system as a reason to walk away from it. Instead, we must focus American engagement on strengthening international institutions and galvanizing the collective action that can serve common interests such as combating violent extremism; stopping the spread of nuclear weapons and securing nuclear materials; achieving balanced and sustainable economic growth; and forging cooperative solutions to the threat of climate change, armed conflict, and pandemic disease.

The starting point for that collective action will be our engagement with other countries. The cornerstone of this engagement is the relationship between the United States and our close friends and allies in Europe, Asia, the Americas, and the Middle East—ties which are rooted in shared interests and shared values, and which serve our mutual security and the broader security and prosperity of the world. We are working to build deeper and more effective partnerships with other key centers of influence—including China, India, and Russia, as well as increasingly influential nations such as Brazil, South Africa, and Indonesia—so that we can cooperate on issues of bilateral and global concern, with the recognition that power, in an interconnected world, is no longer a zero sum game. We are expanding our outreach to emerging nations, particularly those that can be models of regional success and stability, from the Americas to Africa to Southeast Asia. And we will pursue engagement with hostile nations to test their intentions, give their governments the opportunity to change course, reach out to their people, and mobilize international coalitions.

This engagement will underpin our commitment to an international order based upon rights and responsibilities. International institutions must more effectively represent the world of the 21st century, with a broader voice—and greater responsibilities—for emerging powers, and they must be modernized to more effectively generate results on issues of global interest. Constructive national steps on issues ranging from nuclear security to climate change must be incentivized, so nations that choose to do their part see the benefits of responsible action. Rules of the road must be followed, and there must be consequences for those nations that break the rules—whether they are nonproliferation obligations, trade agreements, or human rights commitments.

This modernization of institutions, strengthening of international norms, and enforcement of international law is not a task for the United States alone—but together with like-minded nations, it is a task we can lead. A key source of American leadership throughout our history has been enlightened self-interest. We want a better future for our children and grandchildren, and we believe that their lives will be better if other peoples' children and grandchildren can live in freedom and prosperity. The belief that our own interests are bound to the interests of those beyond our borders will continue to guide our engagement with nations and peoples.

Advancing Top National Security Priorities

Just as our national security strategy is focused on renewing our leadership for the long term, it is also facilitating immediate action on top priorities. This Administration has no greater responsibility than the safety and security of the American people. And there is no greater threat to the American people than weapons of mass destruction, particularly the danger posed by the pursuit of nuclear weapons by violent extremists and their proliferation to additional states.

That is why we are pursuing a comprehensive nonproliferation and nuclear security agenda, grounded in the rights and responsibilities of nations. We are reducing our nuclear arsenal and reliance on nuclear weapons, while ensuring the reliability and effectiveness of our deterrent. We are strengthening the Nuclear Non-Proliferation Treaty (NPT) as the foundation of nonproliferation, while working through the NPT to hold nations like Iran and North Korea accountable for their failure to meet international obligations. We are leading a global effort to secure all vulnerable nuclear materials from terrorists. And we are pursuing new strategies to protect against biological attacks and challenges to the cyber networks that we depend upon.

As we secure the world's most dangerous weapons, we are fighting a war against a far-reaching network of hatred and violence. We will disrupt, dismantle, and defeat al-Qa'ida and its affiliates through a comprehensive strategy that denies them safe haven, strengthens front-line partners, secures our homeland, pursues justice through durable legal approaches, and counters a bankrupt agenda of extremism and murder with an agenda of hope and opportunity. The frontline of this fight is Afghanistan and Pakistan, where we are applying relentless pressure on al-Qa'ida, breaking the Taliban's momentum, and strengthening the security and capacity of our partners. In this effort, our troops are again demonstrating their extraordinary service, making great sacrifices in a time of danger, and they have our full support.

In Iraq, we are transitioning to full Iraqi sovereignty and responsibility—a process that includes the removal of our troops, the strengthening of our civilian capacity, and a long-term partnership to the Iraqi Government and people. We will be unwavering in our pursuit of a comprehensive peace between Israel and its neighbors, including a two-state solution that ensures Israel's security, while fulfilling the Palestinian peoples' legitimate aspirations for a viable state of their own. And our broader engagement with Muslim communities around the world will spur progress on critical political and security matters, while advancing partnerships on a broad range of issues based upon mutual interests and mutual respect.

As we rebuild the economic strength upon which our leadership depends, we are working to advance the balanced and sustainable growth upon which global prosperity and stability depends. This includes steps at home and abroad to prevent another crisis. We have shifted focus to the G-20 as the premier forum for international economic cooperation, and are working to rebalance global demand so that America saves more and exports more, while emerging economies generate more demand. And we will pursue bilateral and multilateral trade agreements that advance our shared prosperity, while accelerating investments in development that can narrow inequality, expand markets, and support individual opportunity and state capacity abroad.

These efforts to advance security and prosperity are enhanced by our support for certain values that are universal. Nations that respect human rights and democratic values are more successful and stronger partners, and individuals who enjoy such respect are more able to achieve their full potential. The United States rejects the false choice between the narrow pursuit of our interests and an endless campaign to impose our values. Instead, we see it as fundamental to our own interests to support a just peace around the world—one in which individuals, and not just nations, are granted the fundamental rights that they deserve.

In keeping with the focus on the foundation of our strength and influence, we are promoting universal values abroad by living them at home, and will not seek to impose these values through force. Instead, we are working to strengthen international norms on behalf of human rights, while welcoming all peaceful democratic movements. We are supporting the development of institutions within fragile democracies, integrating human rights as a part of our dialogue with repressive governments, and supporting the spread of technologies that facilitate the freedom to access information. And we recognize economic opportunity as a human right, and are promoting the dignity of all men and women through our support for global health, food security, and cooperatives responses to humanitarian crises.

Finally, our efforts to shape an international order that promotes a just peace must facilitate cooperation capable of addressing the problems of our time. This international order will support our interests, but it is also an end that we seek in its own right. New challenges hold out the prospect of opportunity, but only if the international community breaks down the old habits of suspicion to build upon common interests. A global effort to combat climate change must draw upon national actions to reduce emissions and a commitment to mitigate their impact. Efforts to prevent conflicts and keep the peace in their aftermath can stop insecurity from spreading. Global cooperation to prevent the spread of pandemic disease can promote public health.

Implementing this agenda will not be easy. To succeed, we must balance and integrate all elements of American power and update our national security capacity for the 21st century. We must maintain our military's conventional superiority, while enhancing its capacity to defeat asymmetric threats. Our diplomacy and development capabilities must be modernized, and our civilian expeditionary capacity strengthened, to support the full breadth of our priorities. Our intelligence and homeland security efforts must be integrated with our national security policies, and those of our allies and partners. And our ability to synchronize our actions while communicating effectively with foreign publics must be enhanced to sustain global support.

However, America's greatest asset remains our people. In an era that will be shaped by the ability to seize the opportunities of a world that has grown more interconnected, it is the American people who will make the difference—the troops and civilians serving within our government; businesses, foundations, and educational institutions that operate around the globe; and citizens who possess the dynamism, drive, and diversity to thrive in a world that has grown smaller. Because for all of its dangers, globalization is in part a product of American leadership and the ingenuity of the American people. We are uniquely suited to seize its promise.

Our story is not without imperfections. Yet at each juncture that history has called upon us to rise to the occasion, we have advanced our own security, while contributing to the cause of human progress. To continue to do so, our national security strategy must be informed by our people, enhanced by the contributions of the Congress, and strengthened by the unity of the American people. If we draw on that spirit anew, we can build a world of greater peace, prosperity, and human dignity.

II. Strategic Approach

"More than at any point in human history—the interests of nations and peoples are shared. The religious convictions that we hold in our hearts can forge new bonds among people, or tear us apart. The technology we harness can light the path

*to peace, or forever darken it. The energy we use can sustain
our planet, or destroy it. What happens to the hope of a single child—anywhere—can enrich our world, or impoverish
it."*

—President Barack Obama,
United Nations General Assembly, September 22, 2009

The United States must renew its leadership in the world by
building and cultivating the sources of our strength and influence.
Our national security depends upon America's ability to leverage
our unique national attributes, just as global security depends upon
strong and responsible American leadership. That includes our military might, economic competitiveness, moral leadership, global
engagement, and efforts to shape an international system that serves
the mutual interests of nations and peoples. For the world has
changed at an extraordinary pace, and the United States must adapt
to advance our interests and sustain our leadership.

American interests are enduring. They are:

- The security of the United States, its citizens, and U.S.
  allies and partners;
- A strong, innovative, and growing U.S. economy in an
  open international economic system that promotes
  opportunity and prosperity;
- Respect for universal values at home and around the
  world; and
- An international order advanced by U.S. leadership
  that promotes peace, security, and opportunity through
  stronger cooperation to meet global challenges.

Currently, the United States is focused on implementing a responsible transition as we end the war in Iraq, succeeding in
Afghanistan, and defeating al-Qa'ida and its terrorist affiliates,
while moving our economy from catastrophic recession to lasting

recovery. As we confront these crises, our national strategy must take a longer view. We must build a stronger foundation for American leadership and work to better shape the outcomes that are most fundamental to our people in the 21st century.

The Strategic Environment—The World as It Is

In the two decades since the end of the Cold War, the free flow of information, people, goods and services has accelerated at an unprecedented rate. This interconnection has empowered individuals for good and ill, and challenged state based international institutions that were largely designed in the wake of World War II by policymakers who had different challenges in mind. Nonstate actors can have a dramatic influence on the world around them. Economic growth has alleviated poverty and led to new centers of influence. More nations are asserting themselves regionally and globally. The lives of our citizens—their safety and prosperity—are more bound than ever to events beyond our borders.

Within this environment, the attacks of September 11, 2001, were a transformative event for the United States, demonstrating just how much trends far beyond our shores could directly endanger the personal safety of the American people. The attacks put into sharp focus America's position as the sole global superpower, the dangers of violent extremism, and the simmering conflicts that followed the peaceful conclusion of the Cold War. And they drew a swift and forceful response from the United States and our allies and partners in Afghanistan. This response was followed by our decision to go to war in Iraq, and the ensuing years have seen America's forces, resources, and national security strategy focused on these conflicts.

The United States is now fighting two wars with many thousands of our men and women deployed in harm's way, and hundreds of billions of dollars dedicated to funding these conflicts. In Iraq, we are supporting a transition of responsibility to the sovereign Iraqi Government. We are supporting the security and prosperity of our partners in Afghanistan and Pakistan as part of a broader campaign to disrupt, dismantle, and defeat al-Qa'ida and its violent extremist affiliates.

Yet these wars—and our global efforts to successfully counter violent extremism—are only one element of our strategic environment and cannot define America's engagement with the world. Terrorism is one of many threats that are more consequential in a global age. The gravest danger to the American people and global security continues to come from weapons of mass destruction, particularly nuclear weapons. The space and cyberspace capabilities that power our daily lives and military operations are vulnerable to disruption and attack. Dependence upon fossil fuels constrains our options and pollutes our environment. Climate change and pandemic disease threaten the security of regions and the health and safety of the American people. Failing states breed conflict and endanger regional and global security. Global criminal networks foment insecurity abroad and bring people and goods across our own borders that threaten our people.

The global economy is being reshaped by innovation, emerging economies, transition to low-carbon energy, and recovery from a catastrophic recession. The convergence of wealth and living standards among developed and emerging economies holds out the promise of more balanced global growth, but dramatic inequality persists within and among nations. Profound cultural and demographic tensions, rising demand for resources, and rapid urbanization could reshape single countries and entire regions. As the world grows more interconnected, more individuals are gaining awareness of their universal rights and have the capacity to pursue them. Democracies that respect the rights of their people remain successful states and America's most steadfast allies. Yet the advance of democracy and human rights has stalled in many parts of the world.

More actors exert power and influence. Europe is now more united, free, and at peace than ever before. The European Union has deepened its integration. Russia has reemerged in the international arena as a strong voice. China and India—the world's two most populous nations—are becoming more engaged globally. From Latin America to Africa to the Pacific, new and emerging powers hold out opportunities for partnership, even as a handful of states endanger regional and global security by flouting international norms. International institutions play a critical role in facilitating cooperation, but at times cannot effectively address new threats or seize new opportunities. Meanwhile, individuals, corporations, and civil society play an increasingly important role in shaping events around the world.

The United States retains the strengths that have enabled our leadership for many decades. Our society is exceptional in its openness, vast diversity, resilience, and engaged citizenry. Our private sector and civil society exhibit enormous ingenuity and innovation, and our workers are capable and dedicated. We have the world's largest economy and most powerful military, strong alliances and a vibrant cultural appeal, and a history of leadership in economic and social development. We continue to be a destination that is sought out by immigrants from around the world, who enrich our society. We have a transparent, accountable democracy and a dynamic and productive populace with deep connections to peoples around the world. And we continue to embrace a set of values that have enabled liberty and opportunity at home and abroad.

Now, the very fluidity within the international system that breeds new challenges must be approached as an opportunity to forge new international cooperation. We must rebalance our long-term priorities so that we successfully move beyond today's wars, and focus our attention and resources on a broader set of countries and challenges. We must seize on the opportunities afforded by the world's interconnection, while responding effectively and comprehensively to its dangers. And we must take advantage of the unparalleled connections that America's Government, private sector, and citizens have around the globe.

The Strategic Approach—The World We Seek

In the past, the United States has thrived when both our nation and our national security policy have adapted to shape change instead of being shaped by it. For instance, as the industrial revolution took hold, America transformed our economy and our role in the world. When the world was confronted by fascism, America prepared itself to win a war and to shape the peace that followed. When the United States encountered an ideological, economic, and military threat from communism, we shaped our practices and institutions at home—and policies abroad—to meet this challenge. Now, we must once again position the United States to champion mutual interests among nations and peoples.

Our national security begins at home. What takes place within our borders has always been the source of our strength, and this is even truer in an age of interconnection.

First and foremost, we must renew the foundation of America's strength. In the long run, the welfare of the American people will determine America's strength in the world, particularly at a time when our own economy is inextricably linked to the global economy. Our prosperity serves as a wellspring for our power. It pays for our military, underwrites our diplomacy and development efforts, and serves as a leading source of our influence in the world. Moreover, our trade and investment supports millions of American jobs, forges links among countries, spurs global development, and contributes to a stable and peaceful political and economic environment.

Yet even as we have maintained our military advantage, our competitiveness has been set back in recent years. We are recovering from underinvestment in the areas that are central to America's strength. We have not adequately advanced priorities like education, energy, science and technology, and health care—all of which are essential to U.S. competitiveness, long-term prosperity, and strength. Years of rising fiscal and trade deficits will also necessitate hard choices in the years ahead.

That is why we are rebuilding our economy so that it will serve as an engine of opportunity for the American people, and a source of American influence abroad. The United States must ensure that we have the world's best-educated workforce, a private sector that fosters innovation, and citizens and businesses that can access affordable health care to compete in a globalized economy. We must transform the way that we use energy— diversifying supplies, investing in innovation, and deploying clean energy technologies. By doing so, we will enhance energy security, create jobs, and fight climate change.

Rebuilding our economy must include putting ourselves on a fiscally sustainable path. As such, implementing our national security strategy will require a disciplined approach to setting priorities and making tradeoffs among competing programs and activities. Taken together, these efforts will position our nation for success in the global marketplace, while also supporting our national security capacity—the strength of our military, intelligence, diplomacy and development, and the security and resilience of our homeland.

We are now moving beyond traditional distinctions between homeland and national security. National security draws on the strength and resilience of our citizens, communities, and economy. This includes a determination to prevent terrorist attacks against the American people by fully coordinating the actions that we take abroad with the actions and precautions that we take at home. It must also include a commitment to building a more secure and resilient nation, while maintaining open flows of goods and people. We will continue to develop the capacity to address the threats and hazards that confront us, while redeveloping our infrastructure to secure our people and work cooperatively with other nations.

America's example is also a critical component of our foundation. The human rights which America has stood for since our founding have enabled our leadership, provided a source of inspiration for peoples around the world, and drawn a clear contrast between the United States and our democratic allies, and those nations and individuals that deny or suppress human rights. Our efforts to live our own values, and uphold the principles of democracy in our own society, underpin our support for the aspirations of the oppressed abroad, who know they can turn to America for leadership based on justice and hope.

Our moral leadership is grounded principally in the power of our example—not through an effort to impose our system on other peoples. Yet over the years, some methods employed in pursuit of our security have compromised our fidelity to the values that we promote, and our leadership on their behalf. This undercuts our ability to support democratic movements abroad, challenge nations that violate international human rights norms, and apply our broader leadership for good in the world. That is why we will lead on behalf of our values by living them. Our struggle to stay true to our values and Constitution has always been a lodestar, both to the American people and to those who share our aspiration for human dignity.

Our values have allowed us to draw the best and brightest to our shores, to inspire those who share our cause abroad, and to give us the credibility to stand up to tyranny. America must demonstrate through words and deeds the resilience of our values and Constitution. For if we compromise our values in pursuit of security, we will undermine both; if we fortify them, we will sustain a key source of our strength and leadership in the world—one that sets us apart from our enemies and our potential competitors.

Pursuing Comprehensive Engagement

Our foundation will support our efforts to engage nations, institutions, and peoples around the world on the basis of mutual interests and mutual respect.

Engagement is the active participation of the United States in relationships beyond our borders. It is, quite simply, the opposite of a self-imposed isolation that denies us the ability to shape outcomes. Indeed, America has never succeeded through isolationism.

As the nation that helped to build our international system after World War II and to bring about the globalization that came with the end of the Cold War, we must reengage the world on a comprehensive and sustained basis.

Engagement begins with our closest friends and allies—from Europe to Asia; from North America to the Middle East. These nations share a common history of struggle on behalf of security, prosperity, and democracy. They share common values and a common commitment to international norms that recognize both the rights and responsibilities of all sovereign nations. America's national security depends on these vibrant alliances, and we must engage them as active partners in addressing global and regional security priorities and harnessing new opportunities to advance common interests. For instance, we pursue close and regular collaboration with our close allies the United Kingdom, France, and Germany on issues of mutual and global concern.

We will continue to deepen our cooperation with other 21st century centers of influence—including China, India, and Russia—on the basis of mutual interests and mutual respect. We will also pursue diplomacy and development that supports the emergence of new and successful partners, from the Americas to Africa; from the Middle East to Southeast Asia. Our ability to advance constructive cooperation is essential to the security and prosperity of specific regions, and to facilitating global cooperation on issues ranging from violent extremism and nuclear proliferation, to climate change, and global economic instability—issues that challenge all nations, but that no one nation alone can meet.

To adversarial governments, we offer a clear choice: abide by international norms, and achieve the political and economic benefits that come with greater integration with the international community; or refuse to accept this pathway, and bear the consequences of that decision, including greater isolation. Through engagement, we can create opportunities to resolve differences, strengthen the international community's support for our actions, learn about the intentions and nature of closed regimes, and plainly demonstrate to the publics within those nations that their governments are to blame for their isolation.

Successful engagement will depend upon the effective use and integration of different elements of American power. Our diplomacy and development capabilities must help prevent conflict, spur economic growth, strengthen weak and failing states, lift people out of poverty, combat climate change and epidemic disease, and strengthen institutions of democratic governance. Our military will continue strengthening its capacity to partner with foreign counterparts, train and assist security forces, and pursue military-to-military ties with a broad range of governments. We will continue to foster economic and financial transactions to advance our shared prosperity. And our intelligence and law enforcement agencies must cooperate effectively with foreign governments to anticipate events, respond to crises, and provide safety and security.

Finally, we will pursue engagement among peoples—not just governments—around the world. The United States Government will make a sustained effort to engage civil society and citizens and facilitate increased connections among the American people and peoples around the world—through efforts ranging from public service and educational exchanges, to increased commerce and private sector partnerships. In many instances, these modes of engagement have a powerful and enduring impact beyond our borders, and are a cost-effective way of projecting a positive vision of American leadership. Time and again, we have seen that the best ambassadors for American values and interests are the American people—our businesses, nongovernmental organizations, scientists, athletes, artists, military service members, and students.

Facilitating increased international engagement outside of government will help prepare our country to thrive in a global economy, while building the goodwill and relationships that are invaluable to sustaining American leadership. It also helps leverage strengths that are unique to America—our diversity and diaspora populations, our openness and creativity, and the values that our people embody in their own lives.

Promoting a Just and Sustainable International Order

Our engagement will underpin a just and sustainable international order—just, because it advances mutual interests, protects the rights of all, and holds accountable those who refuse to meet their responsibilities; sustainable because it is based on broadly shared norms and fosters collective action to address common challenges.

This engagement will pursue an international order that recognizes the rights and responsibilities of all nations. As we did after World War II, we must pursue a rules-based international system that can advance our own interests by serving mutual interests. International institutions must be more effective and representative of the diffusion of influence in the 21st century. Nations must have incentives to behave responsibly, or be isolated when they do not. The test of this international order must be the cooperation it facilitates and the results it generates—the ability of nations to come together to confront common challenges like violent extremism, nuclear proliferation, climate change, and a changing global economy.

That is precisely the reason we should strengthen enforcement of international law and our commitment to engage and modernize international institutions and frameworks. Those nations that refuse to meet their responsibilities will forsake the opportunities that come with international cooperation. Credible and effective alternatives to military action—from sanctions to isolation—must be strong enough to change behavior, just as we must reinforce our alliances and our military capabilities. And if nations challenge or undermine an international order that is based upon rights and responsibilities, they must find themselves isolated.

We succeeded in the post-World War II era by pursuing our interests within multilateral forums like the United Nations—not outside of them. We recognized that institutions that aggregated the national interests of many nations would never be perfect; but we also saw that they were an indispensable vehicle for pooling international resources and enforcing international norms. Indeed, the basis for international cooperation since World War II has been an architecture of international institutions, organizations, regimes, and standards that establishes certain rights and responsibilities for all sovereign nations.

In recent years America's frustration with international institutions has led us at times to engage the United Nations (U.N.) system on an ad hoc basis. But in a world of transnational challenges, the United States will need to invest in strengthening the international system, working from inside international institutions and frameworks to face their imperfections head on and to mobilize transnational cooperation.

We must be clear-eyed about the factors that have impeded effectiveness in the past. In order for collective action to be mobilized, the polarization that persists across region, race, and religion will need to be replaced by a galvanizing sense of shared interest. Swift and effective international action often turns on the political will of coalitions of countries that comprise regional or international institutions. New and emerging powers who seek greater voice and representation will need to accept greater responsibility for meeting global challenges. When nations breach agreed international norms, the countries who espouse those norms must be convinced to band together to enforce them.

We will expand our support to modernizing institutions and arrangements such as the evolution of the G-8 to the G-20 to reflect the realities of today's international environment. Working with the institutions and the countries that comprise them, we will enhance international capacity to prevent conflict, spur economic growth, improve security, combat climate change, and address the challenges posed by weak and failing states. And we will challenge and assist international institutions and frameworks to reform when they fail to live up to their promise. Strengthening the legitimacy and authority of international law and institutions, especially the U.N., will require a constant struggle to improve performance.

Furthermore, our international order must recognize the increasing influence of individuals in today's world. There must be opportunities for civil society to thrive within nations and to forge connections among them. And there must be opportunities for individuals and the private sector to play a major role in addressing common challenges—whether supporting a nuclear fuel bank, promoting global health, fostering entrepreneurship, or exposing violations of universal rights. In the 21st century, the ability of individuals and nongovernment actors to play a positive role in shaping the international environment represents a distinct opportunity for the United States.

Within this context, we know that an international order where every nation upholds its rights and responsibilities will remain elusive. Force will sometimes be necessary to confront threats. Technology will continue to bring with it new dangers. Poverty and disease will not be completely abolished. Oppression will always be with us. But if we recognize these challenges, embrace America's responsibility to confront them with its partners, and forge new cooperative approaches to get others to join us in overcoming them, then the international order of a globalized age can better advance our interests and the common interests of nations and peoples everywhere.

III. Advancing Our Interests

To achieve the world we seek, the United States must apply our strategic approach in pursuit of four enduring national interests:

- *Security:* The security of the United States, its citizens, and U.S. allies and partners.
- *Prosperity:* A strong, innovative, and growing U.S. economy in an open international economic system that promotes opportunity and prosperity.

- *Values:* Respect for universal values at home and around the world.
- *International Order:* An international order advanced by U.S. leadership that promotes peace, security, and opportunity through stronger cooperation to meet global challenges.

Each of these interests is inextricably linked to the others: no single interest can be pursued in isolation, but at the same time, positive action in one area will help advance all four. The initiatives described below do not encompass all of America's national security concerns. However, they represent areas of particular priority and areas where progress is critical to securing our country and renewing American leadership in the years to come.

Security

"We will not apologize for our way of life, nor will we waver in its defense. And for those who seek to advance their aims by inducing terror and slaughtering innocents, we say to you now that our spirit is stronger and cannot be broken—you cannot outlast us, and we will defeat you."
—President Barack Obama,
Inaugural Address, January 20, 2009

The threats to our people, our homeland, and our interests have shifted dramatically in the last 20 years. Competition among states endures, but instead of a single nuclear adversary, the United States is now threatened by the potential spread of nuclear weapons to extremists who may not be deterred from using them. Instead of a hostile expansionist empire, we now face a diverse array of challenges, from a loose network of violent extremists to states that flout international norms or face internal collapse. In addition to facing enemies on traditional battlefields, the United States must now be prepared for asymmetric threats, such as those that target our reliance on space and cyberspace.

This Administration has no greater responsibility than protecting the American people. Furthermore, we embrace America's unique responsibility to promote international security—a responsibility that flows from our commitments to allies, our leading role in supporting a just and sustainable international order, and our unmatched military capabilities.

The United States remains the only nation able to project and sustain large-scale military operations over extended distances. We maintain superior capabilities to deter and defeat adaptive enemies and to ensure the credibility of security partnerships that are fundamental to regional and global security. In this way, our military continues to underpin our national security and global leadership, and when we use it appropriately, our security and leadership is reinforced. But when we overuse our military might, or fail to invest in or deploy complementary tools, or act without partners, then our military is overstretched, Americans bear a greater burden, and our leadership around the world is too narrowly identified with military force. And we know that our enemies aim to overextend our Armed Forces and to drive wedges between us and those who share our interests.

Therefore, we must continue to adapt and rebalance our instruments of statecraft. At home, we are integrating our homeland security efforts seamlessly with other aspects of our national security approach, and strengthening our preparedness and resilience. Abroad, we are strengthening alliances, forging new partnerships, and using every tool of American power to advance our objectives—including enhanced diplomatic and development capabilities with the ability both to prevent conflict and to work alongside our military. We are strengthening international norms to isolate governments that flout them and to marshal cooperation against nongovernmental actors who endanger our common security.

Strengthen Security and Resilience at Home

At home, the United States is pursuing a strategy capable of meeting the full range of threats and hazards to our communities. These threats and hazards include terrorism, natural disasters, large-scale cyber attacks, and pandemics. As we do everything within our power to prevent these dangers, we also recognize that we will not be able to deter or prevent every single threat. That is why we must also enhance our resilience—the ability to adapt to changing conditions and prepare for, withstand, and rapidly recover from disruption. To keep Americans safe and secure at home, we are working to:

Enhance Security at Home: Security at home relies on our shared efforts to prevent and deter attacks by identifying and interdicting threats, denying hostile actors the ability to operate within our borders, protecting the nation's critical infrastructure and key resources, and securing cyberspace. That is why we are pursuing initiatives to protect and reduce vulnerabilities in critical infrastructure, at our borders, ports, and airports, and to enhance overall air, maritime, transportation, and space and cyber security. Building on this foundation, we recognize that the global systems that carry people, goods, and data around the globe also facilitate the movement of dangerous people, goods, and data. Within these systems of transportation and transaction, there are key nodes—for example, points of origin and transfer, or border crossings—that represent opportunities for exploitation and interdiction. Thus, we are working with partners abroad to confront threats that often begin beyond our borders. And we are developing lines of coordination at home across Federal, state, local, tribal, territorial, nongovernmental, and private-sector partners, as well as individuals and communities.

Effectively Manage Emergencies: We are building our capability to prepare for disasters to reduce or eliminate long-term effects to people and their property from hazards and to respond to and recover from major incidents. To improve our preparedness, we are integrating domestic all hazards planning at all levels of government and building key capabilities to respond to emergencies. We continue to collaborate with communities to ensure preparedness efforts are integrated at all levels of government with the private and nonprofit sectors. We are investing in operational capabilities and equipment, and improving the reliability and interoperability of communications systems for first responders. We are encouraging domestic regional planning and integrated preparedness programs and will encourage government at all levels to engage in long-term recovery planning. It is critical that we continually test and improve plans using exercises that are realistic in scenario and consequences.

Empowering Communities to Counter Radicalization: Several recent incidences of violent extremists in the United States who are committed to fighting here and abroad have underscored the threat to the United States and our interests posed by individuals radicalized at home. Our best defenses against this threat are well informed and equipped families, local communities, and institutions. The Federal Government will invest in intelligence to understand this threat and expand community engagement and development programs to empower local communities. And the Federal Government, drawing on the expertise and resources from all relevant agencies, will clearly communicate our policies and intentions, listening to local concerns, tailoring policies to address regional concerns, and making clear that our diversity is part of our strength—not a source of division or insecurity.

Improve Resilience Through Increased Public-Private Partnerships: When incidents occur, we must show resilience by maintaining critical operations and functions, returning to our normal life, and learning from disasters so that their lessons can be translated into pragmatic changes when necessary. The private sector, which owns and operates most of the nation's critical infrastructure, plays a vital role in preparing for and recovering from disasters. We must, therefore, strengthen public-private partnerships by developing incentives for government and the private sector to design structures and systems that can withstand disruptions and mitigate associated consequences, ensure redundant systems where necessary to maintain the ability to operate, decentralize critical operations to reduce our vulnerability to single points of disruption, develop and test continuity plans to ensure the ability to restore critical capabilities, and invest in improvements and maintenance of existing infrastructure.

Engage with Communities and Citizens: We will emphasize individual and community preparedness and resilience through frequent engagement that provides clear and reliable risk and emergency information to the public. A key part of this effort is providing practical steps that all Americans can take to protect themselves, their families, and their neighbors. This includes transmitting information through multiple pathways and to those with special needs. In addition, we support efforts to develop a nationwide public safety broadband network. Our efforts to inform and empower Americans and their communities recognize that resilience has always been at the heart of the American spirit.

Disrupt, Dismantle, and Defeat Al-Qa'ida and its Violent Extremist Affiliates in Afghanistan, Pakistan, and Around the World

The United States is waging a global campaign against al-Qa'ida and its terrorist affiliates. To disrupt, dismantle and defeat al-Qa'ida and its affiliates, we are pursuing a strategy that protects our homeland, secures the world's most dangerous weapons and material, denies al-Qa'ida safe haven, and builds positive partnerships with Muslim communities around the world. Success requires a broad, sustained, and integrated campaign that judiciously applies every tool of American power—both military and civilian—as well as the concerted efforts of like-minded states and multilateral institutions.

We will always seek to delegitimize the use of terrorism and to isolate those who carry it out. Yet this is not a global war against a tactic—terrorism or a religion—Islam. We are at war with a specific network, al-Qa'ida, and its terrorist affiliates who support efforts to attack the United States, our allies, and partners.

Prevent Attacks on and in the Homeland: To prevent acts of terrorism on American soil, we must enlist all of our intelligence, law enforcement, and homeland security capabilities. We will continue to integrate and leverage state and major urban area fusion centers that have the capability to share classified information; establish a nationwide framework for reporting suspicious activity; and implement an integrated approach to our counterterrorism information systems to ensure that the analysts, agents, and officers who protect us have access to all relevant intelligence throughout the government. We are improving information sharing and cooperation by linking networks to facilitate Federal, state, and local capabilities to seamlessly exchange messages and information, conduct searches, and collaborate. We are coordinating better with foreign partners to identify, track, limit access to funding, and prevent terrorist travel. Recognizing the inextricable link between domestic and transnational security, we will collaborate bilaterally, regionally, and through international institutions to promote global efforts to prevent terrorist attacks.

Strengthen Aviation Security: We know that the aviation system has been a particular target of al-Qa'ida and its affiliates. We must continue to bolster aviation security worldwide through a focus on increased information collection and sharing, stronger passenger vetting and screening measures, the development and development of advanced screening technologies, and cooperation with the international community to strengthen aviation security standards and efforts around the world.

Deny Terrorists Weapons of Mass Destruction: To prevent acts of terrorism with the world's most dangerous weapons, we are dramatically accelerating and intensifying efforts to secure all vulnerable nuclear materials by the end of 2013, and to prevent the spread of nuclear weapons. We will also take actions to safeguard knowledge and capabilities in the life and chemical sciences that could be vulnerable to misuse.

Deny Al-Qa'ida the Ability to Threaten the American People, Our Allies, Our Partners and Our Interests Overseas: Al-Qa'ida and its allies must not be permitted to gain or retain any capacity to plan and launch international terrorist attacks, especially against the U.S. homeland. Al Qa'ida's core in Pakistan remains the most dangerous component of the larger network, but we also face a growing threat from the group's allies worldwide. We must deny these groups the ability to conduct operational plotting from any locale, or to recruit, train, and position operatives, including those from Europe and North America.

Afghanistan and Pakistan: This is the epicenter of the violent extremism practiced by al Qa'ida. The danger from this region will only grow if its security slides backward, the Taliban controls large swaths of Afghanistan, and al-Qa'ida is allowed to operate with impunity. To prevent future attacks on the United States, our allies, and partners, we must work with others to keep the pressure on al-Qa'ida and increase the security and capacity of our partners in this region.

In Afghanistan, we must deny al-Qa'ida a safe haven, deny the Taliban the ability to overthrow the government, and strengthen the capacity of Afghanistan's security forces and government so that they can take lead responsibility for Afghanistan's future. Within Pakistan, we are working with the government to address the local, regional, and global threat from violent extremists.

We will achieve these objectives with a strategy comprised of three components.

- First, our military and International Security Assistance Force (ISAF) partners within Afghanistan are targeting the insurgency, working to secure key population centers, and increasing efforts to train Afghan security forces. These military resources will allow us to create the conditions to transition to Afghan responsibility. In July 2011, we will begin reducing our troops responsibly, taking into account conditions on the ground. We will continue to advise and assist Afghanistan's Security Forces so that they can succeed over the long term.

- Second, we will continue to work with our partners, the United Nations, and the Afghan Government to improve accountable and effective governance. As we work to advance our strategic partnership with the Afghan Government, we are focusing assistance on supporting the President of Afghanistan and those ministries, governors, and local leaders who combat corruption and deliver for the people. Our efforts will be based upon performance, and we will measure progress. We will also target our assistance to areas that can make an immediate and enduring impact in the lives of the Afghan people, such as agriculture, while supporting the human rights of all of Afghanistan's people—women and men. This will support our long-term commitment to a relationship between our two countries that supports a strong, stable, and prosperous Afghanistan.

- Third, we will foster a relationship with Pakistan founded upon mutual interests and mutual respect. To defeat violent extremists who threaten both of our countries, we will strengthen Pakistan's capacity to target violent extremists within its borders, and continue to provide security assistance to support those efforts. To strengthen Pakistan's democracy and development, we will provide substantial assistance responsive to the needs of the Pakistani people, and sustain a long-term partnership committed to Pakistan's future. The strategic partnership that we are developing with Pakistan includes deepening cooperation in a broad range of areas, addressing both security and civilian challenges, and we will continue to expand those ties through our engagement with Pakistan in the years to come.

Deny Safe Havens and Strengthen At-Risk States: Wherever al-Qa'ida or its terrorist affiliates attempt to establish a safe haven—as they have in Yemen, Somalia, the Maghreb, and the Sahel—we will meet them with growing pressure. We also will strengthen our own network of partners to disable al-Qa'ida's financial, human, and planning networks; disrupt terrorist operations before they mature; and address potential safe-havens before al-Qa'ida and its terrorist affiliates can take root. These efforts will focus on information-sharing, law enforcement cooperation, and establishing new practices to counter evolving adversaries. We will also help states avoid becoming terrorist safe havens by helping them build their capacity for responsible governance and security through development and security sector assistance.

Deliver Swift and Sure Justice: To effectively detain, interrogate, and prosecute terrorists, we need durable legal approaches consistent with our security and our values. We adhere to several principles: we will leverage all available information and intelligence to disrupt attacks and dismantle al-Qa'ida and affiliated terrorist organizations; we will bring terrorists to justice; we will act in line with the rule of law and due process; we will submit decisions to checks and balances and accountability; and we will insist that matters of detention and secrecy are addressed in a manner consistent with our Constitution and laws. To deny violent extremists one of their most potent recruitment tools, we will close the prison at Guantanamo Bay.

Resist Fear and Overreaction: The goal of those who perpetrate terrorist attacks is in part to sow fear. If we respond with fear, we allow violent extremists to succeed far beyond the initial impact of their attacks, or attempted attacks—altering our society and enlarging the standing of al-Qa'ida and its terrorist affiliates far beyond its actual reach. Similarly, overreacting in a way that creates fissures between America and certain regions or religions will undercut our leadership and make us less safe.

Contrast Al-Qa'ida's Intent to Destroy with Our Constructive Vision: While violent extremists seek to destroy, we will make clear our intent to build. We are striving to build bridges among people of different faiths and regions. We will continue to work to resolve the Arab-Israeli conflict, which has long been a source of tension. We will continue to stand up for the universal rights of all people, even for those with whom we disagree. We are developing new partnerships in Muslim communities around the world on behalf of health, education, science, employment, and innovation. And through our broader emphasis on Muslim engagement, we will communicate our commitment to support the aspirations of all people for security and opportunity. Finally, we reject the notion that al-Qa'ida represents any religious authority. They are not religious leaders, they are killers; and neither Islam nor any other religion condones the slaughter of innocents.

Reverse the Spread of Nuclear and Biological Weapons and Secure Nuclear Materials

The American people face no greater or more urgent danger than a terrorist attack with a nuclear weapon. And international peace and security is threatened by proliferation that could lead to a nuclear exchange. Indeed, since the end of the Cold War, the risk of a nuclear attack has increased. Excessive Cold War stockpiles remain. More nations have acquired nuclear weapons. Testing has continued. Black markets trade in nuclear secrets and materials. Terrorists are determined to buy, build, or steal a nuclear weapon. Our efforts to contain these dangers are centered in a global non-proliferation regime that has frayed as more people and nations break the rules.

That is why reversing the spread of nuclear weapons is a top priority. Success depends upon broad consensus and concerted action, we will move forward strategically on a number of fronts through our example, our partnerships, and a reinvigorated international regime. The United States will:

Pursue the Goal of a World Without Nuclear Weapons: While this goal will not be reached during this Administration, its active pursuit and eventual achievement will increase global security, keep our commitment under the NPT, build our cooperation with Russia and other states, and increase our credibility to hold others accountable for their obligations. As long as any nuclear weapons exist, the United States will sustain a safe, secure, and effective nuclear arsenal, both to deter potential adversaries and to assure U.S. allies and other security partners that they can count on America's security commitments. But we have signed and seek to ratify a landmark New START Treaty with Russia to substantially limit our deployed nuclear warheads and strategic delivery vehicles, while assuring a comprehensive monitoring regime. We are reducing the role of nuclear weapons in our national security approach, extending a negative security assurance not to use or threaten to use nuclear weapons against those nonnuclear nations that are in compliance with the NPT and their nuclear nonproliferation obligations, and investing in the modernization of a safe, secure, and effective stockpile without the production of new nuclear weapons. We will pursue ratification of the Comprehensive Test Ban Treaty. And we will seek a new treaty that verifiably ends the production of fissile materials intended for use in nuclear weapons.

Strengthen the Nuclear Non-Proliferation Treaty: The basic bargain of the NPT is sound: countries with nuclear weapons will move toward disarmament; countries without nuclear weapons will forsake them; and all countries can access peaceful nuclear energy. To strengthen the NPT, we will seek more resources and authority for international inspections. We will develop a new framework for civil nuclear cooperation. As members of the Global Nuclear Energy Partnership have agreed, one important element of an enhanced framework could be cradle-to-grave nuclear fuel management. We will pursue a broad, international consensus to insist that all nations meet their obligations. And we will also pursue meaningful consequences for countries that fail to meet their obligations under the NPT or to meet the requirements for withdrawing from it.

Present a Clear Choice to Iran and North Korea: The United States will pursue the denuclearization of the Korean peninsula and work to prevent Iran from developing a nuclear weapon. This is not about singling out nations—it is about the responsibilities of all nations and the success of the nonproliferation regime. Both nations face a clear choice. If North Korea eliminates its nuclear weapons program, and Iran meets its international obligations on its nuclear program, they will be able to proceed on a path to greater political and economic integration with the international community. If they ignore their international obligations, we will pursue multiple means to increase their isolation and bring them into compliance with international nonproliferation norms.

Secure Vulnerable Nuclear Weapons and Material: The Global Nuclear Security Summit of 2010 rallied 47 nations behind the goal of securing all nuclear materials from terrorist groups. By the end of 2013, we will seek to complete a focused international effort to secure all vulnerable nuclear material around the world through enhanced protection and accounting practices, expanded cooperation with and through international institutions, and new partnerships to lock down these sensitive materials. To detect and intercept nuclear materials in transit, and to stop the illicit trade in these technologies, we will work to turn programs such as the Proliferation Security Initiative and the Global Initiative to Combat Nuclear Terrorism into durable international efforts. And we will sustain broad-based cooperation with other nations and international institutions to ensure the continued improvements necessary to protect nuclear materials from evolving threats.

Support Peaceful Nuclear Energy: As countries move increasingly to tap peaceful nuclear energy to provide power generation while advancing climate goals, the world must develop an infrastructure

in the countries that seek to use nuclear energy for their energy
security needs and climate goals to ensure that nuclear energy is
developed in a safer manner. We will do so by promoting safety
through regulatory bodies and training of operators, promoting
physical security to prevent terrorist acts, and assuring safe and
secure handling of fuel at the front and back ends of the nuclear fuel
cycle.

Counter Biological Threats: The effective dissemination of a
lethal biological agent within a population center would endanger
the lives of hundreds of thousands of people and have unprecedented economic, societal, and political consequences. We must
continue to work at home with first responders and health officials
to reduce the risk associated with unintentional or deliberate outbreaks of infectious disease and to strengthen our resilience across
the spectrum of high-consequence biological threats. We will work
with domestic and international partners to protect against biological threats by promoting global health security and reinforcing
norms of safe and responsible conduct; obtaining timely and accurate insight on current and emerging risks; taking reasonable steps
to reduce the potential for exploitation; expanding our capability
to prevent, attribute, and apprehend those who carry out attacks;
communicating effectively with all stakeholders; and helping to
transform the international dialogue on biological threats.

Advance Peace, Security, and Opportunity
in the Greater Middle East

The United States has important interests in the greater Middle
East. They include broad cooperation on a wide range of issues
with our close friend, Israel, and an unshakable commitment to its
security; the achievement of the Palestinian people's legitimate aspirations for statehood, opportunity, and the realization of their
extraordinary potential; the unity and security of Iraq and the fostering of its democracy and reintegration into the region; the transformation of Iranian policy away from its pursuit of nuclear

weapons, support for terrorism, and threats against its neighbors; nonproliferation; and counterterrorism cooperation, access to energy, and integration of the region into global markets.

At the same time, our engagement must be both comprehensive and strategic. It should extend beyond near-term threats by appealing to peoples' aspirations for justice, education, and opportunity and by pursuing a positive and sustainable vision of U.S. partnership with the region. Furthermore, our relationship with our Israeli and Arab friends and partners in the region extends beyond our commitment to its security and includes the continued ties we share in areas such as trade, exchanges, and cooperation on a broad range of issues.

Complete a Responsible Transition as We End the War in Iraq: The war in Iraq presents a distinct and important challenge to the United States, the international community, the Iraqi people, and the region. America's servicemen and women, along with our coalition partners, have performed remarkably in fighting determined enemies and have worked with our civilians to help the Iraqi people regain control of their own destiny. Going forward, we have a responsibility, for our own security and the security of the region, to successfully end the war through a full transition to Iraqi responsibility. We will cultivate an enduring relationship with Iraq based on mutual interests and mutual respect.

Our goal is an Iraq that is sovereign, stable, and self-reliant. To achieve that goal, we are continuing to promote an Iraqi Government that is just, representative, and accountable and that denies support and safe haven to terrorists. The United States will pursue no claim on Iraqi territory or resources, and we will keep our commitments to Iraq's democratically elected government. These efforts will build new ties of trade and commerce between Iraq and the world, enable Iraq to assume its rightful place in the community of nations, and contribute to the peace and security of the region.

We are pursuing these objectives with a strategy that has three core components.

- **Transition Security:** First, we are transitioning security to full Iraqi responsibility. We will end the combat mission in Iraq by the end of August 2010. We will continue to train, equip, and advise Iraqi Security Forces; conduct targeted counterterrorism missions; and protect ongoing civilian and military efforts in Iraq. And, consistent with our commitments to the Iraqi Government, including the U.S.-Iraq Security Agreement, we will remove all of our troops from Iraq by the end of 2011.

- **Civilian Support:** Second, as the security situation continues to improve, U.S. civilian engagement will deepen and broaden. We will sustain a capable political, diplomatic, and civilian effort to help the Iraqi people as they resolve outstanding differences, integrate those refugees and displaced persons who can return, and continue to develop accountable democratic institutions that can better serve their basic needs. We will work with our Iraqi partners to implement the Strategic Framework Agreement, with the Department of State taking the lead. This will include cooperation on a range of issues including defense and security cooperation, political and diplomatic cooperation, rule of law, science, health, education, and economics.

- **Regional Diplomacy and Development:** Third, we will continue to pursue comprehensive engagement across the region to ensure that our drawdown in Iraq provides an opportunity to advance lasting security and sustainable development for both Iraq and the broader Middle East. The United States will continue to retain a robust civilian presence commensurate with our strategic interests in the country and the region. We are transforming our relationship to one consistent with other strategic partners in the region.

Pursue Arab-Israeli Peace: The United States, Israel, the Palestinians, and the Arab States have an interest in a peaceful resolution of the Arab-Israeli conflict—one in which the legitimate aspirations of Israelis and Palestinians for security and dignity are realized, and Israel achieves a secure and lasting peace with all of its neighbors.

The United States seeks two states living side by side in peace and security—a Jewish state of Israel, with true security, acceptance, and rights for all Israelis; and a viable, independent Palestine with contiguous territory that ends the occupation that began in 1967 and realizes the potential of the Palestinian people. We will continue to work regionally and with like-minded partners in order to advance negotiations that address the permanent-status issues: security for Israelis and Palestinians; borders, refugees, and Jerusalem. We also seek international support to build the institutions upon which a Palestinian state will depend, while supporting economic development that can bring opportunity to its people.

Any Arab-Israeli peace will only be lasting if harmful regional interference ends and constructive regional support deepens. As we pursue peace between Israelis and Palestinians, we will also pursue peace between Israel and Lebanon, Israel and Syria, and a broader peace between Israel and its neighbors. We will pursue regional initiatives with multilateral participation, alongside bilateral negotiations.

Promote a Responsible Iran: For decades, the Islamic Republic of Iran has endangered the security of the region and the United States and failed to live up to its international responsibilities. In addition to its illicit nuclear program, it continues to support terrorism, undermine peace between Israelis and Palestinians, and deny its people their universal rights. Many years of refusing to engage Iran failed to reverse these trends; on the contrary, Iran's behavior became more threatening. Engagement is something we pursue without illusion. It can offer Iran a pathway to a better future, provided Iran's leaders are prepared to take it. But that better pathway can only be achieved if Iran's leaders change course, act to restore the confidence of the international community, and fulfill their obligations. The United States seeks a future in which Iran meets its international responsibilities, takes its rightful place in the community of nations, and enjoys the political and economic opportunities that its people deserve. Yet if the Iranian Government continues to refuse to live up to its international obligations, it will face greater isolation.

Invest in the Capacity of Strong and Capable Partners

Where governments are incapable of meeting their citizens' basic needs and fulfilling their responsibilities to provide security within their borders, the consequences are often global and may directly threaten the American people. To advance our common security, we must address the underlying political and economic deficits that foster instability, enable radicalization and extremism, and ultimately undermine the ability of governments to manage threats within their borders and to be our partners in addressing common challenges. To invest in the capacity of strong and capable partners, we will work to:

Foster Security and Reconstruction in the Aftermath of Conflict: The United States and the international community cannot shy away from the difficult task of pursuing stabilization in conflict and post-conflict environments. In countries like Iraq and Afghanistan, building the capacity necessary for security, economic growth, and good governance is the only path to long term peace and security. But we have also learned that the effectiveness of these efforts is profoundly affected by the capacity of governments and the political will of their leaders. We will take these constraints into account in designing appropriate assistance strategies and will facilitate the kind of collaboration that is essential—within our government and with international organizations—in those instances when we engage in the difficult work of helping to bring conflicts to an end.

Pursue Sustainable and Responsible Security Systems in At-Risk States: Proactively investing in stronger societies and human welfare is far more effective and efficient than responding after state collapse. The United States must improve its capability to strengthen the security of states at risk of conflict and violence. We will undertake long-term, sustained efforts to strengthen the capacity of security forces to guarantee internal security, defend against external threats, and promote regional security and respect for human rights and the rule of law. We will also continue to strengthen the administrative and oversight capability of civilian security sector institutions, and the effectiveness of criminal justice.

Prevent the Emergence of Conflict: Our strategy goes beyond meeting the challenges of today, and includes preventing the challenges and seizing the opportunities of tomorrow. This requires investing now in the capable partners of the future; building today the capacity to strengthen the foundations of our common security, and modernizing our capabilities in order to ensure that we are agile in the face of change. We have already begun to reorient and strengthen our development agenda; to take stock of and enhance our capabilities; and to forge new and more effective means of applying the skills of our military, diplomats, and development experts. These kinds of measures will help us diminish military risk, act before crises and conflicts erupt, and ensure that governments are better able to serve their people.

Secure Cyberspace

Cybersecurity threats represent one of the most serious national security, public safety, and economic challenges we face as a nation. The very technologies that empower us to lead and create also empower those who would disrupt and destroy. They enable our military superiority, but our unclassified government networks are constantly probed by intruders. Our daily lives and public safety depend on power and electric grids, but potential adversaries could use cyber vulnerabilities to disrupt them on a massive scale. The Internet and e-commerce are keys to our economic competitiveness, but cyber criminals have cost companies and consumers hundreds of millions of dollars and valuable intellectual property.

The threats we face range from individual criminal hackers to organized criminal groups, from terrorist networks to advanced nation states. Defending against these threats to our security, prosperity, and personal privacy requires networks that are secure, trustworthy, and resilient. Our digital infrastructure, therefore, is a strategic national asset, and protecting it—while safeguarding privacy and civil liberties—is a national security priority. We will deter, prevent, detect, defend against, and quickly recover from cyber intrusions and attacks by:

Investing in People and Technology: To advance that goal, we are working across the government and with the private sector to design more secure technology that gives us the ability to better protect and to improve the resilience of critical government and industry systems and networks. We will continue to invest in the cutting-edge research and development necessary for the innovation and discovery we need to meet these challenges. We have begun a comprehensive national campaign to promote cybersecurity awareness and digital literacy from our boardrooms to our classrooms and to build a digital workforce for the 21st century.

Strengthening Partnerships: Neither government nor the private sector nor individual citizens can meet this challenge alone—we will expand the ways we work together. We will also strengthen our international partnerships on a range of issues, including the development of norms for acceptable conduct in cyberspace; laws concerning cybercrime; data preservation, protection, and privacy; and approaches for network defense and response to cyber attacks. We will work with all the key players—including all levels of government and the private sector, nationally and internationally—to investigate cyber intrusion and to ensure an organized and unified response to future cyber incidents. Just as we do for natural disasters, we have to have plans and resources in place beforehand.

Prosperity

"The answers to our problems don't lie beyond our reach. They exist in our laboratories and universities; in our fields and our factories; in the imaginations of our entrepreneurs and the pride of the hardest-working people on Earth. Those qualities that have made America the greatest force of progress and prosperity in human history we still possess in ample measure. What is required now is for this country to pull together, confront boldly the challenges we face, and take responsibility for our future once more."
—*President Barack Obama,*
Address to Joint Session of Congress, February 24, 2009

The foundation of American leadership must be a prosperous American economy. And a growing and open global economy serves as a source of opportunity for the American people and a source of strength for the United States. The free flow of information, people, goods, and services has also advanced peace among nations, as those places that have emerged more prosperous are often more stable. Yet we have also seen how shocks to the global economy can precipitate disaster—including the loss of jobs, a decline in standards of living in parts of our country, and instability and a loss of U.S. influence abroad. Meanwhile, growing prosperity around the world has made economic power more diffuse, creating a more competitive environment for America's people and businesses.

To allow each American to pursue the opportunity upon which our prosperity depends, we must build a stronger foundation for economic growth. That foundation must include access to a complete and competitive education for every American; a transformation of the way that we produce and use energy, so that we reduce our dependence on fossil fuels and lead the world in creating new jobs and industry; access to quality, affordable health care so our people, businesses, and government are not constrained by rising costs; and the responsible management of our Federal budget so that we balance our priorities and are not burdened by debt. To succeed, we must also ensure that America stays on the cutting edge of the science and innovation that supports our prosperity, defense, and international technological leadership.

This new foundation must underpin and sustain an international economic system that is critical to both our prosperity and to the peace and security of the world. We must reinvigorate and fortify it for the 21st century: by preventing cycles of boom and bust with new rules of the road at home and abroad; by saving more and spending less; by resisting protectionism and promoting trade that is free and fair; by coordinating our actions with other countries, and reforming international institutions to give emerging economies a greater voice and greater responsibility; and by supporting development that promotes good governance, unleashes the potential of different populations, and creates new markets overseas. Taken together, these actions can ensure inclusive growth that is balanced and sustained.

Strengthen Education and Human Capital

In a global economy of vastly increased mobility and interdependence, our own prosperity and leadership depends increasingly on our ability to provide our citizens with the education that they need to succeed, while attracting the premier human capital for our workforce. We must ensure that the most innovative ideas take root in America, while providing our people with the skills that they need to compete. That means we must:

Improve Education at All Levels: The United States has lost ground in education, even as our competitiveness depends on educating our children to succeed in a global economy based on knowledge and innovation. We are working to provide a complete and competitive education for all Americans, to include supporting high standards for early learning, reforming public schools, increasing access to higher education and job training, and promoting high-demand skills and education for emerging industries. We will also restore U.S. leadership in higher education by seeking the goal of leading the world in the proportion of college graduates by 2020.

Invest in Science, Technology, Engineering, and Math Education (STEM): America's long-term leadership depends on educating and producing future scientists and innovators. We will invest more in STEM education so students can learn to think critically in science, math, engineering, and technology; improve the quality of math and science teaching so American students are no longer outperformed by those in other nations; and expand STEM education and career opportunities for underrepresented groups, including women and girls. We will work with partners—from the private-sector and nonprofit organizations to universities—to promote education and careers in science and technology.

Increase International Education and Exchange: The pervasiveness of the English language and American cultural influence are great advantages to Americans traveling, working, and negotiating in foreign countries. But we must develop skills to help us succeed in a dynamic and diverse global economy. We will support programs that cultivate interest and scholarship in foreign languages and intercultural affairs, including international exchange programs. This will allow our citizens to build connections with peoples overseas and to develop skills and contacts that will help them thrive in the global economy. We must also welcome more foreign exchange students to our shores, recognizing the benefits that can result from deeper ties with foreign publics and increased understanding of American society.

Pursue Comprehensive Immigration Reform: The United States is a nation of immigrants. Our ability to innovate, our ties to the world, and our economic prosperity depend on our nation's capacity to welcome and assimilate immigrants, and a visa system which welcomes skilled professionals from around the world. At the same time, effective border security and immigration enforcement must keep the country safe and deter unlawful entry. Indeed, persistent problems in immigration policy consume valuable resources needed to advance other security objectives and make it harder to focus on the most dangerous threats facing our country. Ultimately, our national security depends on striking a balance between security and openness. To advance this goal, we must pursue comprehensive immigration reform that effectively secures our borders, while repairing a broken system that fails to serve the needs of our nation.

Enhance Science, Technology, and Innovation

Reaffirming America's role as the global engine of scientific discovery and technological innovation has never been more critical. Challenges like climate change, pandemic disease, and resource scarcity demand new innovation. Meanwhile, the nation that leads the world in building a clean energy economy will enjoy a substantial economic and security advantage. That is why the Administration is investing heavily in research, improving education in science and math, promoting developments in energy, and expanding international cooperation.

Transform our Energy Economy: As long as we are dependent on fossil fuels, we need to ensure the security and free flow of global energy resources. But without significant and timely adjustments, our energy dependence will continue to undermine our security and prosperity. This will leave us vulnerable to energy supply disruptions and manipulation and to changes in the environment on an unprecedented scale.

The United States has a window of opportunity to lead in the development of clean energy technology. If successful, the United States will lead in this new Industrial Revolution in clean energy that will be a major contributor to our economic prosperity. If we do not develop the policies that encourage the private sector to seize the opportunity, the United States will fall behind and increasingly become an importer of these new energy technologies.

We have already made the largest investment in clean energy in history, but there is much more to do to build on this foundation.

We must continue to transform our energy economy, leveraging private capital to accelerate deployment of clean energy technologies that will cut greenhouse gas emissions, improve energy efficiency, increase use of renewable and nuclear power, reduce the dependence of vehicles on oil, and diversify energy sources and suppliers. We will invest in research and next-generation technology, modernize the way we distribute electricity, and encourage the usage of transitional fuels, while moving towards clean energy produced at home.

Invest in Research: Research and development is central to our broader national capacity. Incidents like the outbreak of H1N1 influenza and the challenge of identifying new, renewable sources of energy highlight the importance of research in basic and applied science. We are reversing the decades-long decline in federal funding for research, including the single largest infusion to basic science research in American history. Research and innovation is not something government can do on its own, which is why we will support and create incentives to encourage private initiatives. The United States has always excelled in our ability to turn science and technology into engineering and products, and we must continue to do so in the future.

Expand International Science Partnerships: America's scientific leadership has always been widely admired around the world, and we must continue to expand cooperation and partnership in science and technology. We have launched a number of Science Envoys around the globe and are promoting stronger relationships between American scientists, universities, and researchers and their counterparts abroad. We will reestablish a commitment to science and technology in our foreign assistance efforts and develop a strategy for international science and national security.

Employ Technology to Protect our Nation: Our renewed commitment to science and technology—and our ability to apply the ingenuity of our public and private sectors toward the most difficult foreign policy and security challenges of our time—will help us protect our citizens and advance U.S. national security priorities. These include, for example, protecting U.S. and allied forces from asymmetric attacks; supporting arms control and nonproliferation agreements; preventing terrorists from attacking our homeland; preventing and managing widespread disease outbreaks; securing the supply chain; detecting weapons of mass destruction before they reach our borders; and protecting our information, communication, and transportation infrastructure.

Leverage and Grow our Space Capabilities: For over 50 years, our space community has been a catalyst for innovation and a hallmark of U.S. technological leadership. Our space capabilities underpin global commerce and scientific advancements and bolster our national security strengths and those of our allies and partners. To promote security and stability in space, we will pursue activities consistent with the inherent right of self-defense, deepen cooperation with allies and friends, and work with all nations toward the responsible and peaceful use of space. To maintain the advantages afforded to the United States by space, we must also take several actions. We must continue to encourage cutting-edge space technology by investing in the people and industrial base that develops them. We will invest in the research and development of next-generation space technologies and capabilities that benefit our commercial, civil, scientific exploration, and national security communities, in order to maintain the viability of space for future generations. And we will promote a unified effort to strengthen our space industrial base and work with universities to encourage students to pursue space-related careers.

Achieve Balanced and Sustainable Growth

Balanced and sustainable growth, at home and throughout the global economy, drives the momentum of the U.S. economy and underpins our prosperity. A steadily growing global economy means an expanding market for exports of our goods and services. Over time, deepening linkages among markets and businesses will provide the setting in which the energies and entrepreneurship of our private sector can flourish, generating technologies, business growth, and job creation that will boost living standards for Americans. United States economic leadership now has to adapt to the rising prominence of emerging economies; the growing size, speed, and sophistication of financial markets; the multiplicity of market participants around the globe; and the struggling economies that have so far failed to integrate into the global system.

To promote prosperity for all Americans, we will need to lead the international community to expand the inclusive growth of the integrated, global economy. At the same time, we will need to lead international efforts to prevent a recurrence of economic imbalances and financial excesses, while managing the many security threats and global challenges that affect global economic stability. To promote growth that can be balanced and sustained, we will:

Prevent Renewed Instability in the Global Economy: The recent crisis taught us the very high cost of the boom and bust cycle that has plagued the global economy and has served neither the United States nor our international partners. Once Americans found themselves in debt or out of work, our demand for foreign goods fell sharply. As foreign economies weakened, their financial institutions and public finances came under stress too, reinforcing the global slowdown. We must prevent the reemergence of imbalanced growth, with American consumers buying and borrowing, and Asian and other exporting countries selling and accumulating claims. We must pursue reform of the U.S. financial system to strengthen the health of our economy and encourage Americans to save more. And we must prevent the reemergence of excesses in our financial institutions based on irresponsible lending behavior, and abetted by lax and uncoordinated regulation.

Save More And Export More: Striking a better balance at home means saving more and spending less, reforming our financial system, and reducing our long-term budget deficit. With those changes, we will see a greater emphasis on exports that we can build, produce, and sell all over the world, with the goal of doubling U.S. exports by 2014. This is ultimately an employment strategy, because higher exports will support millions of well-paying American jobs, including those that service innovative and profitable new technologies. As a part of that effort, we are reforming our export controls consistent with our national security imperatives.

Shift To Greater Domestic Demand Abroad: For the rest of the world, especially in some emerging market and developing countries, a better balance means placing greater emphasis on increasing domestic demand as the leading driver of growth and opening markets. Those countries will be able to import the capital and technologies needed to sustain the remarkable productivity gains already underway. Rebalancing will provide an opportunity for workers and consumers over time to enjoy the higher standards of living made possible by those gains. As balanced growth translates into sustained growth, middle-income, and poor countries, many of which are not yet sufficiently integrated into the global economy, can accelerate the process of convergence of living standards toward richer countries—a process that will become a driver of growth for the global economy for decades to come.

Open Foreign Markets to Our Products and Services: The United States has long had one of the most open markets in the world. We have been a leader in expanding an open trading system. That has underwritten the growth of other developed and emerging markets alike. Openness has also forced our companies and workers to compete and innovate, and at the same time, has offered market access crucial to the success of so many countries around the world. We will maintain our open investment environment, consistent with our national security goals. In this new era, opening markets around the globe will promote global competition and innovation and will be crucial to our prosperity. We will pursue a trade agenda that includes an ambitious and balanced Doha multilateral trade agreement, bilateral and multilateral trade agreements that reflect our values and interests, and engagement with the transpacific partnership countries to shape a regional agreement with high standards.

As we go forward, our trade policy will be an important part of our effort to capitalize on the opportunities presented by globalization, but will also be part of our effort to equip Americans to compete. To make trade agreements work for Americans, we will take steps to restore confidence, with realistic programs to deal with transition costs, and promote innovation, infrastructure, healthcare reform and education. Our agreements will contain achievable enforcement mechanisms to ensure that the gains we negotiate are in fact realized and will be structured to reflect U.S. interests, especially on labor and environment.

Build Cooperation with Our International Partners: The United States has supported the G-20's emergence as the premier forum for international economic cooperation. This flows from the recognition that we need a broader and more inclusive engagement with the countries responsible for most of global output and trade. U.S. leadership in the G-20 will be focused on securing sustainable and balanced growth, coordinating reform of financial sector regulation, fostering global economic development, and promoting energy security. We also need official international financial institutions to be as modern and agile as the global economy they serve. Through the G-20, we will pursue governance reform at the International Monetary Fund (IMF) and World Bank. We will also broaden our leadership in other international financial institutions so that the rapidly growing countries of the world see their representation increase and are willing to invest those institutions with the authority they need to promote the stability and growth of global output and trade.

Deterring Threats to the International Financial System: Today's open and global financial system also exposes us to global financial threats. Just as we work to make the most of the opportunities that globalization brings, the actors that pose a threat to our national security—terrorists, proliferators, narcotics traffickers, corrupt officials, and others—are abusing the global financial system to raise, move, and safeguard funds that support their illicit activities or from which they derive profit. Their support networks have global reach and are not contained by national borders. Our strategy to attack these networks must respond in kind and target their illicit resources and access to the global financial system through financial measures, administration and enforcement of regulatory authorities, outreach to the private sector and our foreign partners, and collaboration on international standards and information sharing.

Accelerate Sustainable Development

The growth of emerging economies in recent decades has lifted people out of poverty and forged a more interconnected and vibrant global economy. But development has been uneven, progress is fragile, and too many of the world's people still live without the benefits that development affords. While some countries are growing, many lag behind—mired in insecurity, constrained by poor governance, or overly dependent upon commodity prices. But sustained economic progress requires faster, sustainable, and more inclusive development. That is why we are pursuing a range of specific initiatives in areas such as food security and global health that will be essential to the future security and prosperity of nations and peoples around the globe.

Increase Investments in Development: The United States has an interest in working with our allies to help the world's poorest countries grow into productive and prosperous economies governed by capable, democratic, and accountable state institutions. We will ensure a greater and more deliberate focus on a global development agenda across the United States Government, from policy analysis through policy implementation. We are increasing our foreign assistance, expanding our investments in effective multilateral development institutions, and leveraging the engagement of others to share the burden.

Invest in the Foundations of Long-Term Development: The United States will initiate long-term investments that recognize and reward governments that demonstrate the capacity and political will to pursue sustainable development strategies and ensure that all policy instruments at our disposal are harnessed to these ends. And we will provide our support in multiple ways—by strengthening the ability of governments and communities to manage development challenges and investing in strong institutions that foster the democratic accountability that helps sustain development. This will expand the circle of nations—particularly in Africa—who are capable of reaping the benefits of the global economy, while contributing to global security and prosperity.

Exercise Leadership in the Provision of Global Public Goods: Our approach needs to reflect the fact that there are a set of development challenges that strongly affect the likelihood of progress, but cannot be addressed by individual countries acting alone. Particularly in Africa, these challenges—such as adaptation to global warming, the control of epidemic disease, and the knowledge to increase agricultural productivity—are not adequately addressed in bilateral efforts. We will shape the international architecture and work with our global partners to address these challenges, and increase our investments and engagement to transition to a low-carbon growth trajectory, support the resilience of the poorest nations to the effects of climate change, and strengthen food security. We must also pursue potential "game changers" for development such as new vaccines, weather-resistant seed varieties, and green energy technologies.

Spend Taxpayers' Dollars Wisely

The United States Government has an obligation to make the best use of taxpayer money, and our ability to achieve long-term goals depends upon our fiscal responsibility. A responsible budget involves making tough choices to live within our means; holding departments and agencies accountable for their spending and their performance; harnessing technology to improve government performance; and being open and honest with the American people. A responsible budget also depends upon working with our global partners and institutions to share burdens and leverage U.S. investments to achieve global goals. Our national security goals can only be reached if we make hard choices and work with international partners to share burdens.

Reduce the Deficit: We cannot grow our economy in the long term unless we put the United States back on a sustainable fiscal path. To begin this effort, the Administration has proposed a 3-year freeze in nonsecurity discretionary spending, a new fee on the largest financial services companies to recoup taxpayer losses for the Troubled Asset Relief Program (TARP), and the closing of tax loopholes and unnecessary subsidies. The Administration has created a bipartisan fiscal commission to suggest further steps for medium-term deficit reduction and will work for fiscally responsible health insurance reform that will bring down the rate of growth in health care costs, a key driver of the country's fiscal future.

Reform Acquisition and Contracting Processes: Wasteful spending, duplicative programs, and contracts with poor oversight have no place in the United States Government. Cost-effective and efficient processes are particularly important for the Department of Defense, which accounts for approximately 70 percent of all Federal procurement spending. We will scrutinize our programs and terminate or restructure those that are outdated, duplicative, ineffective, or wasteful. The result will be more relevant, capable, and effective programs and systems that our military wants and needs. We are also reforming Federal contracting and strengthening contracting practices and management oversight with a goal of saving Federal agencies $40 billion dollars a year.

Increase Transparency: Americans have a right to know how their tax dollars are spent, but that information can be obscured or unavailable. In some instances, incomplete accounting of the budget has been used to conceal the reality of our fiscal situation. To uphold our commitment to a transparent budget process, we are simultaneously requesting both base budget and overseas contingency operations costs, with the same amount of justification and explanatory material for each, so that Americans can see the true cost of our war efforts and hold leaders accountable for decisions with all of the facts.

Values

"We uphold our most cherished values not only because doing so is right, but because it strengthens our country and keeps us safe. Time and again, our values have been our best national security asset—in war and peace, in times of ease, and in eras of upheaval. Fidelity to our values is the reason why the United States of America grew from a small string of colonies under the writ of an empire to the strongest nation in the world."
—President Barack Obama,
National Archives, May 21, 2009

The United States believes certain values are universal and will work to promote them worldwide. These include an individual's freedom to speak their mind, assemble without fear, worship as they please, and choose their own leaders; they also include dignity, tolerance, and equality among all people, and the fair and equitable administration of justice. The United States was founded upon a belief in these values. At home, fidelity to these values has extended the promise of America ever more fully, to ever more people. Abroad, these values have been claimed by people of every race, region, and religion. Most nations are parties to international agreements that recognize this commonality. And nations that embrace these values for their citizens are ultimately more successful—and friendly to the United States—than those that do not.

Yet after an era that saw substantial gains for these values around the world, democratic development has stalled in recent years.

In some cultures, these values are being equated with the ugly face of modernity and are seen to encroach upon cherished identities. In other countries, autocratic rulers have repressed basic human rights and democratic practices in the name of economic development and national unity. Even where some governments have adopted democratic practices, authoritarian rulers have undermined electoral processes and restricted the space for opposition and civil society, imposing a growing number of legal restrictions so as to impede the rights of people to assemble and to access information. And while there has been substantial progress in combating poverty in many parts of the world, too many of the world's people still lack the dignity that comes with the opportunity to pursue a better life.

The United States supports those who seek to exercise universal rights around the world. We promote our values above all by living them at home. We continue to engage nations, institutions, and peoples in pursuit of these values abroad. And we recognize the link between development and political progress. In doing so, our goals are realistic, as we recognize that different cultures and traditions give life to these values in distinct ways. Moreover, America's influence comes not from perfection, but from our striving to overcome our imperfections. The constant struggle to perfect our union is what makes the American story inspiring. That is why acknowledging our past shortcomings—and highlighting our efforts to remedy them—is a means of promoting our values.

America will not impose any system of government on another country, but our long-term security and prosperity depends on our steady support for universal values, which sets us apart from our enemies, adversarial governments, and many potential competitors for influence. We will do so through a variety of means—by speaking out for universal rights, supporting fragile democracies and civil society, and supporting the dignity that comes with development.

Strengthen the Power of Our Example

More than any other action that we have taken, the power of America's example has helped spread freedom and democracy abroad. That is why we must always seek to uphold these values not just when it is easy, but when it is hard. Advancing our interests may involve new arrangements to confront threats like terrorism, but these practices and structures must always be in line with our Constitution, preserve our people's privacy and civil liberties, and withstand the checks and balances that have served us so well. To sustain our fidelity to our values—and our credibility to promote them around the world—we will continue to:

Prohibit Torture without Exception or Equivocation: Brutal methods of interrogation are inconsistent with our values, undermine the rule of law, and are not effective means of obtaining information. They alienate the United States from the world. They serve as a recruitment and propaganda tool for terrorists. They increase the will of our enemies to fight against us, and endanger our troops when they are captured. The United States will not use or support these methods.

Legal Aspects of Countering Terrorism: The increased risk of terrorism necessitates a capacity to detain and interrogate suspected violent extremists, but that framework must align with our laws to be effective and sustainable. When we are able, we will prosecute terrorists in Federal courts or in reformed military commissions that are fair, legitimate, and effective. For detainees who cannot be prosecuted—but pose a danger to the American people—we must have clear, defensible, and lawful standards. We must have fair procedures and a thorough process of periodic review, so that any prolonged detention is carefully evaluated and justified. And keeping with our Constitutional system, it will be subject to checks and balances. The goal is an approach that can be sustained by future Administrations, with support from both political parties and all three branches of government.

Balance the Imperatives of Secrecy and Transparency: For the sake of our security, some information must be protected from public disclosure—for instance, to protect our troops, our sources and methods of intelligence-gathering or confidential actions that keep the American people safe. Yet our democracy depends upon transparency, and whenever possible, we are making information available to the American people so that they can make informed judgments and hold their leaders accountable. For instance, when we invoke the State Secrets privilege, we will follow clear procedures so as to provide greater accountability and to ensure the privilege is invoked only when necessary and in the narrowest way possible. We will never invoke the privilege to hide a violation of law or to avoid embarrassment to the government.

Protect Civil Liberties, Privacy, and Oversight: Protecting civil liberties and privacy are integral to the vibrancy of our democracy and the exercise of freedom. We are balancing our solemn commitments to these virtues with the mandate to provide security for the American people. Vigorous oversight of national security activities by our three branches of government and vigilant compliance with the rule of law allow us to maintain this balance, affirm to our friends and allies the constitutional ideals we uphold.

Uphold the Rule of Law: The rule of law—and our capacity to enforce it—advances our national security and strengthens our leadership. At home, fidelity to our laws and support for our law enforcement community safeguards American citizens and interests, while protecting and advancing our values. Around the globe, it allows us to hold actors accountable, while supporting both international security and the stability of the global economy. America's commitment to the rule of law is fundamental to our efforts to build an international order that is capable of confronting the emerging challenges of the 21st century.

Draw Strength from Diversity: The United States has benefited throughout our history when we have drawn strength from our diversity. While those who advocate on behalf of extremist ideologies seek to sow discord among ethnic and religious groups, America stands as an example of how people from different backgrounds can be united through their commitment to shared values. Within our own communities, those who seek to recruit and radicalize individuals will often try to prey upon isolation and alienation. Our own commitment to extending the promise of America will both draw a contrast with those who try to drive people apart, while countering attempts to enlist individuals in ideological, religious, or ethnic extremism.

Promote Democracy and Human Rights Abroad

The United States supports the expansion of democracy and human rights abroad because governments that respect these values are more just, peaceful, and legitimate. We also do so because their success abroad fosters an environment that supports America's national interests. Political systems that protect universal rights are ultimately more stable, successful, and secure. As our history shows, the United States can more effectively forge consensus to tackle shared challenges when working with governments that reflect the will and respect the rights of their people, rather than just the narrow interests of those in power. The United States is advancing universal values by:

Ensuring that New and Fragile Democracies Deliver Tangible Improvements for Their Citizens: The United States must support democracy, human rights, and development together, as they are mutually reinforcing. We are working closely with citizens, communities, and political and civil society leaders to strengthen key institutions of democratic accountability—free and fair electoral processes, strong legislatures, civilian control of militaries, honest police forces, independent and fair judiciaries, a free and independent press, a vibrant private sector, and a robust civil society. To do so, we are harnessing our bilateral and multilateral capabilities to help nascent democracies deliver services that respond to the needs and preferences of their citizens, since democracies without development rarely survive.

Practicing Principled Engagement with Non-Democratic Regimes: Even when we are focused on interests such as counterterrorism, nonproliferation, or enhancing economic ties, we will always seek in parallel to expand individual rights and opportunities through our bilateral engagement. The United States is pursuing a dual-track approach in which we seek to improve government-to-government relations and use this dialogue to advance human rights, while engaging civil society and peaceful political opposition, and encouraging U.S. nongovernmental actors to do the same. More substantive government-to-government relations can create permissive conditions for civil society to operate and for more extensive people-to-people exchanges. But when our overtures are rebuffed, we must lead the international community in using public and private diplomacy, and drawing on incentives and disincentives, in an effort to change repressive behavior.

Recognizing the Legitimacy of All Peaceful Democratic Movements: America respects the right of all peaceful, law-abiding, and nonviolent voices to be heard around the world, even if we disagree with them. Support for democracy must not be about support for specific candidates or movements. America will welcome all legitimately elected, peaceful governments, provided they govern with respect for the rights and dignity of all their people and consistent with their international obligations. Those who seek democracy to obtain power, but are ruthless once they do, will forfeit the support of the United States. Governments must maintain power through consent, not coercion, and place legitimate political processes above party or narrow interest.

Supporting the Rights of Women and Girls: Women should have access to the same opportunities and be able to make the same choices as men. Experience shows that countries are more peaceful and prosperous when women are accorded full and equal rights and opportunity. When those rights and opportunities are denied, countries often lag behind. Furthermore, women and girls often disproportionally bear the burden of crises and conflict. Therefore the

United States is working with regional and international organizations to prevent violence against women and girls, especially in conflict zones. We are supporting women's equal access to justice and their participation in the political process. We are promoting child and maternal health. We are combating human trafficking, especially in women and girls, through domestic and international law enforcement. And we are supporting education, employment, and micro-finance to empower women globally.

Strengthening International Norms Against Corruption: We are working within the broader international system, including the U.N., G-20, Organization for Economic Cooperation and Development (OECD), and the international financial institutions, to promote the recognition that pervasive corruption is a violation of basic human rights and a severe impediment to development and global security. We will work with governments and civil society organizations to bring greater transparency and accountability to government budgets, expenditures, and the assets of public officials. And we will institutionalize transparent practices in international aid flows, international banking and tax policy, and private sector engagement around natural resources to make it harder for officials to steal and to strengthen the efforts of citizens to hold their governments accountable.

Building a Broader Coalition of Actors to Advance Universal Values: We are working to build support for democracy, rule of law, and human rights by working with other governments, nongovernmental organizations, and multilateral fora. The United States is committed to working to shape and strengthen existing institutions that are not delivering on their potential, such as the United Nations Human Rights Council. We are working within the broader U.N. system and through regional mechanisms to strengthen human rights monitoring and enforcement mechanisms, so that individuals and countries are held accountable for their violation of international human rights norms. And we will actively support the leadership of emerging democracies as they assume a more active role in advancing basic human rights and democratic values in their regions and on the global stage.

Marshalling New Technologies and Promoting the Right to Access Information: The emergence of technologies such as the Internet, wireless networks, mobile smart-phones, investigative forensics, satellite and aerial imagery, and distributed remote sensing infrastructure has created powerful new opportunities to advance democracy and human rights. These technologies have fueled people-powered political movements, made it possible to shine a spotlight on human rights abuses nearly instantaneously, and increased avenues for free speech and unrestricted communication around the world. We support the dissemination and use of these technologies to facilitate freedom of expression, expand access to information, increase governmental transparency and accountability, and counter restrictions on their use. We will also better utilize such technologies to effectively communicate our own messages to the world.

Promote Dignity by Meeting Basic Needs

The freedom that America stands for includes freedom from want. Basic human rights cannot thrive in places where human beings do not have access to enough food, or clean water, or the medicine they need to survive. The United States has embraced the United Nation's Millennium Development Goals and is working with others in pursuit of the eradication of extreme poverty—efforts that are particularly critical to the future of nations and peoples of Africa. And we will continue to promote the dignity that comes through development efforts such as:

Pursuing a Comprehensive Global Health Strategy: The United States has a moral and strategic interest in promoting global health. When a child dies of a preventable disease, it offends our conscience; when a disease goes unchecked, it can endanger our own health; when children are sick, development is stalled. That is why we are continuing to invest in the fight against HIV/AIDS. Through the Global Health Initiative, we will strengthen health systems and invest in interventions to address areas where progress has lagged, including maternal and child health. And we are also pursuing the goal of reducing the burden of malaria and tuberculosis and seeking the elimination of important neglected tropical diseases.

Promoting Food Security: The United States is working with partners around the world to advance a food security initiative that combats hunger and builds the capacity of countries to feed their people. Instead of simply providing aid for developing countries, we are focusing on new methods and technologies for agricultural development. This is consistent with an approach in which aid is not an end in itself—the purpose of our foreign assistance will be to create the conditions where it is no longer needed.

Leading Efforts to Address Humanitarian Crises: Together with the American people and the international community, we will continue to respond to humanitarian crises to ensure that those in need have the protection and assistance they need. In such circumstances, we are also placing a greater emphasis on fostering long-term recovery. Haiti's devastating earthquake is only the most recent reminder of the human and material consequences of natural disasters, and a changing climate portends a future in which the United States must be better prepared and resourced to exercise robust leadership to help meet critical humanitarian needs.

International Order

"As President of the United States, I will work tirelessly to protect America's security and to advance our interests. But no one nation can meet the challenges of the 21st century on its own, nor dictate its terms to the world. That is why America seeks an international system that lets nations pursue their interests peacefully, especially when those interests diverge; a system where the universal rights of human beings are respected, and violations of those rights are opposed; a system where we hold ourselves to the same standards that we

apply to other nations, with clear rights and responsibilities for all. "

—*President Barack Obama,*
Moscow, Russia, July 7, 2009

The United States will protect its people and advance our prosperity irrespective of the actions of any other nation, but we have an interest in a just and sustainable international order that can foster collective action to confront common challenges. This international order will support our efforts to advance security, prosperity, and universal values, but it is also an end that we seek in its own right. Because without such an international order, the forces of instability and disorder will undermine global security. And without effective mechanisms to forge international cooperation, challenges that recognize no borders—such as climate change, pandemic disease, and transnational crime—will persist and potentially spread.

International institutions—most prominently NATO and the United Nations—have been at the center of our international order since the mid 20th century. Yet, an international architecture that was largely forged in the wake of World War II is buckling under the weight of new threats, making us less able to seize new opportunities. Even though many defining trends of the 21st century affect all nations and peoples, too often, the mutual interests of nations and peoples are ignored in favor of suspicion and self-defeating competition.

What is needed, therefore, is a realignment of national actions and international institutions with shared interests. And when national interests do collide—or countries prioritize their interests in different ways—those nations that defy international norms or fail to meet their sovereign responsibilities will be denied the incentives that come with greater integration and collaboration with the international community.

No international order can be supported by international institutions alone. Our mutual interests must be underpinned by bilateral, multilateral, and global strategies that address underlying sources of insecurity and build new spheres of cooperation. To that end, strengthening bilateral and multilateral cooperation cannot be accomplished simply by working inside formal institutions and frameworks. It requires sustained outreach to foreign governments, political leaderships, and other critical constituencies that must commit the necessary capabilities and resources to enable effective, collective action. And it means building upon our traditional alliances, while also cultivating partnerships with new centers of influence. Taken together, these approaches will allow us to foster more effective global cooperation to confront challenges that know no borders and affect every nation.

Ensure Strong Alliances

The foundation of United States, regional, and global security will remain America's relations with our allies, and our commitment to their security is unshakable. These relationships must be constantly cultivated, not just because they are indispensible for U.S. interests and national security objectives, but because they are fundamental to our collective security. Alliances are force multipliers: through multinational cooperation and coordination, the sum of our actions is always greater than if we act alone. We will continue to maintain the capacity to defend our allies against old and new threats. We will also continue to closely consult with our allies as well as newly emerging partners and organizations so that we revitalize and expand our cooperation to achieve common objectives. And we will continue to mutually benefit from the collective security provided by strong alliances.

Although the United States and our allies and partners may sometimes disagree on specific issues, we will act based upon mutual respect and in a manner that continues to strengthen an international order that benefits all responsible international actors.

Strengthening Security Relationships: Our ability to sustain these alliances, and to build coalitions of support toward common objectives, depends in part on the capabilities of America's Armed Forces. Similarly, the relationships our Armed Forces have developed with foreign militaries are a critical component of our global engagement and support our collective security.

We will continue to ensure that we can prevail against a wide range of potential adversaries—to include hostile states and non-state actors—while broadly shaping the strategic environment using all tools to advance our common security. We will continue to reassure our allies and partners by retaining our ability to bring precise, sustained, and effective capabilities to bear against a wide range of military threats and decisively defeat the forces of hostile regional powers. We will work with our allies and partners to enhance the resilience of U.S. forward posture and facilities against potential attacks. Finally, we will strengthen our regional deterrence postures—for example, through phased, adaptive missile defense architectures—in order to make certain that regional adversaries gain no advantages from their acquisition of new, offensive military capabilities.

European Allies: Our relationship with our European allies remains the cornerstone for U.S. engagement with the world, and a catalyst for international action. We will engage with our allies bilaterally, and pursue close consultation on a broad range of security and economic issues. The North Atlantic Treaty Organization (NATO) is the pre-eminent security alliance in the world today. With our 27 NATO allies, and the many partners with which NATO cooperates, we will strengthen our collective ability to promote security, deter vital threats, and defend our people. NATO's new Strategic Concept will provide an opportunity to revitalize and reform the Alliance. We are committed to ensuring that NATO is able to address the full range of 21st century challenges, while serving as a foundation of European security. And we will continue to anchor our commitment in Article V, which is fundamental to our collective security.

Building on European aspirations for greater integration, we are committed to partnering with a stronger European Union to advance our shared goals, especially in promoting democracy and prosperity in Eastern European countries that are still completing their democratic transition and in responding to pressing issues of mutual concern. We will remain dedicated to advancing stability and democracy in the Balkans and to resolving conflicts in the Caucasus and in Cyprus. We will continue to engage with Turkey on a broad range of mutual goals, especially with regard to pursuit of stability in its region. And we will seek to strengthen existing European institutions so that they are more inclusive and more effective in building confidence, reducing tensions, and protecting freedom.

Asian Allies: Our alliances with Japan, South Korea, Australia, the Philippines, and Thailand are the bedrock of security in Asia and a foundation of prosperity in the Asia-Pacific region. We will continue to deepen and update these alliances to reflect the dynamism of the region and strategic trends of the 21st century. Japan and South Korea are increasingly important leaders in addressing regional and global issues, as well as in embodying and promoting our common democratic values. We are modernizing our security relationships with both countries to face evolving 21st century global security challenges and to reflect the principle of equal partnership with the United States and to ensure a sustainable foundation for the U.S. military presence there. We are working together with our allies to develop a positive security agenda for the region, focused on regional security, combating the proliferation of weapons of mass destruction, terrorism, climate change, international piracy, epidemics, and cybersecurity, while achieving balanced growth and human rights.

In partnership with our allies, the United States is helping to offer a future of security and integration to all Asian nations and to uphold and extend fundamental rights and dignity to all of its people. These alliances have preserved a hard-earned peace and strengthened the bridges of understanding across the Pacific Ocean in the second half of the 20th century, and it is essential to U.S., Asian, and global security that they are as dynamic and effective in the 21st century.

North America: The strategic partnerships and unique relationships we maintain with Canada and Mexico are critical to U.S. national security and have a direct effect on the security of our homeland. With billions of dollars in trade, shared critical infrastructure, and millions of our citizens moving across our common borders, no two countries are more directly connected to our daily lives. We must change the way we think about our shared borders, in order to secure and expedite the lawful and legitimate flow of people and goods while interdicting transnational threat that threaten our open societies.

Canada is our closest trading partner, a steadfast security ally, and an important partner in regional and global efforts. Our mutual prosperity is closely interconnected, including through our trade relationship with Mexico through NAFTA. With Canada, our security cooperation includes our defense of North America and our efforts through NATO overseas. And our cooperation is critical to the success of international efforts on issues ranging from international climate negotiations to economic cooperation through the G-20.

With Mexico, in addition to trade cooperation, we are working together to identify and interdict threats at the earliest opportunity, even before they reach North America. Stability and security in Mexico are indispensable to building a strong economic partnership, fighting the illicit drug and arms trade, and promoting sound immigration policy.

Build Cooperation with Other 21st Century Centers of Influence

The United States is part of a dynamic international environment, in which different nations are exerting greater influence, and advancing our interests will require expanding spheres of cooperation around the word. Certain bilateral relationships—such as U.S. relations with China, India, and Russia—will be critical to building broader cooperation on areas of mutual interest. And emerging powers in every region of the world are increasingly asserting themselves, raising opportunities for partnership for the United States.

Asia: Asia's dramatic economic growth has increased its connection to America's future prosperity, and its emerging centers of influence make it increasingly important. We have taken substantial steps to deepen our engagement in the region, through regional organizations, new dialogues, and high-level diplomacy. The United States has deep and enduring ties with the countries of the region, including trade and investment that drive growth and prosperity on both sides of the Pacific, and enhancing these ties is critical to our efforts to advance balanced and sustainable growth and to doubling U.S. exports. We have increasing security cooperation on issues such as violent extremism and nuclear proliferation. We will work to advance these mutual interests through our alliances, deepen our relationships with emerging powers, and pursue a stronger role in the region's multilateral architecture, including the Association of Southeast Asian Nations (ASEAN), the Asia Pacific Economic Cooperation forum, the Trans-Pacific Partnership, and the East Asia Summit.

We will continue to pursue a positive, constructive, and comprehensive relationship with China. We welcome a China that takes on a responsible leadership role in working with the United States and the international community to advance priorities like economic recovery, confronting climate change, and nonproliferation. We will monitor China's military modernization program and prepare accordingly to ensure that U.S. interests and allies, regionally and globally, are not negatively affected. More broadly, we will encourage China to make choices that contribute to peace, security, and prosperity as its influence rises. We are using our newly established Strategic and Economic Dialogue to address a broader range of issues, and improve communication between our militaries in order to reduce mistrust. We will encourage continued reduction in tension between the People's Republic of China and Taiwan. We will not agree on every issue, and we will be candid on our human rights concerns and areas where we differ. But disagreements should not prevent cooperation on issues of mutual interest, because a pragmatic and effective relationship between the United States and China is essential to address the major challenges of the 21st century.

The United States and India are building a strategic partnership that is underpinned by our shared interests, our shared values as the world's two largest democracies, and close connections among our people. India's responsible advancement serves as a positive example for developing nations, and provides an opportunity for increased economic, scientific, environmental, and security partnership. Working together through our Strategic Dialogue and high-level visits, we seek a broad-based relationship in which India contributes to global counterterrorism efforts, nonproliferation, and helps promote poverty-reduction, education, health, and sustainable agriculture. We value India's growing leadership on a wide array of global issues, through groups such as the G-20, and will seek to work with India to promote stability in South Asia and elsewhere in the world.

Russia: We seek to build a stable, substantive, multidimensional relationship with Russia, based on mutual interests. The United States has an interest in a strong, peaceful, and prosperous Russia that respects international norms. As the two nations possessing the majority of the world's nuclear weapons, we are working together to advance nonproliferation, both by reducing our nuclear arsenals and by cooperating to ensure that other countries meet their international commitments to reducing the spread of nuclear weapons around the world. We will seek greater partnership with Russia in confronting violent extremism, especially in Afghanistan. We also will seek new trade and investment arrangements for increasing the prosperity of our peoples. We support efforts within Russia to promote the rule of law, accountable government, and universal values. While actively seeking Russia's cooperation to act as a responsible partner in Europe and Asia, we will support the sovereignty and territorial integrity of Russia's neighbors.

Emerging Centers of Influence: Due to increased economic growth and political stability, individual nations are increasingly taking on powerful regional and global roles and changing the landscape of international cooperation. To achieve a just and sustainable order that advances our shared security and prosperity, we are, therefore, deepening our partnerships with emerging powers and encouraging them to play a greater role in strengthening international norms and advancing shared interests.

The rise of the G-20, for example, as the premier international economic forum, represents a distinct shift in our global international order toward greater cooperation between traditional major economies and emerging centers of influence. The nations composing the G-20—from South Korea to South Africa, Saudi Arabia to Argentina—represent at least 80 percent of global gross national product, making it an influential body on the world stage. Stabilizing our global economy, increasing energy efficiency around the globe, and addressing chronic hunger in poor countries are only three examples of the broad global challenges that cannot be solved by a few countries alone.

Indonesia—as the world's fourth most populous country, a member of the G-20, and a democracy—will become an increasingly important partner on regional and transnational issues such as climate change, counterterrorism, maritime security, peacekeeping, and disaster relief. With tolerance, resilience, and multiculturalism as core values, and a flourishing civil society, Indonesia is uniquely positioned to help address challenges facing the developing world.

In the Americas, we are bound by proximity, integrated markets, energy interdependence, a broadly shared commitment to democracy, and the rule of law. Our deep historical, familial, and cultural ties make our alliances and partnerships critical to U.S. interests. We will work in equal partnership to advance economic and social inclusion, safeguard citizen safety and security, promote clean energy, and defend universal values of the people of the hemisphere.

We welcome Brazil's leadership and seek to move beyond dated North-South divisions to pursue progress on bilateral, hemispheric, and global issues. Brazil's macroeconomic success, coupled with its steps to narrow socioeconomic gaps, provide important lessons for countries throughout the Americas and Africa. We will encourage Brazilian efforts against illicit transnational networks. As guardian of a unique national environmental patrimony and a leader in renewable fuels, Brazil is an important partner in confronting global climate change and promoting energy security. And in the context of the G-20 and the Doha round, we will work with Brazil to ensure that economic development and prosperity is broadly shared.

We have an array of enduring interests, longstanding commitments and new opportunities for broadening and deepening relationships in the greater Middle East. This includes maintaining a strong partnership with Israel while supporting Israel's lasting integration into the region. The U.S. also will continue to develop our key security relationships in the region with such Arab states as with Egypt, Jordan, and Saudi Arabia and other Gulf Cooperation Council (GCC) countries—partnerships that enable our militaries and defense systems to work together more effectively.

We have a strategic interest in ensuring that the social and economic needs and political rights of people in this region, who represent one of the world's youngest populations, are met. We will continue to press governments in the region to undertake political reforms and to loosen restrictions on speech, assembly and media. We will maintain our strong support for civil society groups and those individuals who stand up for universal rights. And we will continue to foster partnerships in areas like education, economic growth, science, and health to help expand opportunity. On a multilateral basis, we seek to advance shared security interests, such as through NATO's Istanbul Cooperation Initiative with the GCC, and common interests in promoting governance and institutional reform through participating in the Forum for the Future and other regional dialogues.

The diversity and complexity of the African continent offer the United States opportunities and challenges. As African states grow their economies and strengthen their democratic institutions and governance, America will continue to embrace effective partnerships. Our economic, security, and political cooperation will be consultative and encompass global, regional, and national priorities including access to open markets, conflict prevention, global peacekeeping, counterterrorism, and the protection of vital carbon sinks. The Administration will refocus its priorities on strategic interventions that can promote job creation and economic growth; combat corruption while strengthening good governance and accountability; responsibly improve the capacity of African security and rule of law sectors; and work through diplomatic dialogue to mitigate local and regional tensions before they become crises. We will also reinforce sustainable stability in key states like Nigeria and Kenya that are essential subregional linchpins.

The United States will work to remain an attractive and influential partner by ensuring that African priorities such as infrastructure development, improving reliable access to power, and increased trade and investment remain high on our agenda. South Africa's inclusion in the G-20 should be followed by a growing number of emerging African nations who are charting a course toward improved governance and meaningful development. South Africa's vibrant democracy, combined with its regional and global leadership roles, is a critical partner. From peacemaking to climate change to capacity-building, South Africa brings unique value and perspective to international initiatives. With its strong, diversified, well-managed economy, it often serves as a springboard to the entire African continent, and we will work to pursue shared interests in

Africa's security, growth, and the development of Africa's human capital.

Strengthen Institutions and Mechanisms for Cooperation

Just as U.S. foresight and leadership were essential to forging the architecture for international cooperation after World War II, we must again lead global efforts to modernize the infrastructure for international cooperation in the 21st century. Indeed, our ability to advance peace, security, and opportunity will turn on our ability to strengthen both our national and our multilateral capabilities. To solve problems, we will pursue modes of cooperation that reflect evolving distributions of power and responsibility. We need to assist existing institutions to perform effectively. When they come up short, we must seek meaningful changes and develop alternative mechanisms.

Enhance Cooperation with and Strengthen the United Nations: We are enhancing our coordination with the U.N. and its agencies. We need a U.N. capable of fulfilling its founding purpose—maintaining international peace and security, promoting global cooperation, and advancing human rights. To this end, we are paying our bills. We are intensifying efforts with partners on and outside the U.N. Security Council to ensure timely, robust, and credible Council action to address threats to peace and security. We favor Security Council reform that enhances the U.N.'s overall performance, credibility, and legitimacy. Across the broader U.N. system we support reforms that promote effective and efficient leadership and management of the U.N.'s international civil service, and we are working with U.N. personnel and member states to strengthen the U.N.'s leadership and operational capacity in peacekeeping, humanitarian relief, post-disaster recovery, development assistance, and the promotion of human rights. And we are supporting new U.N. frameworks and capacities for combating transnational threats like proliferation of weapons of mass destruction, infectious disease, drug-trafficking, and counterterrorism.

Pursue Decisions though a Wide Range of Frameworks and Coalitions: We need to spur and harness a new diversity of instruments, alliances, and institutions in which a division of labor emerges on the basis of effectiveness, competency, and long-term reliability. This requires enhanced coordination among the United Nations, regional organizations, international financial institutions, specialized agencies, and other actors that are better placed or equipped to manage certain threats and challenges. We are attempting to forge new agreement on common global challenges among the world's leading and emerging powers to ensure that multilateral cooperation reflects the sustained commitment of influential countries. While we are pursuing G-8 initiatives with proven and long-standing partners, have begun to shift the focus of our economic coordination to the G-20, which is more reflective of today's diffusion of power and the need to enlist the efforts of a broader spectrum of countries across Asia to Europe, Africa to the Middle East, and our neighbors in the Americas. We are also renewing U.S. leadership in the multilateral development banks and the IMF, and leveraging our engagement and investments in these institutions to strengthen the global economy, lift people out of poverty, advance food security, address climate and pandemics, and secure fragile states such as Afghanistan and Haiti.

Invest in Regional Capabilities: Regional organizations can be particularly effective at mobilizing and legitimating cooperation among countries closest to the problem. Regional organizations— whether NATO, the Organization for Security Cooperation in Europe, the Organization of the Islamic Conference, the African Union, Organization of American States, or ASEAN, and the Gulf Cooperation Council—vary widely in their membership, constitutions, histories, orientation, and operational capabilities. That variety needs to inform a strategic approach to their evolving roles and relative contributions to global security. The United States is encouraging continued innovation and development of enhanced regional capabilities in the context of an evolving division of labor among local, national, and global institutions that seeks to leverage relative capacities. Where appropriate, we use training and related programs to strengthen regional capacities for peacekeeping and conflict management to improve impact and share burdens. We will also encourage a more comprehensive approach to regional security that brings balanced focus to issues such as food security, global health, and education; access to more affordable and greener forms of energy; access to fair and efficient justice; and a concerted effort to promote transparency at all levels and to fight the corrosive effect of corruption.

Sustain Broad Cooperation on Key Global Challenges

Many of today's challenges cannot be solved by one nation or even a group of nations. The test of our international order, therefore, will be its ability to facilitate the broad and effective global cooperation necessary to meet 21st century challenges. Many of these challenges have been discussed previously, including violent extremism, nuclear proliferation, and promotion of global prosperity. In addition, other key challenges requiring broad global cooperation include:

Climate Change: The danger from climate change is real, urgent, and severe. The change wrought by a warming planet will lead to new conflicts over refugees and resources; new suffering from drought and famine; catastrophic natural disasters; and the degradation of land across the globe. The United States will therefore confront climate change based upon clear guidance from the science, and in cooperation with all nations—for there is no effective solution to climate change that does not depend upon all nations taking responsibility for their own actions and for the planet we will leave behind.

- **Home:** Our effort begins with the steps that we are taking at home. We will stimulate our energy economy at home, reinvigorate the U.S. domestic nuclear industry, increase our efficiency standards, invest in renewable energy, and provide the incentives that make clean energy the profitable kind of energy. This will allow us to make deep cuts in emissions—in the range of 17 percent by 2020 and more than 80 percent by 2050. This will depend in part upon comprehensive legislation and its effective implementation.

- **Abroad:** Regionally, we will build on efforts in Asia, the Americas, and Africa to forge new clean energy partnerships. Globally, we will seek to implement and build on the Copenhagen Accord, and ensure a response to climate change that draws upon decisive action by all nations. Our goal is an effective, international effort in which all major economies commit to ambitious national action to reduce their emissions, nations meet their commitments in a transparent manner, and the necessary financing is mobilized so that developing countries can adapt to climate change, mitigate its impacts, conserve forests, and invest in clean energy technologies. We will pursue this global cooperation through multiple avenues, with a focus on advancing cooperation that works. We accept the principle of common but differentiated responses and respective capabilities, but will insist that any approach draws upon each nation taking responsibility for its own actions.

Peacekeeping and Armed Conflict: The untold loss of human life, suffering, and property damage that results from armed conflict necessitates that all responsible nations work to prevent it. No single nation can or should shoulder the burden for managing or resolving the world's armed conflicts. To this end, we will place renewed emphasis on deterrence and prevention by mobilizing diplomatic action, and use development and security sector assistance to build the capacity of at-risk nations and reduce the appeal of violent extremism. But when international forces are needed to respond to threats and keep the peace, we will work with international partners to ensure they are ready, able, and willing. We will continue to build support in other countries to contribute to sustaining global peace and stability operations, through U.N. peacekeeping and regional organizations, such as NATO and the African Union. We will continue to broaden the pool of troop and police contributors, working to ensure that they are properly trained and equipped, that their mandates are matched to means, and that their missions are backed by the political action necessary to build and sustain peace.

In Sudan, which has been marred by violent conflict for decades, the United States remains committed to working with the international community to support implementation of outstanding elements of the Comprehensive Peace Agreement and ensure that the referendum on the future of Southern Sudan in 2011 happens on time and that its results are respected. In addition, we will continue to engage in the efforts necessary to support peace and stability after the referendum, and continue to work to secure peace, dignity, and accountability in Darfur.

- **Prevent Genocide and Mass Atrocities:** The United States and all member states of the U.N. have endorsed the concept of the "Responsibility to Protect." In so doing, we have recognized that the primary responsibility for preventing genocide and mass atrocity rests with sovereign governments, but that this responsibility passes to the broader international community when sovereign governments themselves commit genocide or mass atrocities, or when they prove unable or unwilling to take necessary action to prevent or respond to such crimes inside their borders. The United States is committed to working with our allies, and to strengthening our own internal capabilities, in order to ensure that the United States and the international community are proactively engaged in a strategic effort to prevent mass atrocities and genocide. In the event that prevention fails, the United States will work both multilaterally and bilaterally to mobilize diplomatic, humanitarian, financial, and—in certain instances—military means to prevent and respond to genocide and mass atrocities.

- **International Justice:** From Nuremberg to Yugoslavia to Liberia, the United States has seen that the end of impunity and the promotion of justice are not just moral imperatives; they are stabilizing forces in international affairs. The United States is thus working to strengthen national justice systems and is maintaining our support for ad hoc international tribunals and hybrid courts. Those who intentionally target innocent civilians must be held accountable, and we will continue to support institutions and prosecutions that advance this important interest. Although the United States is not at present a party to the Rome Statute of the International Criminal Court (ICC), and will always protect U.S. personnel, we are engaging with State Parties to the Rome Statute on issues of concern and are supporting the ICC's prosecution of those cases that advance U.S. interests and values, consistent with the requirements of U.S. law.

Pandemics and Infectious Disease: The threat of contagious disease transcends political boundaries, and the ability to prevent, quickly detect and contain outbreaks with pandemic potential has never been so important. An epidemic that begins in a single community can quickly evolve into a multinational health crisis that causes millions to suffer, as well as spark major disruptions to travel and trade. Addressing these transnational risks requires advance preparation, extensive collaboration with the global community, and the development of a resilient population at home.

Recognizing that the health of the world's population has never been more interdependent, we are improving our public health and medical capabilities on the front lines, including domestic and international disease surveillance, situational awareness, rapid and reliable development of medical countermeasures to respond to public health threats, preparedness education and training, and surge capacity of the domestic health care system to respond to an influx of patients due to a disaster or emergency. These capabilities include our ability to work with international partners to mitigate and contain disease when necessary.

We are enhancing international collaboration and strengthening multilateral institutions in order to improve global surveillance and early warning capabilities and quickly enact control and containment measures against the next pandemic threat. We continue to improve our understanding of emerging diseases and help develop environments that are less conducive to epidemic emergence. We depend on U.S. overseas laboratories, relationships with host nation governments, and the willingness of states to share health data with nongovernmental and international organizations. In this regard, we need to continue to work to overcome the lack of openness and a general reluctance to share health information. Finally, we seek to mitigate other problem areas, including limited global vaccine production capacity, and the threat of emergent and reemergent disease in poorly governed states.

Transnational Criminal Threats and Threats to Governance: Transnational criminal threats and illicit trafficking networks continue to expand dramatically in size, scope, and influence—posing significant national security challenges for the United States and our partner countries. These threats cross borders and continents and undermine the stability of nations, subverting government institutions through corruption and harming citizens worldwide. Transnational criminal organizations have accumulated unprecedented wealth and power through trafficking and other illicit activities, penetrating legitimate financial systems and destabilizing commercial markets. They extend their reach by forming alliances with government officials and some state security services. The crime-terror nexus is a serious concern as terrorists use criminal networks for logistical support and funding. Increasingly, these networks are involved in cyber crime, which cost consumers billions of dollars annually, while undermining global confidence in the international financial system.

Combating transnational criminal and trafficking networks requires a multidimensional strategy that safeguards citizens, breaks the financial strength of criminal and terrorist networks, disrupts illicit trafficking networks, defeats transnational criminal organizations, fights government corruption, strengthens the rule of law, bolsters judicial systems, and improves transparency. While these are major challenges, the United States will be able to devise and execute a collective strategy with other nations facing the same threats.

Safeguarding the Global Commons: Across the globe, we must work in concert with allies and partners to optimize the use of shared sea, air, and space domains. These shared areas, which exist outside exclusive national jurisdictions, are the connective tissue around our globe upon which all nations' security and prosperity depend. The United States will continue to help safeguard access, promote security, and ensure the sustainable use of resources in these domains. These efforts require strong multilateral cooperation, enhanced domain awareness and monitoring, and the strengthening of international norms and standards.

We must work together to ensure the constant flow of commerce, facilitate safe and secure air travel, and prevent disruptions to critical communications. We must also safeguard the sea, air, and space domains from those who would deny access or use them for hostile purposes. This includes keeping strategic straits and vital sea lanes open, improving the early detection of emerging maritime threats, denying adversaries hostile use of the air domain, and ensuring the responsible use of space. As one key effort in the sea domain, for example, we will pursue ratification of the United Nations Convention on the Law of the Sea.

Many of these goals are equally applicable to cyberspace. While cyberspace relies on the digital infrastructure of individual countries, such infrastructure is globally connected, and securing it requires global cooperation. We will push for the recognition of norms of behavior in cyberspace, and otherwise work with global partners to ensure the protection of the free flow of information and our continued access. At all times, we will continue to defend our digital networks from intrusion and harmful disruption.

Arctic Interests: The United States is an Arctic Nation with broad and fundamental interests in the Arctic region, where we seek to meet our national security needs, protect the environment, responsibly manage resources, account for indigenous communities, support scientific research, and strengthen international cooperation on a wide range of issues.

IV. Conclusion

"It's easy to forget that, when this war began, we were united, bound together by the fresh memory of a horrific attack and by the determination to defend our homeland and the values we hold dear. I refuse to accept the notion that we cannot summon that unity again. I believe with every fiber of my being that we, as Americans, can still come together behind a common purpose, for our values are not simply words written into parchment. They are a creed that calls us together and that has carried us through the darkest of storms as one nation, as one people."

—*President Barack Obama,*
West Point, New York, December 2, 2009

This strategy calls for a comprehensive range of national actions, and a broad conception of what constitutes our national security. Above all, it is about renewing our leadership by calling upon what is best about America—our innovation and capacity; our openness and moral imagination.

Success will require approaches that can be sustained and achieve results. One of the reasons that this nation succeeded in the second half of the 20th century was its capacity to pursue policies and build institutions that endured across multiple Administrations, while also preserving the flexibility to endure setbacks and to make necessary adjustments. In some instances, the United States has been able to carry forward this example in the years since the Cold War. But there are also many open questions, unfinished reforms, and deep divisions—at home and abroad—that constrain our ability to advance our interests and renew our leadership.

To effectively craft and implement a sustainable, results-oriented national security strategy, there must be effective cooperation between the branches of government. This Administration believes that we are strong when we act in line with our laws, as the Constitution itself demands. This Administration is also committed to active consultation with Congress, and welcomes robust and effective oversight of its national security policies. We welcome Congress as a full partner in forging durable solutions to tough challenges, looking beyond the headlines to take a long view of America's interests. And we encourage Congress to pursue oversight in line with the reforms that have been enacted through legislation, particularly in the years since 9/11.

The executive branch must do its part by developing integrated plans and approaches that leverage the capabilities across its departments and agencies to deal with the issues we confront. Collaboration across the government—and with our partners at the state, local, and tribal levels of government, in industry, and abroad—must guide our actions.

This kind of effective cooperation will depend upon broad and bipartisan cooperation. Throughout the Cold War, even as there were intense disagreements about certain courses of action, there remained a belief that America's political leaders shared common goals, even if they differed about how to reach them. In today's political environment, due to the actions of both parties that sense of common purpose is at times lacking in our national security dialogue. This division places the United States at a strategic disadvantage. It sets back our ability to deal with difficult challenges and injects a sense of anxiety and polarization into our politics that can affect our policies and our posture around the world. It must be replaced by a renewed sense of civility and a commitment to embrace our common purpose as Americans.

Americans are by nature a confident and optimistic people. We would not have achieved our position of leadership in the world without the extraordinary strength of our founding documents and the capability and courage of generations of Americans who gave life to those values—through their service, through their sacrifices, through their aspirations, and through their pursuit of a more perfect union. We see those same qualities today, particularly in our young men and women in uniform who have served tour after tour of duty to defend our nation in harm's way, and their civilian counterparts.

This responsibility cannot be theirs alone. And there is no question that we, as a nation, can meet our responsibility as Americans once more. Even in a world of enormous challenges, no threat is bigger than the American peoples' capacity to meet it, and no opportunity exceeds our reach. We continue to draw strength from those founding documents that established the creed that binds us together. We, too, can demonstrate the capability and courage to pursue a more perfect union and—in doing so—renew American leadership in the world.

Strengthening National Capacity—A Whole of Government Approach

To succeed, we must update, balance, and integrate all of the tools of American power and work with our allies and partners to do the same. Our military must maintain its conventional superiority and, as long as nuclear weapons exist, our nuclear deterrent capability, while continuing to enhance its capacity to defeat asymmetric threats, preserve access to the global commons, and strengthen partners. We must invest in diplomacy and development capabilities and institutions in a way that complements and reinforces our global partners. Our intelligence capabilities must continuously evolve to identify and characterize conventional and asymmetric threats and provide timely insight. And we must integrate our approach to homeland security with our broader national security approach.

We are improving the integration of skills and capabilities within our military and civilian institutions, so they complement each other and operate seamlessly. We are also improving coordinated planning and policymaking and must build our capacity in key areas where we fall short. This requires close cooperation with Congress and a deliberate and inclusive interagency process, so that we achieve integration of our efforts to implement and monitor operations, policies, and strategies. To initiate this effort, the White House merged the staffs of the National Security Council and Homeland Security Council.

However, work remains to foster coordination across departments and agencies. Key steps include more effectively ensuring alignment of resources with our national security strategy, adapting the education and training of national security professionals to equip them to meet modern challenges, reviewing authorities and mechanisms to implement and coordinate assistance programs, and other policies and programs that strengthen coordination.

Defense: We are strengthening our military to ensure that it can prevail in today's wars; to prevent and deter threats against the United States, its interests, and our allies and partners; and prepare to defend the United States in a wide range of contingencies against state and nonstate actors. We will continue to rebalance our military capabilities to excel at counterterrorism, counterinsurgency, stability operations, and meeting increasingly sophisticated security threats, while ensuring our force is ready to address the full range of military operations. This includes preparing for increasingly sophisticated adversaries, deterring and defeating aggression in anti-access environments, and defending the United States and supporting civil authorities at home. The most valuable component of our national defense is the men and women who make up America's all-volunteer force. They have shown tremendous resilience, adaptability, and capacity for innovation, and we will provide our service members with the resources that they need to succeed and rededicate ourselves to providing support and care for wounded warriors, veterans, and military families. We must set the force on a path to sustainable deployment cycles and preserve and enhance the long-term viability of our force through successful recruitment, retention, and recognition of those who serve.

Diplomacy: Diplomacy is as fundamental to our national security as our defense capability. Our diplomats are the first line of engagement, listening to our partners, learning from them, building respect for one another, and seeking common ground. Diplomats, development experts, and others in the United States Government must be able to work side by side to support a common agenda. New skills are needed to foster effective interaction to convene, connect, and mobilize not only other governments and international organizations, but also nonstate actors such as corporations, foundations, nongovernmental organizations, universities, think tanks, and faith-based organizations, all of whom increasingly have a distinct role to play on both diplomatic and development issues. To accomplish these goals our diplomatic personnel and missions must be expanded at home and abroad to support the increasingly transnational nature of 21st century security challenges. And we must provide the appropriate authorities and mechanisms to implement and coordinate assistance programs and grow the civilian expeditionary capacity required to assist governments on a diverse array of issues.

Economic: Our economic institutions are crucial components of our national capacity and our economic instruments are the bedrock of sustainable national growth, prosperity and influence. The Office of Management and Budget, Departments of the Treasury, State, Commerce, Energy, and Agriculture, United States Trade Representative, Federal Reserve Board, and other institutions help manage our currency, trade, foreign investment, deficit, inflation, productivity, and national competitiveness. Remaining a vibrant 21st century economic power also requires close cooperation between and among developed nations and emerging markets because of the interdependent nature of the global economy. America—like other nations—is dependent upon overseas markets to sell its exports and maintain access to scarce commodities and resources. Thus, finding overlapping mutual economic interests with other nations and maintaining those economic relationships are key elements of our national security strategy.

Development: Development is a strategic, economic, and moral imperative. We are focusing on assisting developing countries and their people to manage security threats, reap the benefits of global economic expansion, and set in place accountable and democratic institutions that serve basic human needs. Through an aggressive and affirmative development agenda and commensurate resources, we can strengthen the regional partners we need to help us stop conflicts and counter global criminal networks; build a stable, inclusive global economy with new sources of prosperity; advance democracy and human rights; and ultimately position ourselves to better address key global challenges by growing the ranks of prosperous, capable, and democratic states that can be our partners in the decades ahead. To do this, we are expanding our civilian development capability; engaging with international financial institutions that leverage our resources and advance our objectives; pursuing a development budget that more deliberately reflects our policies and our strategy, not sector earmarks; and ensuring that our policy instruments are aligned in support of development objectives.

Homeland Security: Homeland security traces its roots to traditional and historic functions of government and society, such as civil defense, emergency response, law enforcement, customs, border patrol, and immigration. In the aftermath of 9/11 and the foundation of the Department of Homeland Security, these functions have taken on new organization and urgency. Homeland security, therefore, strives to adapt these traditional functions to confront new threats and evolving hazards. It is not simply about government action alone, but rather about the collective strength of the entire country. Our approach relies on our shared efforts to identify and interdict threats; deny hostile actors the ability to operate within our borders; maintain effective control of our physical borders; safeguard lawful trade and travel into and out of the United States; disrupt and dismantle transnational terrorist, and criminal organizations; and ensure our national resilience in the face of the threat and hazards. Taken together, these efforts must support a homeland that is safe and secure from terrorism and other hazards and in which American interests, aspirations, and way of life can thrive.

Intelligence: Our country's safety and prosperity depend on the quality of the intelligence we collect and the analysis we produce, our ability to evaluate and share this information in a timely manner, and our ability to counter intelligence threats. This is as true for the strategic intelligence that informs executive decisions as it is for intelligence support to homeland security, state, local, and tribal governments, our troops, and critical national missions. We are working to better integrate the Intelligence Community, while also enhancing the capabilities of our Intelligence Community members. We are strengthening our partnerships with foreign intelligence services and sustaining strong ties with our close allies. And we continue to invest in the men and women of the Intelligence Community.

Strategic Communications: Across all of our efforts, effective strategic communications are essential to sustaining global legitimacy and supporting our policy aims. Aligning our actions with our words is a shared responsibility that must be fostered by a culture of communication throughout government. We must also be more effective in our deliberate communication and engagement and do a better job understanding the attitudes, opinions, grievances, and concerns of peoples—not just elites around the world. Doing so allows us to convey credible, consistent messages and to develop effective plans, while better understanding how our actions will be perceived. We must also use a broad range of methods for communicating with foreign publics, including new media.

The American People and the Private Sector: The ideas, values, energy, creativity, and resilience of our citizens are America's greatest resource. We will support the development of prepared, vigilant, and engaged communities and underscore that our citizens are the heart of a resilient country. And we must tap the ingenuity outside government through strategic partnerships with the private sector, nongovernmental organizations, foundations, and community-based organizations. Such partnerships are critical to U.S. success at home and abroad, and we will support them through enhanced opportunities for engagement, coordination, transparency, and information sharing.

Use of Force

Military force, at times, may be necessary to defend our country and allies or to preserve broader peace and security, including by protecting civilians facing a grave humanitarian crisis. We will draw on diplomacy, development, and international norms and institutions to help resolve disagreements, prevent conflict, and maintain peace, mitigating where possible the need for the use of force. This means credibly underwriting U.S. defense commitments with tailored approaches to deterrence and ensuring the U.S. military continues to have the necessary capabilities across all domains—land, air, sea, space, and cyber. It also includes helping our allies and partners build capacity to fulfill their responsibilities to contribute to regional and global security.

While the use of force is sometimes necessary, we will exhaust other options before war whenever we can, and carefully weigh the costs and risks of action against the costs and risks of inaction. When force is necessary, we will continue to do so in a way that reflects our values and strengthens our legitimacy, and we will seek broad international support, working with such institutions as NATO and the U.N. Security Council.

The United States must reserve the right to act unilaterally if necessary to defend our nation and our interests, yet we will also seek to adhere to standards that govern the use of force. Doing so strengthens those who act in line with international standards, while isolating and weakening those who do not. We will also outline a clear mandate and specific objectives and thoroughly consider the consequences—intended and unintended—of our actions. And the United States will take care when sending the men and women of our Armed Forces into harm's way to ensure they have the leadership, training, and equipment they require to accomplish their mission.

NOTES

Chapter 1

1. "Barack Obama's Feb. 5 Speech," *New York Times*, February 5, 2008; available at: http://www.nytimes.com/2008/02/05/us/politics/05text-obama.html [accessed July 13, 2010].
2. Ibid.
3. Tim Jones, "Barack Obama: Mother not just a girl from Kansas," *Chicago Tribune,* March 27, 2007; available at: http://www.chicagotribune.com/news/politics/obama/chi-0703270151mar27-archive,0,5853572,full.story [accessed July 13, 2010].
4. Barack Obama, *Dreams from My Father* (New York: Crown Publishers, 1995, 2004), 50.
5. Aaron Klein, "Obama tied to Ayers...at age 11," *WorldNet Daily*, June 19, 2009; available at: http://www.wnd.com/?pageId=101566 [accessed July 13, 2010].

6. Barack Obama is perhaps the first president in history to have written two autobiographies before the age of fifty—and before he'd achieved anything of substance.

7. Barack Obama, *Dreams from My Father*, 76–77.

8. Ibid.

9. Toby Harnden, "Frank Marshall Davis, alleged Communist, was early influence on Barack Obama," *Telegraph*, August 22, 2008; available at: http://www.telegraph.co.uk/news/worldnews/north-america/usa/barackobama/2601914/Frank-Marshall-Davis-alleged-Communist-was-early-influence-on-Barack-Obama.html [accessed July 13, 2010].

10. Barack Obama, *Dreams from My Father*, 100–1.

11. Saul D. Alinsky, *Rules for Radicals: A Practical Primer for Realistic Radicals* (New York: Vintage Books, 1989), xiii.

12. Ibid.

13. Ibid.

14. Peter Slevin, "For Clinton and Obama, a Common Ideological Touchstone," *Washington Post*, March 25, 2007; available at: http://www.washingtonpost.com/wp-dyn/content/article/2007/03/24/AR2007032401152.html [accessed July 13, 2010].

15. Saul D. Alinsky, *Rules for Radicals*, 113.

16. Richard Poe, *Turrish Weekly*, "The Chicago Connection: Hillary, Obama and the cult of Alinsky," CatholicCitizens.org, March 2, 2008; available at: http://www.catholiccitizens.org/platform/platformview.asp?c=45262 [accessed July 13, 2010].

17. L. David Alinsky, Letter to the Editor, "Son sees father's handiwork in convention," *Boston Globe*, August 31, 2008; available at: http://www.boston.com/bostonglobe/editorial_opinion/letters/articles/2008/08/31/son_sees_fathers_handiwork_in_convention/ [accessed July 13, 2010].

18. "Transcript: Obama and Clinton Debate," *ABC News*; available at: http://abcnews.go.com/Politics/DemocraticDebate/story?id=4670271&page=2 [accessed July 13, 2010].

19. See for instance Jack Cashill, "Book Confirms: Ayers wrote Obama's book," *WorldNetDaily*, September 23, 2009; available at:

http://www.wnd.com/index.php?pageId=110781 [accessed July 13, 2010].

20. Scott Swett and Roger Canfield, "Obama's Foul Weather Friends," *American Thinker*, September 16, 2008; available at: http://www.americanthinker.com/2008/09/obamas_foul_weather_fri ends.html [accessed July 13, 2001].

21. Ronald Radosh, "Don't Need a Weatherman," *Weekly Standard*, October 8, 2001, vol. 7, issue 4; available at: http://www.weeklystandard.com/Content/Public/Articles/000/000/00 0/267rdlhy.asp [accessed July 13, 2010].

22. Dinitia Smith, "No Regrets for a Love of Explosives; In a Memoir of Sorts, a War Protestor Talks of Life with the Weathermen," *New York Times*, September 11, 2001; available at: http://www.nytimes.com/2001/09/11/books/no-regrets-for-love-explosives-memoir-sorts-war-protester-talks-life-with.html [accessed July 13, 2010].

23. Hope Reeves, "The Way We Live Now: 9-16-01: Questions for Bill Ayers; Forever Rad," *New York Times Magazine*, September 16, 2001; available at: http://www.nytimes.com/2001/09/16/ maga-zine/the-way-we-live-now-9-16-01-questions-for-bill-ayers-forever-rad.html?ref=william_c_ayers [accessed July 13, 2010].

24. Sasha Issenberg, "Pride in the name of self-love," *Boston Globe*, February 18, 2008; available at: http://www.boston.com/news/ poli-tics/politicalintelligence/2008/02/pride_in_the_na.html [accessed July 13, 2010].

25. Duncan Campbell, "Most Wanted," *The Guardian*, October 18, 2001.

26. David Horowitz, "Allies in War," FrontPageMagazine.com, September 17, 2001; available at: http://97.74.65.51/readArticle.aspx? ARTID=24446 [accessed July 13, 2010].

27. Judi McLeod, "Stopping the Revolution in its tracks," *Canada Free Press*, November 2, 2008; available at: http://www.canadafreepress.com/index.php/article/5991 [accessed July 13, 2010].

28. John Howard, "Exclusive: Obama – The One They've Been Waiting For (Part One of Two)," Family Security Matters, October14, 2008; available at: http://www.familysecuritymatters.org/publications/ id.1458/pub_detail.asp [accessed July 13, 2010].

29. Jack Kelly, "Obama's Fishy Associations," *Pittsburgh Post-Gazette*, October 12, 2008; available at: http://www.post-gazette.com/pg/08286/919158-373.stm [accessed July 13, 2010].

30. Fred Lucas, "Despite Campaign Claim, Obama Told Paper He Attended Trinity Church 'Every Week,'" CNS News, November 13, 2008; available at: http://www.cnsnews.com/public/content/ article.aspx?RsrcID=39273 [accessed July 13, 2010].

31. Tom Baldwin, "Barack Obama distances himself from pastor who denounced 'racist' US," *The Sunday Times*, March 15, 2008; available at: http://www.timesonline.co.uk/tol/news/world/us_-and_americas/us_elections/article3555561.ece [accessed July 13, 2010].

32. Jeremiah A. Wright, Jr., biography, http://www.discoverthe networks.org/individualProfile.asp?indid=2307 [accessed July 13, 2010].

33. Victor Davis Hanson, "A Weird Campaign Gets Weirder," *National Review Online*, the Corner, October 11, 2008; available at: http://www.nationalreview.com/corner/171830/weird-campaign-gets-weirder/victor-davis-hanson [accessed July 13, 2010].

34. Steve Waldman, "Obama's Fascinating Interview with Cathleen Falsani," *Christianity Today*, November 11, 2008; available at: http://blog.christianitytoday.com/ctpolitics/2008/11/obamas_fascinat.html [accessed July 13, 2010].

35. Paul Sperry, "Obama's 9/11 Prism," *Front Page Magazine*, September 11, 2009; available at: http://97.74.65.51/readArticle.aspx?ARTID=36247 [accessed July 13, 2010].

36. Brian Ross and Rehab El-Buri, "Obama's Pastor: God Damn America, U.S. to Blame for 9/11," *ABC News,* The Blotter, March 13, 2008; available at: http://abcnews.go.com/Blotter/DemocraticDebate/story?id=4443788&page=1 [accessed July 13, 2010].

37. Ron Kessler, "Obama Minister's Hatred of America," NewsMax.com, March 6, 2008; available at: http://www.newsmax.com/RonaldKessler/obama-minister-wright/2008/03/06/id/323105 [accessed July 13, 2010].

38. See the Code Pink Website, http://www.codepink4peace.org/ article.php?list=type&type=3.

39. Kristinn Taylor and Andrea Shea King, "A Name Americans Should Know—Jodie Evans and the Obama-Hollywood-Terrorist Connection," BigGovernment.com, October 23, 2009; available at: http://biggovernment.com/taylorking/2009/10/23/a-name-americans should-know-jodie-evans-and-the-obama-hollywood-terrorist-connection/ [accessed July 13, 2010].

40. Ibid.

41. Wesley Pruden, "Back to the old days, if only for a minute," *Jewish World Review*, September 22, 2006; available at: http://jewishworldreview.com/cols/pruden092206.php3 [accessed July 13, 2010].

42. Kristinn Taylor and Andrea Shea King, "Obama Ally Code Pink Invites Muslim Brotherhood: 'Join Us in Cleansing Our Country,'" BigGovernment.com, January 11, 2010; available at: http://biggovernment.com/taylorking/2010/01/11/obama-ally-code-pink-invites-muslim-brotherhood-join-us-in-cleansing-our-country/ [accessed July 13, 2010].

43. Iraq Occupation Watch (IOW), biography, http://www.discoverthe networks.org/groupProfile.asp?grpid=6785.

44. "Jodie Evans: Witnessing the U.S. Occupation of Iraq," *Revolutionary Worker*, August 17, 2003; available at: http://www.revcom.us/a/1210/codepink-iraq.htm [accessed July 13, 2010].

45. Tariq Ali, biography, http://www.discoverthenetworks.org /individualProfile.asp?indid=898.

46. Ben Johnson, "Obama's Bundler, Osama's Enabler," *Front Page Magazine*, June 20, 2008; available at: http://97.74.65.51/readArticle.aspx?ARTID=31412 [accessed July 13, 2010].

47. "Relatives of US Servicemen Killed in Iraq to Hold Vigil on Jordan Border," *Agence France–Presse*, December 31, 2004.

48. Adam Wild Aba, "Bereaved US Families Share Iraqis Agonies of War," January 4, 2005, IslamOnline.net; available at: http://www.islamonline.net/English/News/2005-01/04/article05.shtml [accessed July 13, 2010].

49. Ibid.

50. Biography, Middle East Children's Alliance (MECA), http://www.discoverthenetworks.org/groupProfile.asp?grpid=6158.

51. Kristinn Taylor and Andrea Shea-King, "A Name Americans Should Know-Jodie Evans and the Obama-Hollywood-Terrorist Connection," *op. cit.*

52. Marc Morano, "Anti-War Protests Target Wounded at Army Hospital," CNS News, August 25, 2005.

53. Ibid.

54. Kristinn Taylor and Andrea Shea King, "Obama Ally Code Pink Targets Children of Military Families for Psychological Abuse," BigGovernment.com; available at: http://biggovernment.com/taylorking /2009/11/09/obama-ally-code-pink-targets-children-of-military-families-for-psychological-abuse/ [accessed July 13, 2010].

55. Ibid.

56. John Steele Gordon, "Bring back the old glory: It's time to rescue the idea that America is exceptional, says historian," *New York Daily News*, July 4, 2010; available at: http://www.nydailynews.com/opinions/2010/07/04/2010-07-04_bring_back_the_old_glory_its_time_to_rescue_the_idea_that_america_is_exceptional.html [accessed July 13, 2010].

Chapter 2

1. Laura Blumenfeld, "Soros Deep Pockets vs. Bush Financier Contributes $5 Million More in Effort to Oust President," *Washington Post*, November 11, 2003; available at: http://www.washingtonpost.com/ac2/wp-dyn/A24179-2003Nov10?language=printer [accessed July 22, 2010].

2. Jim O'Neill, "Soros: Public Enemy # 1," *Canada Free Press*, September 15, 2009; available at: http://www.canadafreepress.com/index.php/article/14700 [accessed July 22, 2010].

3. Michael McKee, "Soros Says Kerry's Failings Undermined Campaign Against Bush," Bloomberg, January 30, 2005; available at: http://www.bloomberg.com/apps/news?pid=newsarchive&refer=top _world_news&sid=aqkoN4tLMDv8 [accessed July 22, 2010].

4. "Shadow Party defined," http://www.discoverthenetworks.org/ viewSubCategory.asp?id=842 [accessed July 22, 2010].

5. "Guide to the George Soros Network," http://www.discoverthenetworks.org/viewSubCategory.asp?id=589 [accessed July 22, 2010].

6. George Soros biography, http://www.discoverthenetworks.org/ printindividualProfile.asp?indid=977 [accessed July 22, 2010].

7. "Profile of Barack Obama, from Birth through Election Day 2008," http://www.discoverthenetworks.org/individualProfile.asp?indid=15 11 [accessed July 22, 2010].

8. Center for American Progress (CAP) biography, http://www.discoverthenetworks.org/groupProfile.asp?grpid=6709 [accessed July 22, 2010].

9. Matt Bai, "Notion Building," *New York Times* magazine, October 12, 2003; available at http://www.nytimes.com/2003/10/12/ magazine/12PODESTA.html [accessed July 22, 2010].

10. Edward Chen, "Soros-Funded Democratic Idea Factory Becomes Obama Policy Font," Bloomberg, November 18, 2008; available at: http://www.bloomberg.com/apps/news?pid=washingtonstory&sid=a F7fB1PF0NPg [accessed July 22, 2010].

11. "Obama Declares His Candidacy," *ABC News*, February 10, 2007; available at: http://abcnews.go.com/GMA/Politics/ story?id=2865196&page=1 [accessed July 22, 2010].

12. Kyle-Anne Shiver, "What Soros Wanted, Obama Delivers," *American Thinker*, October 14, 2009; available at: http://www.americanthinker.com/2009/10/what_soros_wanted_oba ma_delive.html [accessed July 22, 2010].

13. "MoveOn Endorsement Throws Progressive Weight Behind Barack Obama," MoveOn.org, February 1, 2008; available at: http://moveon.org/press/pr/obamaendorsementrelease.html [accessed July 22, 2010].

14. Richard Baehr, "Soros and Hillary: Partner's on Israel?" *The American Thinker*, May 10, 2007; available at: http://www.americanthinker.com/2007/05/the_soros_political_machi ne.html [accessed July 22, 2010].

15. Van Jones biography, http://www.discoverthenetworks.org /individualProfile.asp?indid=2406 [accessed July 22, 2010].

16. Jeff Zeleny, "Obama Weighs Quick Undoing of Bush Policy," *New York Times*, November 9, 2008; available at: http://www.nytimes.com/2008/11/10/us/politics/10obama.html [accessed July 22, 2010].

Chapter 3

1. Dennis Miller, *The O'Reilly Factor*, Fox News Network, May 31, 2010; available at: http://www.foxnews.com/story/ 0,2933,584177,00.html [accessed July 16, 2010].

2. Mike Glover, Associated Press, "Gingrich Weighing Run for White House," *Washington Times*, July 12, 2010; available at: http://www.washingtontimes.com/news/2010/jul/12/gingrich-weigh-ing-run-for-white-house/ [accessed July 16, 2010].

3. Charles Krauthammer, "Obama: Modest about U.S., not Himself," *Chicago Tribune*, July 12, 2010; available at: http://articles.chicagotribune.com/2010-07-12/news/ct-oped-0712-krauthammer-20100712_1_american-exceptionalism-equivalence-charles-bolden [accessed July 16, 2010].

4. You can find Jeane Kirkpatrick's speech online at http://www.cnn.com/ALLPOLITICS/1996/conventions/san.diego/-facts/GOP.speeches.past/84.kirkpatrick.shtml [accessed July 16, 2010].

5. Tim Reid, "Barack Obama's 'guns and religion' blunder gives Hillary Clinton a chance," *The Times* of London, April 14, 2008; available at: http://www.timesonline.co.uk/tol/news/ world/us_and_americas/us_elections/article3740080.ece [accessed July 16, 2010].

6. Toby Young, "President Barack Obama; America has been 'arrogant and dismissive' towards Europe," *The Daily Telegraph,* April 3, 2009; available at: http://www.telegraph.co.uk/news/ world-news/northamerica/usa/barackobama/5101244/President-Barack-Obama-America-has-been-arrogant-and-dismissive-towards-Europe. html [accessed July 16, 2010].

7. Jim Hoft, "Obama Bashes Bush in France—Apologizes for Liberat-ing Iraq," *First Things,* April 3, 2009; available at: http://gatewaypundit.firstthings.com/2009/04/obama-bashes-bush-in-france-apologizes-for-liberating-iraq/ [accessed July 16, 2010].

8. Jim Hoft, "Stunner… Obama Apologizes for America Again at the United Nations," *First Things,* September 23, 2009; available at: http://gatewaypundit.firstthings.com/2009/09/stunner-obama-apolo-gizes-for-america-again-at-united-nations/ [accessed July 16, 2010].

9. Nile Gardiner, "The UN loves Barack Obama because he is weak," *The London Daily Telegraph,* September 23, 2009; available at: http://www.telegraph.co.uk/news/worldnews/northamerica/usa/bara ckobama/6221379/The-UN-loves-Barack-Obama-because-he-is-weak.html [accessed July 16, 2010].

10. "Top 10 Obama Apologies," *Human Events,* June 17, 2009; available at: http://www.humanevents.com/article.php?id=32296 [accessed July 16, 2010].

11. David Limbaugh, "Obama's Alternative Foreign Policy Universe," *Townhall,* January 15, 2010; available at: http://townhall.com/columnists/DavidLimbaugh/2010/01/15/o-bamas_alternative_foreign_policy_universe/page/full [accessed July 16, 2010].

12. Marc Thiessen, "The Good and Bad in Obama's Cairo Address," *National Review Online,* The Corner, June 4, 2009; available at: http://corner.nationalreview.com/post/?q=NWMzOTJiMDFmYmQ2 OTQwODZjMjkxNzcyMjQ4ZTUwMjk= [accessed July 16, 2010].

13. Letter written by Bill Clinton to Colonel Eugene Holmes, 1969.

14. Barack Obama, "Breaking the War Mentality," *Sundial,* March 10, 1983.

15. Ibid.

16. Barack Obama, *Dreams from My Father* (New York: Crown Publishers, 1995, 2004), xi.

17. "Obama Pledges Cuts in Missile Defense, Space, and Nuclear Weapons Programs," MissileThreat.com, February 29, 2008; available at: http://missilethreat.com/archives/id.7086/detail.asp [accessed July 16, 2010].

18. "Obama Mispronounces 'Corpsman' At Prayer Breakfast," *Real Clear Politics,* February 4, 2010; video available at: http://www.realclearpolitics.com/video/2010/02/04/obama_mispron ounces_corpsman_at_prayer_breakfast.html [accessed July 16, 2010].

19. Victor Davis Hanson, "Victory—How Quaint an Idea!" *National Review Online,* February 10, 2010; available at: http://article.nationalreview.com/424518/victory-how-quaint-an-idea/victor-davis-hanson [accessed July 16, 2010].

20. "Remarks by the President and Vice President at Signing of the Health Insurance Reform Bill," WhiteHouse.gov, March 23, 2010;

available at: http://www.whitehouse.gov/the-press-office/remarks-president-and-vice-president-signing-health-insurance-reform-bill [accessed July 16, 2010].

21. A term coined by James Delingpole in his eerily prescient and very funny book *Welcome to Obamaland: I Have Seen Your Future and It Doesn't Work* (Washington, D.C.: Regnery, 2009).

22. "VIDEO: Wrong red button," *Politico*, March 6, 2009; available at: http://www.politico.com/news/stories/0309/19719.html [accessed July 16, 2010].

23. Karen DeYoung, "More Troops Headed to Afghanistan," *Washington Post*, February 18, 2009; available at: http://www.washingtonpost.com/wp-dyn/content/article/2009/02/17/AR2009021702411.html [accessed July 16, 2010].

24. "Iran responds to Barack Obama's video appeal with nuclear pledge," *Washington Post*, March 20, 2009; available at: http://www.telegraph.co.uk/news/worldnews/northamerica/usa/barackobama/5021796/Iran-responds-to-Barack-Obamas-video-appeal-with-nuclear-pledge.html [accessed July 16, 2010].

25. "Top 10 Obama Apologies," *op. cit.*

26. Marc Thiessen, *Courting Disaster: How the CIA Kept America Safe and How Barack Obama Is Inviting the Next Attack* (Regnery, 2010). The quote comes from p. 12, but the entire book is a must read.

27. "Top 10 Obama Apologies," *op. cit.*

28. Victor Davis Hanson, "Our historically challenged president," SFGate.com, June 12, 2009; available at: http://articles.sfgate.com/2009-06-12/opinion/17207887_1_obama-s-image-obama-team-cairo-speech [accessed July 16, 2010].

29. Eliot Cohen, "Taking the Measure of Obama's Foreign Policy," *The Wall Street Journal*, January 11, 2010; available at: http://online.wsj.com/article/SB10001424052748703481004574-646080636258614.html [accessed July 16, 2010].

30. Robert J. Lieber, "Obama's can't-do style," *Los Angeles Times*, January 4, 2010; available at: http://articles.latimes.com/2010/jan/04/opinion/la-oe-lieber4-2010jan04 [accessed July 16, 2010].

31. "French Atomic Pique," *Wall Street Journal*, September 29, 2009; available at: http://online.wsj.com/article/SB100014240527487 04471504574441402775482322.html [accessed July 16, 2010].

32. "Obama's Speech on Nuclear Proliferation," *Real Clear Politics*, April 5, 2009; available at: http://www.realclearpolitics.com /articles/2009/04/obama_nuclear_proliferation.html [accessed July 16, 2010].

33. Mark Steyn, "The Very Model of a Modern Major Generalist," *National Review Online*, June 12, 2010; available at: http://article.nationalreview.com/436145/the-very-model-of-a-mod-ern-major-generalist/mark-steyn [accessed July 16, 2010].

34. Robert J. Lieber, "Obama's can't-do style," *op. cit.*

35. Charles Bremner, "Barack and Michelle Obama decline dinner with the Sarkozys," *The Times* of London, June 5, 2009; available at: http://www.timesonline.co.uk/tol/news/world/europe/article6434141 .ece [accessed July 16, 2010].

36. John O'Sullivan, "Divided by an Ocean," *National Review Online*, March 30, 2010; available at: http://article.nationalreview.com/ 429778/divided-by-an-ocean/john-osullivan [accessed July 16, 2010].

37. Ibid.

38. Charles Krauthammer, "Obama's policy of slapping allies," *Washington Post*, April 2, 2010; available at: http://www.washingtonpost.com/wp-dyn/content/article/ 2010/04/01/AR2010040102805.html [accessed July 16, 2010].

Chapter 4

1. Winston Churchill, *The River War: An Historical Account of the Reconquest of the Sudan*, 1899, Vol II (London: Longmans, Green, & Co., Ltd., 1899), 248–50.

2. The evidence for this is fast becoming encyclopedic, but see, for instance, Thomas E. Woods, *How the Catholic Church Built Western Civilization* (Washington, D.C.: Regnery, 2005). See also many of the books by the priest and scientist Stanley Jaki, or by the sociologist turned historian Rodney Stark, or James Hannam's book *God's Philosophers*. Hannam, an Oxford and Cambridge-educated scientist and historian, is soon to have *God's Philosophers* reissued

under the title *The Genesis of Science*. His book proves beyond doubt, at least to this layman, that the Christian Middle Ages laid the foundations for modern science.

3. John McCormack, "Obama Quietly Issues Statement on Terrorist Attack in Arkansas," *The Weekly Standard*, June 3, 2009; available at: http://www.weeklystandard.com/weblogs/TWSFP/2009/06/o-bama_quietly_issues_statement_1.asp [accessed July 19, 2010].

4. "Cops: Religion Fueled Army Office Slay," *CBS News*, June 2, 2009; available at: http://www.cbsnews.com/stories/2009/06/02/national/main5056232.shtml [accessed July 19, 2010].

5. Emily Friedman, Richard Esposito, Ethan Nelson, and Desiree Adib, "Fort Hood Gunman Who Killed 12, Wounded 30 Survived Gun Battle," *ABC News*, November 5, 2009; available at: http://abcnews.go.com/WN/fort-hood-shooting-army-doctor-leaves-12-dead/story?id=9007938 [accessed July 19, 2010].

6. Adam Gadahn: "A Call to Arms," the NEFA Foundation, March 7, 2010; available at: http://www.nefafoundation.org/miscellaneous/nefagadahn0210.pdf [accessed July 19, 2010].

7. "General Casey: diversity shouldn't be casualty of Fort Hood," Reuters, November 8, 2009; available at: http://blogs.reuters.com/frontrow/2009/11/08/general-casey-diversity-shouldnt-be-casualty-of-fort-hood/ [accessed July 19, 2010].

8. Interview with Homeland Security Secretary Janet Napolitano, "'Away From the Politics of Fear,'" *Spiegel*, March 16, 2009; available at: http://www.spiegel.de/international/world/0,1518,613330,00.html [accessed July 19, 2010].

9. The report is quoted in Audrey Hudson and Eli Lake "Napolitano Stands by Controversial Report," *Washington Times,* April 16, 2009; available at: http://www.washingtontimes.com/news/2009/apr/16/napolitano-stands-rightwing-extremism/ [accessed July 19, 2010].

10. Robert B. Patterson, *Dereliction of Duty* (Washington, D.C.: Regnery, 2003), 134.

11. Attorney General Eric Holder at the Press Conference Regarding the Times Square Attempted Bombing, May 4, 2010; available at: http://www.justice.gov/ag/speeches/2010/ag-speech-100504.html [accessed July 19, 2010].

12. "The Criminal Justice System as a Counterterrorism Tool," U.S. Department of Justice, http://www.justice.gov/cjs/ [accessed July 19, 2010].

13. Stephen Dinan, "Holder balks at blaming 'radical Islam,'" *Washington Times,* May 14, 2010; available at: http://www.washingtontimes.com/news/2010/may/14/holder-balks-at-blaming-radical-islam/ [accessed July 19, 2010].

14. Rowan Scarborough, "Obama Cleanses the Terrorism Glossary," *Human Events*, July 13, 2010; available at: http://www.humanevents.com/article.php?id=38019 [accessed July 19, 2010].

15. Ibid.

16. Michael B. Mukasey, "Shahzad and the Pre-9/11 Paradigm," *Wall Street Journal*, May 12, 2010; available at: http://online.wsj.com/article/SB10001424052748703880304575-236303698836186.html [accessed July 19, 2010].

17. Arthur Herman, "Obama at West Point: Lessons Unlearned," *National Review Online*, May 24, 2010; available at: http://article.nationalreview.com/434778/obama-at-west-point-lessons-unlearned/arthur-herman [accessed July 19, 2010].

18. Rowan Scarborough, "America Less Safe after Obama's First Year," *Human Events*, January 20, 2010; available at: http://www.humanevents.com/article.php?id=35248 [accessed July 19, 2010].

19. Samuel P. Huntington, *The Clash of Civilizations and the Remaking of World Order* (Austin, TX: Touchstone Publishing, 1997), 256–58.

20. Victor Davis Hanson, "The Paranoid Style," *National Review Online*, August 26, 2005; available at: http://article.nationalreview.com/276534/the-paranoid-style/victor-davis-hanson [accessed July 19, 2010].

21. Bernard Lewis, "The Roots of Muslim Rage," *The Atlantic Monthly*, September 1990; available at: http://www.theatlantic.com/past/docs/issues/90sep/rage.htm [accessed July 19, 2010].

22. His complete remarks can be read here: http://frwebgate.access.gpo.gov/cgi-bin/getpage.cgi?dbname=2005 _record&page=S6594&position=all [accessed July 19, 2010].

23. "Durbin Revises and Extends Gitmo Remarks," FOX News, June 17, 2005; available at: http://www.foxnews.com/story/ 0,2933,159844,00.html [accessed July 19, 2010].

24. Robert B. Patterson, *War Crimes: The Left's Campaign to Destroy Our Military and Lose the War on Terror* (New York: Crown Forum, 2007), 162.

25. Author interview with Major Eric Egland, September 16, 2005.

26. Author interview with U.S. Army specialist, Camp Victory, Baghdad, Iraq, July 14, 2005.

27. Gordon Cucullu, "Gitmo Jive," *American Enterprise*, September 2005.

28. Gordon Cucullu, "Mothering Terrorists at Gitmo," Democracy Project, June 28, 2005; available at: http://democracy-project.com/?p=1348 [accessed July 19, 2010].

29. Marc Thiessen, *Courting Disaster: How the CIA Kept America Safe and How Barack Obama Is Inviting the Next Attack* (Washington, D.C.: Regnery, 2010), 193.

30. Associated Press, "Pentagon: More return to fight after leaving Gitmo," *USA Today*, January 7, 2010; available at: http://www.usatoday.com/news/washington/2010-01-06-Guantanamo_N.htm [accessed July 19, 2010].

31. Marc Thiessen, *Courting Disaster*, see for instance pp. 89–90.

32. Ibid.

Chapter 5

1. "Obama: We are 5 days from FUNDAMENTALLY transforming America"; video available at: http://www.youtube.com/ watch?v=_cqN4NIEtOY [accessed July 20, 2010].

2. "Dwight D. Eisenhower Quotes," http://www.eisenhower.archives. gov/all_about_ike/Quotes/Quotes.html [accessed July 20, 2010].

3. "Gays-Military Chronology," Associated Press News Service, December 22, 1993.

4. Section 654, Title 10, U.S.C., *The Military Personnel Eligibility Act of 1993*.

5. Robert Maginnis, "The 'Don't Ask' Trojan Horse Strategy," *Human Events*, July 15, 2010; available at: http://www.humanevents.com/article.php?id=38066 [accessed July 20, 2010].

6. Tommy Sears, "Congress Moves Military Toward the LGBT Left," *Richmond Times Dispatch*, July 9, 2010; available at: http://www2.timesdispatch.com/news/2010/jul/09/ed-sears09-ar-267680/ [accessed July 20, 2010].

7. Frank Gaffney, "Obama's Wrecking Ball Swings at Military," Newsmax, March 29, 2010; available at: http://www.newsmax.com/FrankGaffney/Obama-gays-military-Alinksy/2010/03/29/id/354105 [accessed July 20, 2010].

8. Robert Bork, *Slouching Towards Gomorrah: Modern Liberalism and American Decline* (New York: Regan Books, 1996), 88.

9. Richard Grenier, "Bill Clinton's Armchair Warriors, *Washington Times*, November 18, 1997.

10. Ibid.

11. Nile Gardiner, "Rosa Brooks: The Pentagon's Far Left Advisor," *The Telegraph*, April 16, 2009; available at: http://blogs.telegraph.co.uk/news/nilegardiner/9534208/Rosa_Brooks_the_Pentagon%C3%A2s_far_left_adviser/ [accessed July 20, 2010].

12. Rowan Scarborough, "Soros Invades Pentagon," *Human Events*, April 21, 2009; available at: http://www.humanevents.com /article.php?id=31525 [accessed July 20, 2010].

13. Alan Gomez and Oren Dorell, "Absence of U.S. flag in Haiti sparks controversy," *USA Today*, March 15, 2010; available at: http://www.usatoday.com/news/world/2010-03-14-haiti-flag-flap_N.htm [accessed July 20, 2010].

14. Associated Press, "Obama: U.S. Troops in Afghanistan Must Do More Than Kill Civilians," FOX News, August 14, 2007; available at: http://www.foxnews.com/story/0,2933,293187,00.html [accessed July 20, 2010].

15. Remarks of Barack Obama U.S. Senator (D–ILL), Reunion & Commencement 2008; available at: http://www.wesleyan.edu/ news-rel/announcements/rc_2008/obama_speech.html [accessed July 20, 2010].

16. Jason Gutierrez, "US Casualties in Afghanistan Provoke Rage and Frustration, *Telegraph*, February 1, 2010; available at: http://www.telegraph.co.uk/expat/expatnews/7127365/US-casualties-in-Afghanistan-provoke-rage-and-frustration.html [accessed July 20, 2010].

17. Elena Kagan biography, http://www.discoverthenetworks.org /individualProfile.asp?indid=2398 [accessed July 20, 2010].

18. Ibid.

19. Robert B. Patterson, *War Crimes* (New York: Crown Forum, 2007), 59.

20. Harris Poll, Harris Confidence Index, January 22, 2003.

21. Institute of Politics, Harvard University, "A National Survey of College Undergraduates," (Cambridge, MA: Harvard University, 2002), 2.

22. Gordon Trowbridge, "2003 Military Times Poll—We Asked, You Answered," *Army Times*, December 29, 2003; available at: http://www.armytimes.com/legacy/new/0-292925-2513919.php [accessed July 20, 2010].

23. Jeff Nuding, "It Is Well with My Soul," dadmanly.com, June 14, 2005; available at: http://dadmanly.blogspot.com/2005/06/it-is-well-with-my-soul.html [accessed July 20, 2010].

24. Author interviews conducted at Camp Victory, Baghdad, Iraq, July11 to 14, 2005.

25. Daniel Ford, "God-Fearing Spartans," *Wall Street Journal*, September 22, 2005; available at: http://online.wsj.com/article/SB112734409995747956.html [accessed July 20, 2010].

26. Karl Zinsmeister, "Facts v. Fiction: A Report from the Front," *American Enterprise*, January 2006.

INDEX

ABOUT THE AUTHOR

Lieutenant Colonel Robert "Buzz" Patterson, United States Air Force (Retired), is the author of *New York Times* best sellers, *Dereliction of Duty: The Eyewitness Account of How Bill Clinton Compromised America's National Security; Reckless Disregard: How Liberal Democrats Undercut Our Military, Endanger Our Soldiers, and Jeopardize Our Security;* and *War Crimes: The Left's Campaign to Destroy the Military and Lose the War on Terror.*

Patterson served twenty years as a pilot on active duty in the United States Air Force and saw tours of duty world-wide, including combat operations in Grenada, Somalia, Rwanda, Haiti, and Bosnia. From 1996 to 1998, Colonel Patterson was the Senior Military Aide to President Bill Clinton. During that time he was responsible for the President's Emergency Satchel, otherwise known as the "Nuclear Football," the black bag with the nation's nuclear capability that accompanies the president at all times. In addition, Colonel Patterson was operational commander for all military units assigned to the White House, which included Air Force One, Marine One, Camp David, White House Transportation Agency, and White House Mess. Among his many military commendations, Patterson received the Defense Superior Service Medal for accomplishments while at the White House and was awarded the Air Force Air Medal for flying fifteen combat support missions into then-besieged Sarajevo, Bosnia-Herzegovina in 1994. He retired in 2001 to pursue a career as a commercial airline pilot, writer, and conservative speaker.

He is a frequent guest on talk shows across the country, including television appearances on *Hannity and Colmes, The O'Reilly Factor, CBS Morning Show, Fox and Friends, Hardball with Chris Matthews, The Dennis Miller Show,* C-SPAN's *Book Notes,* Joe Scarborough, *Heartland with John Kasich,* and MSNBC News. He's also been heard on radio shows ranging from Rush Limbaugh, Sean Hannity, Laura Ingraham, Michael Savage, and G. Gordon Liddy to Hugh Hewitt. Patterson was born in Chapel Hill, North Carolina, on October 5, 1955. He is a Distinguished Graduate from the Air Command and Staff College. He has his Bachelor's Degree in Political Science from Virginia Tech University, and a Master's in Business Administration from Webster University in St. Louis, Missouri. He and his family currently reside in California.